The Courts, the Ballot Box,
& Gay Rights

The Courts, the Ballot Box, & Gay Rights

HOW OUR GOVERNING INSTITUTIONS SHAPE THE SAME-SEX MARRIAGE DEBATE

Joseph Mello

University Press of Kansas

Published by the University Press of Kansas (Lawrence, Kansas 66045), which was organized by the Kansas Board of Regents and is operated and funded by Emporia State University, Fort Hays State University, Kansas State University, Pittsburg State University, the University of Kansas, and Wichita State University

Library of Congress Cataloging-in-Publication Data

Names: Mello, Joseph, author.

Title: The courts, the ballot box, and gay rights : how our governing institutions shape the same-sex marriage debate / Joseph Mello.

Description: Lawrence, Kansas : University Press of Kansas, 2016. | Includes bibliographical references and index.

Identifiers: LCCN 2016014265 | ISBN 9780700622917 (cloth : alk. paper) | ISBN 9780700622924 (ebook)

Subjects: LCSH: Same-sex marriage—Law and legislation—United States.

Classification: LCC KF539 .M45 2016 | DDC 346.7301/68—dc23

LC record available at http://lccn.loc.gov/2016014265.

British Library Cataloguing-in-Publication Data is available.

Printed in the United States of America

10 9 8 7 6 5 4 3 2 1

The paper used in this publication is recycled and contains 30 percent postconsumer waste. It is acid free and meets the minimum requirements of the American National Standard for Permanence of Paper for Printed Library Materials Z39.48-1992.

Contents

Acknowledgments, *vii*

1 The Mobilization of Bias, *1*

2 Citizens or Deviants? Rights and the Construction of
Gay Identities, *18*

3 Sites of Conflict: How Institutions Shape the Same-Sex
Marriage Debate, *43*

4 No Right to Object? Opposition to Same-Sex Marriage in the
Golden State, *72*

5 "A Place Apart": Opposition to Same-Sex Marriage in Maine, *111*

6 Taking (or Leaving) the Initiative Process, *149*

Appendix A. Same-Sex Marriage Ballot Measures, *167*

Appendix B. Individualism Master Frame Logit Regression, *169*

Appendix C. Religion, Threat, or Slippery Slope Subframe Logit
Regression, *171*

Notes, *173*

Works Cited, *193*

Cases Cited, *221*

Index, *223*

Acknowledgments

This book would not have been possible without the help of many people. I benefited immensely from the insights of Jeff Dudas, David Yalof, Kristen Kelly, Virginia Hettinger, and the late Howard Reiter during the earliest stages of developing this project. I am particularly thankful to Jeff for introducing me to the field of law and society and for helping me craft a bunch of jumbled ideas into a coherent narrative. Jeff has also been a great mentor and general sounding board for me over the years. I could not have done this without him. I would also like to thank the various discussants, conference participants, journal editors, and workshop coordinators who read portions of this project over the years and provided useful commentary—in particular Anna-Maria Marshall, for her feedback on the California case study at the Law and Society Association's Early Career Workshop, and Joshua Wilson, for his insights on the Maine case study. Also thanks of course to Chuck Myers and his editorial staff at the University Press of Kansas for believing in this project and for helping to steer it to completion.

I have had so many great colleagues and mentors who have provided me support while working on this project. I would like to thank my colleagues at DePaul for creating a wonderful and engaging environment to work in every day, and Wayne Steger in particular for being a great mentor to me during the first few years of my career. Also thanks to Renee Cramer for giving me my first real academic job at Drake University and for being such a great source of support and advice. I developed many of the ideas for this project while in graduate school at the University of Connecticut. I would like to thank all of the people who helped make that experience more enjoyable. Special thanks to the contingent of law and society scholars in my cohort, including Sarah Hampson, Jamie Huff, Allyson Yankle, Dan Tagliarina, and Corinne Tagliarina. I am sure that many of the insights they shared with me during class, or over beers, have made their way into this book in one way or another. Also, thanks to Jason Charrette for helping code the dataset used in Chapter 3 of this book. Finally, I have to thank Richard Ellis at Willamette University for encouraging me to go to graduate school in the first place. Richard saw potential in a young scholar who was, in his words, "a total slacker." He also saved me from becoming a lawyer by pulling me into his office during my senior year at

Willamette and encouraging me to get a PhD instead. Richard continues to be a great source of advice and encouragement. His career is an inspiration to me as well—if I can be half as prolific a scholar as he has been, I will feel like I am doing pretty well for myself.

Last, but certainly not least, I must thank my family for supporting me as I worked through this project. My wife, Brianna Mello, is probably the only person other than me who has read every word of this book. Bri is an extremely talented copy editor, and this book's arguments are presented much more clearly and succinctly thanks to her efforts. Perhaps most importantly, though, she provided me the emotional (and financial) support I needed to get through the difficult times during graduate school. I do not know how I would have been able to cope with the crippling amount of uncertainty and anxiety that all academics must face during the first few years of their career without her. I would also like to thank my parents, Frank and Jeannie Mello, for always encouraging me to pursue my education and for enthusiastically supporting my decision to go to graduate school, even after I told them how long it would take to get my PhD and how little money political scientists actually make. Finally, I would like to thank my children, Elizabeth and Everett, for providing a needed distraction from the occasional drudgery of academic work, and Brent and Karen White for occasionally relieving me from watching them so that I could finish writing this book.

1. The Mobilization of Bias

The majority today . . . seizes for itself a question the
Constitution leaves to the people, at a time when the people
are engaged in a vibrant debate on that question. . . . I
have no choice but to dissent. . . . This dissent . . . is not
about whether, in my judgment, the institution of marriage
should be changed to include same-sex couples. It is instead
about whether, in our democratic republic, that decision
should rest with the people . . . or with five lawyers who
happen to hold commissions authorizing them to resolve
legal disputes according to law. The Constitution leaves no
doubt about the answer.

   —CHIEF JUSTICE JOHN ROBERTS
     (Dissenting opinion, *Obergefell v. Hodges* 2015)

The idea of the Constitution "was to withdraw certain
subjects from the vicissitudes of political controversy, to
place them beyond the reach of majorities and officials
and to establish them as legal principles to be applied by
the courts." . . . This is why "fundamental rights may not
be submitted to a vote; they depend on the outcome of no
elections."

   —JUSTICE ANTHONY KENNEDY
     (*Obergefell v. Hodges* 2015)

The US Supreme Court's landmark decision in *Obergefell v. Hodges* (2015) effectively ended an intense nationwide debate over the proper definition of marriage by legalizing same-sex marriage in all fifty states. Although much of this nearly two-decades-long debate was spent weighing the substantive implications of continuing to define marriage as a union of one man and one woman, the case itself touched not just on the question of what the definition of marriage should be but also on who should be charged with determining that definition—the courts or "the people." The question of who should decide issues of fundamental rights has been a recurring point of reflection for the Supreme Court justices of late. In 2014 they issued an emphatic defense of Michigan's right to determine affirmative action policy through the ballot measure process (*Schuette v. Coalition to Defend Affirmative Action* 2014).[1] The following term, the Court heard two cases involving the constitutionality of laws passed through popular referendum. In *Obergefell* it invalidated the laws of twenty-eight states that had passed ballot measures defining marriage as between one man and one woman (*Obergefell v. Hodges* 2015), but just a few days later it issued an opinion that upheld Arizona voters' right to alter their redistricting policy through popular referendum (*Arizona State Legislature v. Arizona Independent Redistricting Commission* 2015). Clearly the Court has not yet developed a consistent answer to the question of whether citizens should be able to vote directly on issues of fundamental rights.

Increasingly, some of the most salient rights-based issues of our time, including same-sex marriage,[2] affirmative action,[3] abortion,[4] immigration,[5] and drug policy[6] are being decided through the ballot measure process. Yet, discussions of the merits of deciding these issues in this environment have tended to focus on the same well-worn theoretical debates. Proponents of the ballot measure process argue that it is the most democratic way to decide difficult moral questions (Schmidt 1989, 25–40). This echoes the sentiments of the progressive reformers who originally pushed for the expansion of the initiative and referendum process in the early twentieth century. They saw this process as a way for citizens to regulate the power of special interests and check the influence of corrupt elites (Cronin 1989, 43–59; Schmidt 1989, 6–10). In contrast, courts have often been regarded as antidemocratic institutions because they are, by design, insulated from the influences of popular will (Bickel 1962). Critics of the ballot measure process have responded by pointing out that it has often been used as a tool of retrenchment to roll back minority rights (Bell 1978; Cronin 1989, 90–124; Gamble 1997; Miller 2001). These critics question the value of endorsing a strictly majoritarian definition of democracy and contend that protecting vulnerable or unpopular minorities requires that we place some rights outside of the purview of potentially hostile and discriminatory majorities (Cronin 1989, 7–37).

These scholars raise valid concerns, but such arguments oversimplify this issue somewhat by focusing too much on the question of who should decide and not enough on how these different institutional environments affect the structure and tenor of these debates. This is important because institutions do more than just aggregate the individual preferences of the actors working within them; they consist of norms and constraints that structure individual behavior and help determine outcomes (Riker 1980; March and Olsen 1984; Smith 1988; Gillman and Clayton 1999). As a result, moving this debate from one institutional environment to another does not just change the audience, it alters the entire nature of the debate itself in some fundamental, and often surprising, ways.

In this book, I seek to better understand how institutional norms and constraints shape debates over fundamental rights. Using conservative[7] opposition[8] to same-sex marriage as an extended case study, I analyze arguments made by opponents of marriage equality both inside and outside of the courtroom. I find that conservative opponents of same-sex marriage were able to use rights language to effectively argue against marriage equality in ballot measure campaigns but that they typically avoided using the language of rights to frame their arguments after the debate moved inside the courtroom. This finding is counterintuitive given that the language of rights would seem well suited for a legal environment. This raises two important questions that motivate the inquiry conducted in this book: Why did conservative opponents of same-sex marriage enjoy such an advantage when debating this issue in the popular arena of a ballot measure campaign? And why were they less successful at mobilizing the language of rights when arguing against it in more elite-centered environments?

Although most early scholarship on rights-based social movements was focused on efforts to bring about social change, rights discourse is also frequently used by conservatives as a means of protecting status-quo power structures (Goldberg-Hiller and Milner 2003; Haltom and McCann 2004; Dudas 2008). During same-sex marriage ballot measure campaigns, conservatives often used the discourse of parental rights and religious liberty to counter the rights-based appeals of marriage equality activists. An activist working to pass California's Proposition 8 in 2008 summed up the opinions of many opponents of marriage equality when he argued:

> The marriage controversy has been contaminated by the language of rights. We must remember there are other groups and other people who also have their own rights besides gays. We have to think about children, their right to be raised by a mother and a father. We have to think about religious groups that believe that marriage is an institution established by God who are right now are [sic] having their rights violated by the supposed rights of the gay portion of our society. (Miranda 2008, 53)

Jim Garlow, a pastor at Skyline Church in San Diego, expressed a similar sentiment in a speech he gave to opponents of same-sex marriage at a rally in support of Proposition 8:

> Rights have been crushed under every time same-sex marriage is legal. Some pastors have been threatened with jail. Many have been muzzled and silenced. Churches have been threatened and intimidated and parents . . . and business persons [*sic*] as well. . . . This is ultimately really not about marriage and homosexuality at its core. At its core is they have found a loophole hiding under the guise of civil rights by which they can put underfoot and crush underfoot the rights of every person who has a Biblical worldview. That is what is at stake. (2008a, 45–46)

This language is incredibly powerful. Using rights discourse in this way allowed conservative opponents of same-sex marriage to construct an identity of themselves as victims of oppression and to construct gays and lesbians as oppressors. Such logic mobilized conservative activists and helped them appeal to a wider audience as well. Although one must be careful not to assign too much instrumental importance to the use of rights language, it is notable that conservatives won thirty-four of the thirty-nine same-sex marriage ballot measure campaigns that took place from 1998 to 2012.

Yet despite their considerable emotional appeal, such arguments were almost never used by conservatives when arguing this issue in a courtroom environment. I argue that this is because our modern conception of law as an "arena of reason" (Fitzpatrick 1992; Darian-Smith 2010) has shaped courtroom procedures, ensuring that the claims of conservatives will be subjected to a level of scrutiny inside the courtroom that they do not receive in more popular arenas. Though this conservative rights language is not overtly discriminatory, these arguments rely on an implicit assumption that gays and lesbians are "dangerous" and "deviant" others whose selfish and excessive rights claims threaten the legitimate rights of the majority of Americans (Schacter 1994; Goldberg-Hiller and Milner 2003; Dudas 2008). This logic builds on a long-standing conception of citizenship in which individuals must prove they deserve equal rights by disciplining what are thought to be deviant sexual urges (Foucault 1990; Comaroff and Comaroff 1991, 365–404; Merry 2000, 221–257). Although these arguments would be rejected by many if made explicitly, when masked by the secular discourse of rights, these implicit moral assumptions are free to operate at a subconscious level, feeding on latent stereotypes and helping to foment popular opposition to same-sex marriage. In this way, rights discourse is used as a means of transforming arguments based on moral assumptions into something acceptable to a more secular audience (Schacter 1994, 289–290; Herman 1997, 115, 144; Hardisty 1999, 114).

Litigation has proven an effective tactic for advocates of gay and lesbian rights in part because the courtroom environment allows them to move beyond simple sound bites and more successfully challenge the arguments of their opponents (Gerstmann 1999, 99–127; Andersen 2005, 143–174). Requirements such as the need to support claims with evidence; to subject them to more dispassionate scrutiny from experts; and to show how the law in question furthers a legitimate, secular, government interest all work to unmask the discriminatory stereotypes that underlie many of the rights-based arguments made by conservative opponents of same-sex marriage. As a result, I find that the same arguments that work so effectively for conservatives in a popular environment frequently become a liability for them when the debate over marriage equality moves inside the courtroom.

LAW AS AN ARENA OF REASON

The insights provided in this book have been influenced by "new institutional" approaches to social science inquiry.[9] This scholarship argues that institutions consist of norms and constraints that shape how individuals react to different types of political issues, structure conflicts, and determine outcomes (Riker 1980; March and Olsen 1984; Smith 1988; Gillman and Clayton 1999). As E. E. Schattschneider famously asserted, "All forms of political organization have a bias in favor of the exploitation of some kinds of conflict and the suppression of others because *organization is the mobilization of bias.* Some issues are organized into politics while others are organized out" (1960, 69).[10] This "mobilization of bias" represents what some have called "the second face of power" (Bachrach and Baratz 1962; Gaventa 1980, 8–11). According to this conception, institutional norms are a source of power because they determine how disputes must be structured—placing those who adhere to this structure at an advantage and disadvantaging those either unable or unwilling to do so.

Contemporary US legal disputes are shaped by our modern conception of law as an objective, unbiased, and rational process. This conception of law emerged in the West during the Enlightenment era, when new scientific discoveries and an emphasis on reason began to challenge entrenched religious authority. These changes caused law to be seen as an exercise of science and logic, a break from previous conceptions of law as a product of divine inspiration and a reflection of religious beliefs (Fitzpatrick 1992; Darian-Smith 2010). This led to the creation of a "positivist" conception of law as a form of decision making that exists outside the realm of politics or morality. Legal positivism argues that judicial decisions should be the product of careful, unbiased, legal reasoning untainted by individual moral or political beliefs (Austin 1879). Although the idea that it is possible to remove politics and morality from law has been thoroughly disputed (see, for example, Holmes 1897), the belief that law is an objective and reasoned process persists (Fitzpatrick 1992).

In an attempt to ensure that legal decision making is a product of reason, a number of norms and procedures have been established that govern the actions of courtroom officials. Arguments made in court are required to be supported with evidence, they must be based on legal reasoning, and they must be subjected to scrutiny from opponents as part of an "adversarial process." These requirements have been formalized through a system of legal education that imparts these values to budding legal professionals. Law school trains students to use the "case study method" and reinforces expectations that lawyers and judges will "think logically," carefully scrutinize arguments, and make dispassionate decisions based on evidence. Though these procedures have fallen well short of accomplishing the goals of legal positivism, this does not mean they are irrelevant. As we shall see, these constraints have had an important impact on the debate over same-sex marriage. They limit the value of specious arguments, which cannot be supported with credible evidence, and they lessen the impact of arguments based solely on individual moral values or discriminatory stereotypes.

The norm of impartiality in law sets the courtroom apart from other institutional environments. In the legislative arena, for example, no such assumptions exist. Instead, these institutions celebrate partisan bias and encourage individual actors to pursue their own self-interest. Here, individuals make decisions typically based not on notions of fundamental rights but on narrow self-interested goals, such as winning reelection (Downs 1957; Mayhew 1974) or advancing up the ranks of the party hierarchy (Cox and McCubbins 1993). These unique institutional norms can diminish the impact rights discourse has on legislative officials. This has, we will see, a dramatic impact on the way debates over same-sex marriage play out in the legislative arena.

In contrast to the elite-centered environments of the courtroom and the legislature, ballot measure campaigns are a more wide-open affair. Every state has some mechanism that allows citizens to vote on issues directly.[11] Although states carefully regulate the process of qualifying measures for the ballot, they generally allow discourse used during ballot measure campaigns to operate without restrictions. Arguments for and against ballot measures are typically presented to the public through short television advertisements and thirty-second sound bites. As we shall see, these arguments often contain conceptions of individual rights that rest on discriminatory stereotypes. Because these arguments are targeted at a "rationally ignorant" popular audience that is typically unable, or unwilling, to subject them to extensive scrutiny, the moral assumptions that underlie this rights discourse go largely unchallenged during these campaigns.

In this book, I examine how these different institutional norms and constraints have shaped the debate over marriage equality by conducting comparative analyses of arguments used by opponents of same-sex marriage in different institutional environments. This approach offers an opportunity to empirically test what have often been necessarily theoretical ideas about how different institutional environments might affect the efficacy of social movements.[12] Social scientists do not have the luxury of creating controlled experiments. They cannot replay historical events to see what might have happened had movement activists pursued their cause in a different institutional venue. The same-sex marriage debate was, however, carried out in a variety of different institutional contexts. Focusing on this issue provides a unique opportunity to examine how institutional frameworks have affected the way opponents of same-sex marriage think and talk about their cause while holding other factors such as region, culture, and time frame constant.

SOCIAL MOVEMENTS, RIGHTS TALK, AND LAW

This book is also grounded in scholarship that uses a sociolegal approach to study the relationship between law and social movements. Legal scholars working within the interdisciplinary field of law and society have long studied how members of social movements mobilize the law in order to bring about or resist social change (Scheingold 1974; Zemans 1983; Burstein 1991; McCann 1994; Engel and Munger 2003; Epp 2009). This scholarship has often challenged what Stuart Scheingold (1974) called the "myth of rights," which holds that social change can be brought about directly through litigation. This popular belief can result in frustration for social movement activists because legal victories typically fail to deliver tangible change immediately (Rosenberg 1991). Scheingold argued instead that rights should be understood as resources that can be used by activists to bring about change indirectly. In what he called the "politics of rights" activists use legal symbols and discourse to lend legitimacy to their positions, mobilize supporters, and agitate for social change both inside and outside of formal legal environments.

This approach challenges us to expand our view of the law beyond the walls of the courtroom. This is important because most studies of law and social movements have focused on the actions of formal legal actors—primarily the US Supreme Court. This can have the effect of artificially separating the "political" and the "legal," missing the way in which politics are frequently imbued with legal symbols and discourse and reinforcing the conventional legal formalist view of law as distinct from politics.[13] Law and society scholars have long recognized, however, that the United States has a "plural legal order" and that legal meaning is frequently constructed outside of formal legal institutions (Merry 1988). In light of this fact, they have called for a more expansive view of legal phenomena that moves beyond the courtroom and examines the "common place of the law" (Ewick and Silbey 1998). This book builds on that tradition by examining how legal discourse is employed not just inside the courtroom but also in ballot measure campaigns and legislative arenas—institutions that, with a few notable exceptions (Gerstmann 1999, 99–127; Andersen 2005, 143–174; Stone 2012) have not received much attention from sociolegal scholars.

Another key insight provided by law and society scholars is an understanding of how movement activists and average citizens use "rights talk" to create frames of collective meaning favorable to their cause. Scholars who study this phenomenon have worked to unpack the instrumental and constitutive implications of rights discourse (Ewick and Silbey 1998; Gilliom 2001; Passavant 2002; Engel and Munger 2003; Goldberg 2007; Dudas 2008; Lovell 2012; Wilson 2013). Rights carry with them substantial symbolic power in the United States. As a result, framing one's cause as a rights-based issue can lend considerable legitimacy to it (Glendon 1993). Activists may capitalize on this fact by using rights discourse to "expand the sphere" of a conflict and broaden their appeal beyond their base of supporters (Schattschneider 1960).[14] Scholars have shown, for example, that members of the religious right will often couch moral arguments in the language of rights in an attempt to appeal to more secular individuals (Schacter 1994, 289–290; Herman 1997, 115, 144; Hardisty 1999, 114).[15]

Framing one's cause using the language of rights also has constitutive impact on the identity of the speaker. Rights are often popularly conceived of as assets available to everyone equally without conditions, but this has not proven true historically.[16] Instead, rights should be understood as contingent resources given only to those who demonstrate that they deserve them by exhibiting behavior deemed acceptable by the majority (Goldberg 2007). Making a valid rights claim does more than just allow an individual to "do something"; it also entitles her to "be someone"—to be considered a legitimate, virtuous US citizen (Passavant 2002; Engel and Munger 2003; Dudas 2008). Examining the debate over same-sex marriage through this prism makes it clear that activists engaged in this issue are offering competing conceptions of identity. Proponents of same-sex marriage have used rights language to argue that gays and lesbians are full and equal citizens entitled to the same treatment as everyone else (Hull 2006; Richman 2014). In contrast, opponents of same-sex marriage argue that gays and lesbians are deviant others whose values pose a threat to the legitimate rights of the majority (Schacter 1994; Goldberg-Hiller and Milner 2003).

I find that this perspective has important constitutive implications for conservative opponents of same-sex marriage. These activists typically view the push for marriage equality as a "zero-sum game" in which granting rights to gays and lesbians necessarily means infringing on the existing rights of the majority. Using rights discourse in this way creates an inversion process whereby gays and lesbians become the oppressors seeking to infringe on individual rights, and conservatives become victims of oppression (Goldberg-Hiller and Milner 2003). Adopting such a perspective personalizes opposition to same-sex marriage, transforming it from a fight to protect the somewhat abstract institution of marriage to a personal defense of one's individual rights. Using the discourse of rights in this way causes opponents of same-sex marriage to see themselves as "cultural warriors" fighting to preserve fundamental rights and values threatened by the "excessive" and "unnecessary" rights claims of gays and lesbians.

These conceptions of rights still motivate conservative opponents of same-sex marriage today, despite the fact that these positions have been repeatedly invalidated by the courts. This shows that the constitutive power of this conservative rights discourse is incredibly resilient. Unfavorable legal decisions are often thought to repudiate existing interpretations of the law and kill alternative legal meanings that develop outside of the courtroom (Cover 1983). However, the "deployment of legal claims is not always a one-way process in which government officials impose their vision of law on a passive population" (Lovell 2006, 285). Conservatives have always treated formal legal actors with a great deal of skepticism, particularly with regard to what they consider moral or cultural issues. This approach seems to inoculate them against unfavorable judicial decisions, easily dismissed as "judicial activism." As a result, the conceptions of individual rights advanced by conservative opponents of same-sex marriage continue to thrive despite the fact that these conceptions have been ignored or even outright rejected by formal legal actors. This suggests that the *Obergefell* decision might have altered the dynamics of the marriage equality debate in some fundamental ways, but it is unlikely to have ended it altogether.

RIGHTS ON THE RIGHT

Finally, this book is focused on understanding how conservative activists mobilize legal symbols and discourse in order to oppose social change. In doing so I build on the insights of scholars who have studied the growing conservative legal movement in the United States (Brown 2002; Heinz et al. 2003; Hacker 2005; Hatcher 2005; den Dulk 2006, 2008; Dudas 2008; Southworth 2008; Teles 2008; Wilson 2013). Much of this scholarship has been influenced by the work of Charles Epp (1998), who showed how the development of progressive legal organizations helped to spark the "rights revolution." These scholars pick up where Epp left off, documenting how New Right[17] conservative activists sought to counter this rights revolution by building stronger legal organizations during the 1980s and 1990s (Stefancic and Delgado 1996; Brown 2002; Hacker 2005; Southworth 2008; Teles 2008). Organizations formed during this time, such as the Federalist Society, the Alliance Defense Fund, and the American Center for Law and Justice, helped to provide training and resources to lawyers interested in pursuing conservative causes and worked to appoint judges sympathetic to the conservative point of view. Many scholars have credited these legal organizations with recent gains made by conservatives on economic issues, such as free enterprise, economic deregulation, and property rights (Southworth

2008; Teles 2008), as well as social issues, such as religious liberty and abortion (Brown 2002; Hacker 2005; den Dulk 2006; Southworth 2008).

This focus on conservative law use is a necessary perspective because rights have traditionally been understood as a tool the politically powerless can, in theory, use to challenge status-quo power structures (Scheingold 1974; Zemans 1983; Burstein 1991; McCann 1994; Engel and Munger 2003). The marriage equality debate in particular has received considerable attention from legal scholars of late. However, with a few notable exceptions (Goldberg-Hiller 2002; Klarman 2012), most of this work has focused primarily on the efforts of marriage equality activists and given little attention to their opponents (see, for example, Andersen 2005; Hull 2006; Pinello 2006; Gerstmann 2008; Smith 2008; Hirshman 2012; Richman 2014).

Scholarly inattention to this conservative rights use can result in a skewed perspective of US history and an overly optimistic view of the country's future. An exclusive focus on progressive rights use tells a tale of a nation driven by a common creed of equal treatment for all citizens to consistently expand the rights of once-marginalized populations (Myrdal 1944). Such a view lends an air of inevitability to the cause of social movements that advocate on behalf of oppressed groups. However, as scholars such as Rogers Smith have noted, the "dynamics of American development cannot simply be seen as a rising tide of liberalizing forces progressively submerging contrary beliefs and practices" (Smith 1993, 558–559). The findings of this book underscore the fact that there is nothing inherently liberating about rights. They are, instead, indeterminate or "contingent" resources (Scheingold 1974, 7). Rights are given meaning by the parties who seek to use them and by the institutional contexts in which they are advanced. As such, rights can be used just as effectively to preserve entrenched hierarchies as they can to challenge them. There is nothing inevitable about calls to extend rights to marginalized populations. Instead, appeals to particular notions of individual rights will continue to be used as a means of preserving existing power dynamics or as instruments of retrenchment used to roll back newly won concessions.

ON METHODS

This book is focused on understanding the use and effectiveness of legal symbols and discourse. As such, it is theoretically and methodologically informed by interpretive social science. Scholarship oriented by interpretive epistemology begins with the assumption that reality is socially constructed and that the meaning we give to the world around us is necessarily mediated by cultural and linguistic understandings and normative assumptions (McCann 1996, 463; Hawkesworth 2006, 31; Yanow 2006, 75). According to this conception, language does not merely describe reality but actually constitutes it. As a result, meaning construction is seen as a complex, indeterminate, mutually constitutive, and hotly contested process. The complex nature of this process frustrates attempts to isolate the impact of individual variables, requiring that scholars instead explore how social, legal, institutional, and cultural norms work together to shape our understanding of the world (Rabinow and Sullivan 1988, 14; McCann 1996, 463).

In order to overcome these inherent difficulties, I examine conservative rights discourse using a variety of different methodological techniques. This mixed-methods approach is common in interpretive work. Because interpretation is such a complex and interrelated process, and because all interpretations are necessarily partial and incomplete (McCann 1994, 14–16), interpretive scholars frequently use a variety of methods to ensure their findings conform to rigorous scholarly standards (McCann 1994, 1996, 477; Yanow 2006, 77). I follow this model by studying conservative opposition to same-sex marriage using a "quantitative" content analysis of discourse used by opponents of marriage equality in different institutional environments (Chapter 3), and two "qualitative," bounded, comparative case studies (Chapters 4 and 5).

Texts are used as the unit of analysis throughout this project. By "texts" I mean anything written down or recorded in some way. This would include, for example, speeches transcribed and made available to the public, amicus curiae briefs submitted in court cases, documents made available on organization websites, statements made before a legislative body, and television advertisements used in statewide ballot measure campaigns. I have chosen to use written texts as opposed to other forms of data, such as interviews, because this project is focused on understanding the implications of the rights discourse of conservative activists. Understanding these implications requires the researcher to focus on the text itself rather than determine the intentions of the author. This is because as soon as a speaker has finished speaking (or writing), she loses control of the meaning of her words. The audience members are free to interpret them however they see fit, regardless of intentions. Thus, when interpreting the meaning of a text, it is more important to look to the text itself than it is to consider the motivations of the author who wrote it (Ricouer 1973, 113; Rabinow and Sullivan 1988, 13).

CHAPTER OVERVIEW

In Chapter 2 I begin my analysis of conservative opposition to same-sex marriage by examining the history of the gay rights movement in the United States and the conservative countermobilization against it. I focus in particular on how conservatives have used rights discourse to construct gays and lesbians as deviant and how proponents of gay rights have sought to challenge this conception. Examining this history is crucial for understanding the current debate over same-sex marriage because this dispute is built on an existing framework of cultural traditions and mediated by frames of collective meaning established during these previous conflicts. The historical analysis conducted in this chapter provides the necessary context for understanding conservative opposition to same-sex marriage today.

I begin by exploring the movement-countermovement dynamics of the early gay rights movement. For much of US history, gays and lesbians have been targets of discrimination and violence. This discriminatory treatment has been fueled in large part by popular conceptions of gays and lesbians as "sick" and "depraved" individuals who are unable to control their own sexual impulses and who often seek to prey on children (Fejes 2008). In the 1970s, members of a nascent gay rights movement began challenging these conceptions and arguing that they deserved equal rights. Conservatives responded to this movement by using the ballot measure process as a tool of retrenchment. Antigay activists such as Anita Bryant argued that local gay rights ordinances normalized "homosexuality" and made it easier for gays to "recruit" children into their "sinful" lifestyle. These arguments worked well with a popular audience because they played on long-standing conceptions of gays and lesbians as sexual deviants. The success of Bryant's strategy proved to be short-lived, however. She often aggressively denounced homosexuality by using overtly religious and homophobic language to characterize gays and lesbians as dangerous and sinful predators. Although this discourse resonated with many in the conservative base, it alienated more moderate voters.

I conclude the chapter by examining how, during the 1990s, antigay activists began eschewing the more overtly discriminatory and homophobic language of these earlier campaigns in favor of a more rights-based approach. This strategy was used most successfully to pass Colorado's Amendment 2 in 1992 (Herman 1997, 137–169; Gerstmann 1999, 99–127; Andersen 2005, 143–174). During this campaign, conservatives convinced voters to pass a constitutional amendment prohibiting gays and lesbians from being recognized as a "protected class" by framing gay rights as excessive, "special rights." Although this discourse refrains from using overtly homophobic language, it still communicates the message that gays and lesbians are deviant others pushing for excessive rights that infringe on the legitimate rights of responsible, disciplined citizens (Schacter 1994; Goldberg-Hiller and Milner 2003).

In Chapter 3, I provide a "big-picture" overview of opposition to same-sex marriage in the United States and begin my empirical analysis of the impact of institutional environments on the use and effectiveness of conservative rights discourse. I begin by examining the structures of the local and national organizations that led the fight against same-sex marriage. I then conduct a quantitative content analysis of discourse used by opponents of marriage equality in a variety of different institutional contexts. This analysis reveals that conservative rights discourse is much more prevalent outside of the courtroom than inside it and suggests that the use of this rights discourse was crucial to the success opponents of same-sex marriage had in statewide ballot measure campaigns.

Chapter 4 focuses on conservative opposition to same-sex marriage in California. I begin this chapter with a brief overview of the political development of California. This historical analysis traces the development of the state's political culture and institutions and examines how this dynamic affected the debate over marriage equality in that state. I then conduct an in-depth analysis of the 2008 Proposition 8 campaign. This analysis begins by describing the organizational structure and strategy of the campaign. Finally, I use interpretive textual analysis to explore the constitutive and instrumental implications of arguments used in support of the measure. I conclude the chapter with an analysis of the *Perry v. Schwarzenegger* trial (2010). Here I examine arguments made during the trial and show how institutional norms and constraints present inside the courtroom made it difficult for conservatives to effectively mobilize rights discourse in that environment.

The results of this analysis show that conservatives have been able to employ rights discourse instrumentally to influence ballot measure campaigns. Framing their arguments using the discourse of rights, and minimizing the use of moral or religious appeals, allows conservatives to connect with a more secular audience and helps them build popular support for their cause. In addition to its instrumental implications, this discourse also has constitutive impact on opponents of same-sex marriage. Thinking about their cause using the discourse of rights helps mobilize opposition to marriage equality. This language lends increased legitimacy to the arguments of conservatives. It allows them to see themselves not as a recalcitrant majority stubbornly opposing the rights of gays and lesbians but as victims of oppression standing up against the excessive and unnecessary rights claims of subversive elites.

After the debate over same-sex marriage moved inside the courtroom, however, these conservative rights claims became much less effective. Conservatives attempted to downplay the rights-based arguments they had used during the Proposition 8 campaign when arguing against same-sex marriage during the *Perry* trial. However, proponents of marriage equality made the Yes on 8 campaign's arguments a centerpiece of their case. They used expert testimony to expose the stereotypes underlying advertisements run by conservatives in support of Proposition 8 and showed that the law was motivated by a discriminatory intent, not a compelling government interest. This strategy proved successful because the court largely agreed with this analysis. Thus, the rights-based arguments used by conservatives during the Proposition 8 campaign were not merely ineffective in this environment, they actually became liabilities.

Chapter 5 focuses on conservative opposition to same-sex marriage in Maine. I begin my analysis by briefly discussing New England's political development and examining how the region's institutional environment shaped the same-sex marriage debate. Although the citizens' initiative process is a staple of politics in many parts of the nation, political systems in northeastern states tend to be much more elite-centered. I argue that this dynamic placed conservatives at a disadvantage when debating this issue in this region and explain why the marriage equality movement was able to gain an early foothold there. Maine is an exception to this rule, however. It is the one New England state with a robust citizens' initiative process, and as a result, opponents of same-sex marriage were able to resist marriage equality more aggressively there.

After discussing the development of New England's political institutions, I conduct an in-depth exploration of the passage of LD 1020, a bill legalizing same-sex marriage in Maine in 2009. I show that marriage equality activists were able to capitalize on the fact that Democrats had won significant majorities in Maine's state legislature in 2008 by pushing for the passage of a marriage equality bill. Conservatives had a difficult time opposing these efforts because legislative officials are primarily concerned with winning reelection and currying favor with members of their own political party. This makes them less receptive to rights discourse than a popular audience. The success of LD 1020 proved short-lived for marriage equality advocates, however. Opponents of same-sex marriage placed a measure seeking to repeal the legislation before voters in 2009. During the campaign over what came to be known as Question 1, conservatives used the same tactics employed during the Proposition 8 campaign in California to mobilize their own counter-rights discourse and successfully repeal LD 1020.

The chapter concludes by examining Maine's 2012 Question 1 campaign. During this campaign, advocates of marriage equality successfully convinced voters to legalize same-sex marriage using the ballot measure process. Maine is one of only three states to have done so. I find that marriage equality activists succeeded in 2012 by avoiding the language of rights, choosing instead to frame support for same-sex marriage using the language of family. I speculate that this approach might have proven successful in part because it caused voters to stop thinking about this issue as a debate between competing rights claims, a dynamic that seems to favor conservatives. This suggests that rights language can actually be counterproductive to efforts to bring about social change when used in a popular arena. Though avoiding this rights discourse had instrumental value for proponents of marriage equality, this strategy has problematic constitutive implications. Most of the arguments made by the Yes on 1 campaign in 2012 were presented by heterosexual individuals who talked about what family meant to them. Gays and lesbians were largely kept in the background of the campaign. This suggests that many voters are willing to support same-sex marriage but only if gays and lesbians are made to appear less threatening to them by not making "aggressive" rights claims and by not being the face of the campaign.

Chapter 6 is the conclusion. In this chapter I highlight the key findings of this book. I then expand the scope of this project and consider the broader implications of these insights. I show that institutional environments have shaped a number of important cultural conflicts in ways similar to the debate over same-sex marriage. These debates frequently end up being decided in the popular arena through the ballot measure process. Rights discourse often plays a central role in these campaigns, but I argue that it does not necessarily add value to these debates. On the contrary, the results of this study suggest that the institutional norms and constraints present in this environment make it more likely that rights claims will be used to obfuscate these issues than to enrich this discussion. This suggests that the results of ballot measure campaigns are not a reflection of popular will, as so many of their most ardent supporters suggest, but rather a distortion of it. This may lead us to question the wisdom of allowing so many important cultural questions to be decided in this environment.

2. Citizens or Deviants?
Rights and the Construction
of Gay Identities

In this chapter I begin my analysis of conservative opposition to same-sex marriage by examining the history of the gay rights movement in the United States and the countermobilization against it. I focus in particular on how debates over gay rights have historically featured competing conceptions of identity and on the roles different institutional environments have played in shaping these debates. Examining this history is crucial for understanding the more recent debate over same-sex marriage because this dispute has not occurred on a tabula rasa. It has instead been built on an existing framework of cultural traditions and has been mediated by frames of collective meaning established during previous conflicts. The historical analysis I conduct in this chapter will provide the necessary context for understanding conservative opposition to same-sex marriage today. Subsequent chapters will show how opponents of marriage equality adapted these long-standing conceptions of gays and lesbians, and popular notions of acceptable rights use, to fit the current debate over same-sex marriage.

I begin this chapter by examining the origins of the gay rights movement in the United States. For much of US history, gays and lesbians have been targets of discrimination and violence. This discriminatory treatment has been fueled in large part by popular conceptions of gays and lesbians as "sick" and "depraved" individuals who are unable to control their own sexual impulses and who seek to prey on children (Jenkins 2004; Fejes 2008). In the 1970s a nascent gay rights movement began challenging these conceptions and arguing that gays and lesbians were deserving of equal rights. These activists succeeded in passing laws outlawing discrimination based on sexual orientation in cities such as San Francisco, where the presence of a large gay community allowed them to exert considerable political power at the local level.

Next, I explore how conservatives responded to these early victories by using the ballot measure process as a tool of retrenchment. Moving the debate over gay rights away from the elite-centered environment of the city council or the state legislature into a more popular arena allowed conservatives to make arguments that capitalized on common conceptions of gays and lesbians as deviant. Antigay activists such as Anita Bryant argued that local gay rights ordinances normalized homosexuality and made it easier for gays and lesbians to "recruit" children into their "sinful" lifestyle. These arguments played on long-standing conceptions of gays and lesbians as sexual deviants who seek to prey on children. Bryant proved to be an incredibly divisive figure, however. Her opposition to gay rights was fueled primarily by her evangelical Christian beliefs, and she often aggressively denounced homosexuality by using overtly religious and homophobic language to characterize gays and lesbians as dangerous predators. Although this discourse resonated with many in the conservative base, it often alienated more moderate voters.

In the final sections of this chapter I explore how in the 1990s anti-gay-rights activists began eschewing the more overtly discriminatory and homophobic language of these earlier campaigns and instead sought to frame their cause using the secular language of rights. This strategy was used most successfully to pass Colorado's Amendment 2 in 1992 (Herman 1997, 137–169). During this campaign, conservatives convinced voters to pass a constitutional amendment prohibiting gays and lesbians from being recognized as a protected class by framing gay rights as excessive, "special rights." Although these arguments were made without using overtly homophobic language, they still communicated the message that gays and lesbians were deviant others, pushing for special privileges that infringed on the legitimate rights of responsible, disciplined citizens (Schacter 1994; Goldberg-Hiller and Milner 2003). Gay rights advocates countered by shifting the debate to the courtroom, where they could more easily unpack the discriminatory logic underlying conservative rights discourse (Gerstmann 1999, 99–127; Andersen 2005, 143–174). This approach proved successful—the Supreme Court struck down Amendment 2 as unconstitutional before it went into effect (*Romer v. Evans* 1996). As we shall see, this dynamic has shaped the more recent debate over marriage equality as well.

SEX PERVERTS AND CRIMES AGAINST NATURE

In the Western legal tradition, being viewed as a responsible citizen deserving of equal rights has required one to discipline her sexuality (Foucault 1990).

Typically, this has meant confining sexual activity to the boundaries of heterosexual marriage. Those who do not do this have traditionally been seen by the state as morally inferior or deviant and thus undeserving of equal citizenship status (Merry 2000, 221–257; Darian-Smith 2010, 115–147). Early in the nation's history, homosexuality was just one of a number of "deviant" sexual practices prohibited by the state. American colonies adopted English laws against sodomy, or "buggery," and other "crimes against nature." These laws criminalized not just homosexual acts but all sex that took place outside of marriage along with all nonreproductive sex—even when it occurred between married, consenting adults.

Laws prohibiting homosexuality were harsh—in many cases the penalty for a violation was death. Their effectiveness against gays and lesbians was minimal, though, because homosexuality was a taboo subject, and few people risked identifying themselves publicly as gay at that time. Furthermore, early America was a sparsely populated, largely agrarian society. This made it difficult for gays and lesbians to meet each other and kept gay life invisible to most Americans. It was only after the Industrial Revolution spurred the growth of large, cosmopolitan cities that visible gay subcultures began to emerge in places such as New York's Greenwich Village (Chauncey 1995). Here gay individuals could, for the first time, interact with each other as openly gay.[1] This allowed for the creation of a positive sense of gay identity and the development of a community support structure that would be crucial to later efforts to agitate for equal rights.

These gay communities were tolerated during the late nineteenth and early twentieth century, but in the aftermath of the Great Depression, gays and lesbians began to be seen by many as a symptom of the country's moral decline (Charles 2015). As a result, laws against sodomy and other forms of "sexual perversion" began to be more aggressively enforced against them (Chauncey 2004, 5–22). Inspired by the work of earlier moral crusaders such as Anthony Comstock, who founded the New York Society for the Suppression of Vice and was responsible for passing federal laws against "obscene" materials being sent through the mail, reformers started to crack down on gay establishments and individuals. Many government entities passed laws against sodomy and began prohibiting bars from selling alcohol to gay individuals during this time. Police used these laws as a pretext for harassing and arresting gays and lesbians. They repeatedly raided establishments where gays and lesbians were known to congregate and closed down gay bars. Undercover officers often infiltrated gay establishments and arrested individuals for kissing, holding hands, or dancing with members of the same gender.

Those suspected of homosexual activity risked jail or, perhaps worse, being publicly exposed as gay. Having their sexual orientation revealed publicly could result in individuals having to register as sex offenders, being ostracized by friends and family, being evicted from their homes, and losing their jobs. Most professions openly discriminated against gays and lesbians at that time. Gays were prohibited from serving in the military, and professional licensing laws were designed to prevent them from becoming doctors, dentists, pharmacists, lawyers, and teachers in most states (Berube 2010). During the Cold War era, concerns that the government could be infiltrated by Communist sympathizers led President Dwight D. Eisenhower to issue an executive order prohibiting the hiring of federal employees who committed acts of "sexual perversion." The government used this provision to fire any worker suspected of being gay. It was believed that these "sex perverts" were security risks whose questionable moral standards made them vulnerable to manipulation and disloyalty. During the height of the Red Scare more people lost their jobs under suspicion of being gay than for being Communist (Johnson 2004).

This crackdown on gays and lesbians was justified by popular conceptions of them as "perverts" and "sex deviants" (Fejes 2008, 11–52). Of particular concern were fears that gays and lesbians sought to prey on children. In the decades following World War II, moral panic over child sex crimes gripped the nation. News outlets sensationalized cases of child molestation and abuse. Gays and lesbians were often identified as the perpetrators of these crimes, with many stories portraying them as violent predators who lurked in the shadows and sought to prey on innocent children (Jenkins 2004). This coverage skewed public perception of child molestation, making these relatively rare occurrences seem more prevalent and ignoring the fact that child sex crimes are most often committed by friends or family members, not strangers.

Combating these negative stereotypes was made difficult by discriminatory policies, such as the Motion Picture Production Code, that prevented positive images of gays and lesbians from being presented to the public. Popularly known as the "Hays Code" after Hollywood censor William H. Hays, this code prohibited the subject of homosexuality from being openly broached in film, television, or radio from 1934 to 1968 (Russo 1987).[2] During this time, any mention of homosexuality was deemed obscene and thus unfit for public consumption. Films and literature with gay themes were destroyed or censored.

This policy reinforced the idea that homosexuality was an extreme perversion, not to be discussed publicly, even in a nonsexual manner. Limiting the visibility of gay life also made it easier to depict gays and lesbians as deviants who lived a shadowy lifestyle on the margins of society.

These harmful stereotypes were further perpetrated by the medical and psychiatric community. Psychiatrists had historically viewed homosexuality as a mental disorder and developed various treatments designed to "help" gay individuals overcome their sexual urges.[3] In 1952, the American Psychiatric Association released its first *Diagnostic and Statistical Manual of Mental Disorders* (*DSM-I*). It listed homosexuality as a mental illness caused by poor parenting or individual maladjustment (American Psychiatric Association 1952).[4] As a result of these views, gays and lesbians were deemed "mental defectives" by the medical community. Those suspected of engaging in homosexual activity were often required by law to see a therapist who would provide treatment. They could even be legally confined to mental institutions for indefinite periods. In addition to subjecting gays and lesbians to unwanted and unnecessary medical procedures, the designation of homosexuality as a mental disorder also created a perception that being gay was something one could develop (or grow out of) over time, not something that was innate.[5] This logic created a popular concern that anyone could potentially be at risk of becoming gay and fed fears that gays and lesbians would try to recruit unwitting children into their ranks.

THE BIRTH OF THE GAY RIGHTS MOVEMENT

According to popular mythology, the gay rights movement began with the 1969 riots at the Stonewall Inn in New York City (see, for example, Carter 2004).[6] Before then, the story goes, there was little organized resistance to the discriminatory treatment of gays and lesbians. Most gay individuals were afraid to push aggressively for rights at that time because they did not want to risk having their sexual orientation disclosed publicly. Stonewall was a dramatic departure from this norm. The riots began after New York police raided the Stonewall Inn, a popular meeting spot for gays and lesbians in Greenwich Village. Such raids were fairly commonplace during this time because New York law prohibited bars from serving alcohol to gay men or lesbians. Patrons of these bars typically complied with police demands in hopes that they could deal with the issue quietly, either by being given a warning or at worst having to pay a small fine. An arrest for "sexual perversion" was a minor offense, and disputing it risked publicly exposing one's sexual orientation, which had more serious consequences. On this day, however, frustration with police harassment boiled over. As the raid commenced, an angry crowd began to gather outside of the bar. Some of Stonewall's patrons resisted arrest, and the police responded with brutality. This sparked the crowd to riot and fueled violent protests that lasted three days. In the aftermath of these riots, members of the gay community began organizing, using the moment as a catalyst for a larger gay rights movement.

This depiction of events makes for a compelling story, but it greatly exaggerates the impact of the Stonewall riots. A number of scholars have shown that the gay rights movement did not emerge spontaneously in reaction to this event, as is popularly believed, but was painstakingly built by activists who had begun fighting against discrimination long before the riots took place (D'Emilio 1983; Armstrong 2002). Much of this activism occurred not in New York City, as the Stonewall narrative suggests, but in California, where many gay rights activists were initially unaware of, or deeply ambivalent about, the riots (Armstrong and Crage 2006, 741–743). Instead of viewing Stonewall as the inspiration for the radical gay rights activism of the late 1960s and early 1970s, it should be more properly understood as a product of this activism. Radical gay rights activists living in New York City at the time of Stonewall fanned the flames of the riots, helping to create the event in the first place. Afterward, they recognized the potential symbolic significance of Stonewall and made a concerted effort to mythologize it (Armstrong and Crage 2006). The annual gay pride events commemorating the riots are primarily responsible for perpetuating the legendary status of Stonewall today.

A more accurate portrayal of the origins of the gay rights movement must begin nearly two decades before Stonewall. This early gay rights activism was conducted in large part by "homophile" organizations such as the Mattachine Society, founded by a group of gay men in Los Angeles in 1950, and the Daughters of Bilitis, founded by lesbians in San Francisco in 1955. These organizations had to contend with a society extremely hostile to them as well as a gay population that did not really see itself as a distinct minority group and was largely ambivalent about the idea of openly challenging discriminatory treatment (Armstrong 2002, 31–55). As such, they struggled to attract members and had to take extraordinary measures to preserve their anonymity. These were fairly conservative organizations with modest goals. They were primarily focused on increasing tolerance for gays and lesbians rather than gaining widespread acceptance. Most of the members of this early homophile movement wanted only to be able to live a quiet, closeted lifestyle, relatively free from police harassment. They did not seek to challenge the established order (Adam 1987, 60–68). Despite these limitations, the homophile movement played a critical role in laying the groundwork for the more radical gay activism that would emerge during the late 1960s. They succeeded in promoting the idea that gays and lesbians were a minority group entitled to the same basic rights to meet collectively and promote their viewpoints as members of other minority groups. This might seem like a small victory, but for a gay population whose very right to exist was typically denied by state actors at the time, it was a crucial achievement (Armstrong 2002, 38–41).

In the late 1960s more radical activists began questioning the conservative approach of these homophile organizations. Groups championing the cause of "gay liberation" began advocating for a positive image of gays and lesbians as a means of challenging discriminatory treatment and ending antigay harassment. In contrast to the homophile organizations that came before them, leaders of this movement sought to make homosexuality more visible and more acceptable. They encouraged gay individuals to "come out" to friends and family so that they could challenge popular conceptions of themselves as deviant (Armstrong 2002, 56–80). Calls for "gay liberation" or "gay power" were inspired by New Left organizations prominent at the time, including black nationalist groups such as the Black Liberation Front. The new gay advocacy groups typically argued for a distinctive and positive conception of gay identity. They aggressively challenged established norms of gender and sexual expression (Wittman 1970; Kissack 1995).

Many activists who would go on to lead the gay rights movement, including some involved in the older homophile movement, saw this approach as too radical. They sought instead to counter conceptions of gays and lesbians as deviant by minimizing their distinctiveness—depicting themselves as normal, hardworking Americans with the same goals and values as everyone else.[7] This approach would eventually win out, in large part because its more moderate ideals were less threatening to the established order and thus held more political promise than that of the radical reformers (Armstrong 2002, 81–96).

The gay rights movement that emerged out of the early 1970s had two primary goals: repealing laws against sodomy and prohibiting discrimination based on sexual orientation. These rights for gays and lesbians were painfully slow in coming, however. Illinois became the first state to repeal its law against sodomy in 1962, but no other state did so until the early 1970s, and fourteen states still had such laws on the books when the Supreme Court ruled them unconstitutional in 2003 (*Lawrence v. Texas*). Some cities began passing municipal ordinances protecting gays and lesbians from discrimination in the late 1970s. However, no protections existed at the state level until Wisconsin passed a law in 1982 prohibiting both public and private companies from discriminating against individuals on the basis of sexual orientation. Most of the movement's earliest victories came by way of statutes passed in large cities with sizable gay and lesbian populations or in small, liberal "college towns." These modest achievements provoked a quick response from the religious right.

ANITA BRYANT AND THE COUNTERMOBILIZATION AGAINST GAY RIGHTS

The first antigay activist to gain national prominence was Anita Bryant, who would become the face of the 1977 campaign against Miami-Dade County's antidiscrimination ordinance. This conflict began in 1976, after a small coalition of activists placed a proposal for a law protecting gays and lesbians from discrimination in housing and employment before the Miami-Dade County Board of Commissioners. A preliminary version of the bill was unanimously approved by the nine-member board, and a public hearing and final vote on the measure was set to take place in January of the following year. This vote was expected to be largely perfunctory—similar laws had been passed without incident in other locations, and there was little reason to believe Miami would be any different. Things changed, though, after Bryant, a popular singer and former beauty pageant winner who had become a national celebrity as a spokesperson for Florida orange juice, learned of the board's decision. Bryant was a political neophyte who had shown little interest in local issues before.[8] However, after being informed of the bill by her pastor, she said that she felt compelled by God to do something to stop it. She took part in the public hearing on the law, and her passionate opposition to it caught the attention of Robert Brake, a local activist preparing a ballot measure designed to repeal the ordinance. After the board passed the bill by a vote of five to three, Brake asked Bryant to lead his campaign. She immediately agreed.

Bryant's opposition to gay rights was motivated by her strong evangelical Christian faith. She believed that the Bible condemned homosexuality as sinful. She saw laws protecting gays and lesbians from discrimination as providing approval for their deviant lifestyle and infringing on her right to be protected from such activities. Bryant was particularly concerned with how such laws would affect children. She thought gays and lesbians sought to prey on innocent children and believed that any law that lent them legitimacy would encourage this abhorrent behavior.

Religious beliefs are often cited as justification for opposition to gay rights today, but at the time such arguments were less common. Christian leaders such as Jerry Falwell and James Dobson began encouraging their flocks to take a more active role in politics during the 1970s, but the religious right was still in its infancy as a political movement at this time (Diamond 1995). Many Americans thought of religion as a deeply personal matter that should be kept separate from the political realm and found the cavalier way with which Bryant openly mixed religion and politics somewhat distasteful (Fejes 2008, 71–88). Bryant's association of religion with antigay discourse was also a bit of a novelty at the time. Those religious individuals who had begun taking a more active role in politics were, at this point, focused primarily on issues such as school prayer and abortion. Although most churches deemed acts of "sexual deviance" immoral, they had no defined policy against homosexuality.[9] Antigay politics would not become a focal point of the religious right until the 1980s (Herman 1997, 25–59).

Brake and Bryant orchestrated a well-organized and effective campaign in Miami. Following the bill's passage, Bryant founded Save Our Children Inc., an organization dedicated to opposing the antidiscrimination ordinance, and began gathering signatures for a ballot measure designed to repeal it. She needed 10,000 signatures to qualify the measure for a special election—she got more than 60,000. Save Our Children drew on Miami's evangelical community to build a base of enthusiastic supporters. This core of dedicated supporters allowed the campaign members to raise more money than their opponents and ensured that they would have an effective "get-out-the-vote" effort on Election Day. This was a particularly important factor given that the vote would take place during a local, special election—the type of event that typically garners very low voter turnout.

The campaign developed a message designed to cause voters to see homosexuality not as a benign activity but as a dangerous threat. As the name of Bryant's organization suggests, this message emphasized the ordinance's supposedly negative impact on children. The law's primary purpose was to protect gays and lesbians from discrimination, a purpose that does not seem to have an obvious relationship to children. However, Bryant, whose children attended a local parochial school in Miami-Dade County, feared that this new law would require such institutions to hire openly gay schoolteachers. She argued that this would infringe on her parental right to direct her children's moral education and put them at risk of abuse. In making this argument, the campaign constructed a familiar image of gays and lesbians as dangerous sexual predators. An advertisement sponsored by Save Our Children that ran in the *Miami Herald* during the campaign highlighted many of these concerns:

> THERE IS NO "HUMAN RIGHT" TO CORRUPT OUR CHILDREN. . . . Many parents are
> confused and don't know the real dangers posed by many homosexuals—and
> perceive them as all being gentle, non-aggressive types. THE OTHER SIDE OF THE
> HOMOSEXUAL COIN IS A HAIR-RAISING PATTERN OF RECRUITMENT AND OUTRIGHT
> SEDUCTION AND MOLESTATION, A GROWING PATTERN THAT PREDICTABLY WILL
> INTENSIFY IF SOCIETY APPROVES LAWS GRANTING LEGITIMACY TO THE SEXUALLY
> PERVERTED. (as quoted in Clendinen and Nagourney 1999, 304)

This portrayal taps into long-standing discriminatory stereotypes of gays and lesbians as child molesters who seek to recruit children into their deviant lifestyle. It casts sexual orientation as a learned behavior, not something innate. According to this conception, older gays and lesbians seek to prey on vulnerable young children in much the same way a drug dealer might encourage a new client to experiment with drugs. In fact, Bryant compared gays and lesbians to "prostitutes, pimps, and drug pushers" at several points during the campaign (Fejes 2008, 113). These arguments resonated with many voters in large part because they repeated familiar tropes about gays and lesbians well known in the popular culture at the time.

Bryant reinforced these arguments when talking to the press during the campaign. She read a number of carefully prepared statements that emphasized the recruitment concern. She argued that because "homosexuals cannot procreate, the only way to increase their numbers is to recruit, and what better place to do this than in the schools?" and that "some of the stories I could tell you of child recruitment and child abuse by homosexuals would turn your stomach" (as quoted in Clendinen and Nagourney 1999, 303). Her unscripted remarks were even more inflammatory. During the campaign she referred to gays and lesbians as "human garbage," said that the Miami ordinance would allow them to have "intercourse with beasts," proclaimed that God had inflicted a drought on California because the state was tolerant of gays, and said that "gay folks [would] just as soon kill you as look at you" (as quoted in Clendinen and Nagourney 1999, 306). Despite these overtly discriminatory appeals, the initiative passed overwhelmingly, with nearly 70 percent voting to repeal the antidiscrimination law.

The success of Bryant's Miami campaign sent a troubling signal to advocates of gay rights. Many interpreted this success as a sign that the public was not yet ready to accept gay rights. Bryant herself seemed to interpret her victory this way. Buoyed by her success in Miami, she began to challenge antidiscrimination laws in a host of other cities as well. Bryant proved to be an incredibly divisive figure, however. Although she spurred the initial movement against gay rights, her tendency to make extreme comments and rely on overtly discriminatory stereotypes made her a bit of a liability for opponents of gay rights. Many Americans saw her as a symbol of bigotry, and her presence often drew angry crowds of opponents. In light of this, members of campaigns against antidiscrimination ordinances in cities such as Eugene, Oregon, and Wichita, Kansas, asked that she not appear at their events (Clendinen and Nagourney 1999, 328–330). With Bryant sitting on the sidelines, Minneapolis–St. Paul, Wichita, and Eugene all repealed antidiscrimination ordinances in 1978 through the ballot measure process.

Bryant remains a controversial figure today. She is regarded as a pioneer by many who oppose gay rights and as a villain by those who support them. Her strategy of using church networks and religious arguments to mobilize antigay sentiment was used heavily by conservatives in the debate over marriage equality. Although more recent campaigns against gay rights have toned down Bryant's extremist rhetoric, her arguments remain influential for many opponents of same-sex marriage. As we shall see, arguments made in favor of Proposition 8 in California and Question 1 in Maine featured many of the same themes used by Bryant in 1977.

Bryant's influence might be a bit overstated, though. Although her strategy led to victory in Miami, opponents of gay rights struggled to duplicate these results (Stone 2012, 12–23). In retrospect, Bryant's victory seems less the product of a brilliant campaign strategy and more the result of her having faced an opposition with considerable limitations. There was very little in the way of an organized gay rights movement in Miami in 1977. The organizations that did exist spent most of their time arguing with each other about how best to respond to Bryant (Fejes 2008, 115–151). This made it very difficult for the campaign to present a united front. Although national gay rights activists were brought in to assist the campaign, their efforts were often frustrated by local members who made radical statements questioning the value of the nuclear family and promoting "alternative lovestyles" such as "swinging" (Fejes 2008, 70). This had the effect of alienating more moderate voters and lent credence to Bryant's conception of gays and lesbians as sexual deviants seeking to foist a radically different lifestyle on the public. Bryant's approach worked well in this environment. Her extreme rhetoric energized her base of evangelical supporters, and her disorganized opponents were unable to match these efforts. However, states with more established gay rights organizations were much better prepared to combat this approach.

JOHN BRIGGS AND THE LIMITS OF ANTIGAY DISCOURSE

Inspired by Bryant's campaign, John Briggs, a state senator from Orange County, California, introduced Proposition 6 in 1978. Popularly known as the "Briggs Initiative," Proposition 6 sought to allow public school boards to dismiss teachers who "publicly admit to being homosexual or promote a homosexual lifestyle." Briggs's motivation for offering the initiative is not completely clear. Whereas Bryant was driven to oppose gay rights by her sincere religious beliefs, Briggs appears to have been much more of an opportunist. He had designs on the governorship and saw this initiative as a way to gain national attention and propel himself to higher office.[10] Briggs remained an outspoken critic of gay rights even after the conclusion of his campaign, however, suggesting that his motivations were not purely political. He would go on to help form the Traditional Values Coalition, which continues to be a prominent national organization opposing gay rights today, with more than 31,000 churches as members (McGirr 2001, 259).

Briggs, who had worked with Bryant during her Miami campaign, adopted a similar strategy to build support for Proposition 6. He used religious appeals to help mobilize his base of supporters in California's sizable evangelical community and worked to depict gays and lesbians as threats to children. Briggs named the committee he formed in support of his initiative Defend

Our Children and developed campaign arguments that emphasized gays and lesbians' supposed desire to recruit and molest children. During the campaign Briggs wrote a column for the *Los Angeles Times,* "Deviants Threaten the American Family," that contained many familiar themes:

> Children in this country spend more than 1,200 hours a year in classrooms. A teacher who is a known homosexual will automatically represent that way of life to young, impressionable students at a time when they are struggling with their own critical choice of sexual orientation. When children are constantly exposed to such homosexual role models, they may well be inclined to experiment with a lifestyle that could lead to disaster for themselves and ultimately, for society as a whole. (as quoted in Clendinen and Nagourney 1999, 381)

This approach seemed effective, initially. The initiative enjoyed considerable support from conservative Christians based primarily in Southern California and looked to have strong support statewide as well. Early polls showed it passing with as much as 70 percent of the vote. Many in California's gay and lesbian community resigned themselves to defeat.

Opposition to the initiative would be much stronger and more effective in California than it had been in Miami, however. Bryant's campaign had struck down a law that benefited a county with a fairly small and politically apathetic gay community; Briggs's law would affect all of California, a large state at the center of the gay rights movement. California was home to a sizable gay community with many powerful gay rights activists who were veterans of previous campaigns. Prominent leaders such as Harvey Milk—the first openly gay man elected to public office in California—worked tirelessly in opposition to the measure, organizing rallies, giving speeches, and challenging Briggs's arguments directly during numerous debates held over the course of the campaign.[11]

Gay rights activists had learned some important lessons from their failed fight against Bryant in Miami. One such lesson was the need for a much more professional and disciplined campaign dedicated to presenting a "nonthreatening" image of gays and lesbians to the average voter. As part of this effort, many leaders insisted that gays and lesbians should play a less visible role in the campaign. David Goodstein, chair of the board for the *Advocate,* the largest gay newsmagazine in the country, and also one of the principal financiers of the No on 6 campaign, wrote a column arguing forcefully for such an approach:

The "gay extremists" and "hedonists"—the drag queens, the advocates of man-boy sex, the feminist-separatists, the leather enthusiasts, the sexual liberationists, the Marxists—must keep out of sight and leave it to the professionals to try to salvage the campaign. Straight people are put off by homosexuals. . . . Almost all gay people could help best by maintaining low profiles. . . . Let our friends and allies speak to the non-gay issues. . . . We can do a lot to assist John Briggs by being visible and in any way stereotypical." (as quoted in Clendinen and Nagourney 1999, 382)

This controversial position directly contradicted the radical calls for gay liberation and gay pride, a prominent part of the early gay liberation movement. Many in the gay community bristled at being told to stay in the background, believing that increasing their visibility was key to the long-term success of the movement. As we shall see in Chapter 5 of this book, this tension would reemerge during the most recent debate over same-sex marriage.

In addition to minimizing the visibility of the more radical elements of the gay community, opponents of Proposition 6 also chose to break from previous campaigns that had typically framed gay rights as "human rights." Those in charge of the campaign argued that voters had not seemed responsive to these rights claims in the past and advocated instead for a strategy that framed their cause using the discourse of "privacy." Focusing on privacy would, they reasoned, allow them to capitalize on the overly broad language used in the hastily crafted initiative. Briggs might have intended for his law to apply only to those who were openly gay, but the wording of Proposition 6 allowed school boards to dismiss anyone who "publicly supported homosexuality." This could result in anyone who said anything that could be construed as supportive of gays and lesbians being dismissed from her job, even those who were not gay themselves. This sweeping impact would, opponents argued, violate privacy and undermine school discipline. It might even allow students to blackmail their teachers by threatening to accuse them of being gay or supporting homosexuality.

These arguments proved compelling to moderate voters who might not have been comfortable with the concept of homosexuality but who were troubled by the potentially sweeping impact of the initiative. Perhaps most importantly, these arguments proved compelling to the extremely popular former California governor and future US president Ronald Reagan. He agreed to a meeting with opponents of Proposition 6 and afterward released a statement denouncing the initiative. In his statement, Reagan argued that Proposition 6 was "unnecessary" because legal protections for children already existed and that it had the "potential of infringing on basic rights of privacy and perhaps even constitutional rights" (Clendinen and Nagourney 1999, 387). Other political leaders followed Reagan's lead, and public opinion quickly swung against the initiative.

As the campaign wore on, it became clear that Proposition 6 was going to fail. Mainstream political figures from both parties began speaking out against the initiative. Briggs became increasingly desperate, and his arguments became even more inflammatory. He said that "homosexuality is like a creeping disease," that homosexuals have a "proclivity for having sex with young boys," and that "20 percent of the teachers in Los Angeles were practicing homosexuals" (Clendinen and Nagourney 1999, 388). California's gay rights activists were able to capitalize on these overtly homophobic and discriminatory arguments. Milk and others like him calmly and effectively countered these increasingly outlandish claims, contrasting these extreme arguments with the more measured and professional tone of the No on 6 campaign. They portrayed Briggs and Bryant as hateful extremists pushing laws that were hurtful and unnecessary (Stone 2012, 41–62). This proved an effective strategy—the initiative would ultimately fail by more than 1 million votes.

Bryant showed that religious language could be used to effectively mobilize a base of evangelical Christian supporters against gay rights. Briggs showed, however, that an ability to effectively mobilize supporters is not the only requirement for a successful ballot measure campaign. Successful campaigns must also be able to develop a message that appeals to moderate and undecided voters. Although the overtly discriminatory language of Bryant and Briggs did a good job of accomplishing the former goal, their strategy worked against the latter. This was particularly problematic in a state such as California, where a well-organized gay rights movement was able to launch a sophisticated and effective campaign in opposition to the measure. The No on 6 campaign was further aided by support from the powerful California Teachers Union and endorsements from prominent politicians such as Reagan, then-president Jimmy Carter, and former president Gerald Ford.

THE HIV/AIDS EPIDEMIC

During the 1970s, the drive for gay rights grew into a powerful national movement. Gay rights activists won a number of victories at the local level and successfully fended off attacks from their opponents. The 1980s should have been a time in which this budding movement would finally be able to make major breakthroughs at the state and national level—but it was not to be. Instead, efforts to agitate on behalf of gay rights became supplanted by efforts to raise awareness of and fight against a worsening HIV/AIDS epidemic. The disease probably set the cause of gay rights back decades—subjecting the community to increased stigma, completely dominating the time and resources of the movement, and killing many of its brightest leaders.

HIV/AIDS also had a profound impact on how many gays and lesbians viewed themselves and their movement. Seeing their friends and loved ones die of this disease radicalized many previously apathetic individuals in the gay and lesbian community. The experience of being denied the right to make medical decisions for a partner dying of AIDS or to administer her estate after death would cause many gays and lesbians to push more aggressively for the legalization of same-sex marriage in the 1990s (Chauncey 2004). The revelation that the disease was sexually transmitted led a number of activists within the gay community to criticize the central role sexual promiscuity and experimentation had come to play in the lives of many gay men in particular (Kramer 1985; Shilts 1987). This critique exacerbated the familiar fissure between more moderate assimilationists and more radical liberation-minded activists—a fissure that has continued to have enormous impact on the long-term trajectory of the gay rights movement.

With the gay rights movement increasingly focused on combating the HIV/AIDS epidemic, the 1980s could have been an opportune time for their opponents to push for more draconian laws against them. The disease caused widespread panic in the general public. Little was known about it initially, other than that it was most common within the gay population and that it was fatal. Yet, opponents of gay rights had few successes during that time. This might be because antigay activism had not yet grown into an organized national movement. The campaigns of the 1970s had been led primarily by local leaders and one national celebrity—Bryant. When Bryant was forced to retreat from the national spotlight in the face of growing outrage over her extreme positions[12] and a messy divorce from her husband, antigay activism lost considerable momentum. It would not be until the 1990s, when organizations such as Dobson's Focus on the Family and Pat Robertson's Christian Coalition started funding efforts to oppose gay rights, that antigay activism would begin to grow into an organized national movement.

In addition to their organizational issues, opponents of gay rights also continued to marginalize themselves with their use of overtly homophobic and discriminatory appeals. At this time, most ardent opponents of gay rights were motivated primarily by their religious beliefs, and they made little effort to hide that fact. Many saw the HIV/AIDS epidemic as "God punishing homosexuals" for their "sinful" lifestyle (Clendinen and Nagourney 1999, 472–493). In the handful of ballot measure campaigns that took place during that period, opponents of gay rights typically described gays and lesbians as "dirty" or "diseased" and depicted them as a threat to public health. One such initiative was California's Proposition 64 in 1986. The measure proposed that individuals with HIV or AIDS be forced to register with the state of California, allowed them to be quarantined from the general public, and restricted the types of occupations in which they could participate. Lyndon LaRouche, the initiative's sponsor, used extreme, scientifically unfounded arguments to defend his initiative, arguing that a "person with AIDS running around is like a person with a machine gun running around shooting up the neighborhood" (as quoted in Stone 2012, 17–18). The initiative was easily defeated 71 percent to 29 percent. It was placed back on the ballot by LaRouche two years later, when it was defeated again.

GAY RIGHTS AS "SPECIAL RIGHTS"

During the 1990s opposition to gay rights grew into a more disciplined national movement, led by activists who would increasingly come to see their cause not just as a religious issue but also as one involving fundamental rights. These changes did not happen overnight, however. Beginning in the late 1980s, opponents of gay rights became increasingly divided over how best to frame their positions. Members of one camp continued to present their opposition to gay rights using primarily religious and moral language. Others thought the movement could benefit from a more secular, rights-based approach. This divide was seen most clearly in the different tactics of two groups agitating against gay rights at the time, the Oregon Citizens Alliance (OCA) and Colorado for Family Values (CFV).

The OCA was founded by Lon Mabon in 1986. Mabon was a conservative Christian who used the OCA as a vehicle for launching a series of failed senatorial campaigns and as a means of placing antigay and antiabortion ballot measures before voters. During the 1980s and 1990s the OCA sponsored a number of antigay ballot measures in Oregon. These campaigns were notable for their reliance on overtly discriminatory and homophobic arguments. The OCA's greatest victory came in 1988, when it successfully passed Measure 8. The measure repealed an executive order prohibiting discrimination against gay employees in state government and prohibited such protections from being granted in the future.[13] In 1992 the OCA sponsored Ballot Measure 9, which sought to amend the state's constitution to prohibit gays and lesbians from being granted protections from discrimination. The OCA framed its support for Measure 9 using overtly homophobic and moralistic language. Arguments made by the OCA during the campaign explicitly linked homosexuality to pedophilia, promiscuity, and a propensity to murder (Schacter 1994, 285; Douglass 1997). The wording of the amendment itself reflected this approach. It stated in part that the "State Department of Higher Education . . . recognizes homosexuality, pedophilia, sadism, and masochism as abnormal, wrong, unnatural, and perverse and that these behaviors are to be discouraged and avoided" (Oregon State Library 1992). Measure 9 lost 56 percent to 44 percent.[14] The OCA would sponsor two more statewide antigay ballot measures in 1994, one in Oregon and one in the neighboring state of Idaho—both failed.

The same year the OCA introduced Ballot Measure 9 in Oregon, CFV introduced Amendment 2 in Colorado. This amendment was placed on the ballot after antidiscrimination ordinances were passed in the cities of Aspen, Boulder, and Denver. As was the case with the Oregon measure, proponents of Amendment 2 saw it as a means of reversing these gains and preventing the passage of any new antidiscrimination laws. In contrast to the Oregon campaign, however, proponents of Amendment 2 were careful to frame their arguments using the language of rights and to avoid the use of moral appeals or discriminatory stereotypes (Herman 1997, 137–169). In contrast to the inflammatory language of Measure 9, the wording of Amendment 2 was much more legalistic. It stated that the amendment would "prohibit the state of Colorado . . . from adopting or enforcing any law or policy which provides that homosexual, lesbian, or bisexual orientation, conduct, or relationships constitutes or entitles a person to claim any minority or protected status, quota preferences, or discrimination" (Colorado State Legislative Council 1992).

CFV built its campaign in support of Amendment 2 around the argument that antidiscrimination laws provided excessive, "special rights" to gays and lesbians. This strategy was the brainchild of Tony Marco, an evangelical Christian who helped found CFV in Colorado. Marco had long argued for a more rights-based approach to opposing gay rights, believing that it would lead to greater electoral success. Not everyone in CFV agreed with him, however. The decision was the subject of much internal debate, with many arguing that abandoning the moral arguments of previous campaigns would make it difficult for them to excite their base of evangelical supporters (Herman 1997, 144).[15] However, the rights-based approach of CFV proved successful. Colorado voters passed Amendment 2 by 54 percent to 46 percent. This strategy was copied by activists working in other states as well. Opponents of gay rights in Cincinnati used the same approach to pass Ballot Issue 3 the following year (Dugan 2005), and activists in Maine used this strategy to convince voters to repeal newly passed gay rights ordinances both in 1998 and in 2000.[16]

This transition to a more rights-based approach had a profound effect on the conservative activists who would come to lead the fight against same-sex marriage.[17] Consequently, the logic of "special rights" is worth exploring in a bit more detail here. Supporters of gay rights have long used a civil rights model to agitate for greater equality. This model argues that because gays and lesbians are members of a historically oppressed minority group, they will never achieve equal rights if they do not have antidiscrimination statutes to protect them. Such a strategy draws explicit parallels between the plight of gays and lesbians and the plight of other historically oppressed groups, such as African Americans and women (Gerstmann 1999). The logic of special rights offers a direct challenge to this model. It argues that gays and lesbians are not like other minority groups and are thus not in need of government protections. According to this conception, antidiscrimination laws do not grant gays and lesbians "equal rights" but instead give them "special" advantages not enjoyed by others (Schacter 1997).

In order to deny the equal rights frame to gays and lesbians, antigay activists make a distinction between them and other minority groups such as African Americans, typically viewed as entitled to some government protections (Schacter 1994; Herman 1997, 128–136). For example, they often depict gays and lesbians as members of a powerful, economically privileged class, distinct from other minority groups (Schacter 1994, 292; Hardisty 1999, 112–114; Herman 2000, 145).[18] They also argue that gays and lesbians are not politically powerless because they have undue influence in the media, are favored by "activist" judges, and have powerful allies within the Democratic Party (Herman 1997, 119–120).[19] Another popular tactic used to distinguish the legitimate civil rights claims of African Americans from the "illegitimate" rights claims of gays and lesbians is to argue that, although race and gender are immutable characteristics, homosexuality is a chosen behavior and is thus outside the realm of constitutional protection (Sprigg 2007).[20]

Using these rights-based arguments has both instrumental and constitutive implications for antigay activists. From an instrumental perspective, using this language might have allowed them to broaden their appeal and increase support for their cause. Shifting away from religious and moralistic language allowed opponents of gay rights to reach out to more moderate and secular voters, many of whom felt alienated by the tenor of their earlier campaigns (Herman 1997, 144). Although the implicit assumptions of these arguments continued to rest on an image of gays and lesbians as dangerous or threatening, the absence of overtly discriminatory stereotypes obscured this logic, increasing the legitimacy of these appeals. Depicting gays and lesbians as a privileged class also allowed antigay activists to drive a wedge between them and members of other racial and ethnic minority groups who might otherwise be sympathetic to calls for equal rights (Hardisty 1999, 101; Herman 2000, 145).[21]

These arguments also had powerful constitutive impact on the identity of opponents of gay rights. Using rights talk in this way gave them a sense of purpose by creating what Michael Rogin (1986) calls a "counter-subversive mentality." Framing their cause using the logic of special rights helps transform opponents of gay rights from a recalcitrant majority stubbornly opposing the rights of others to "cultural warriors" seeking to protect their own fundamental rights and values (Dudas 2008). The logic of special rights depicts gays and lesbians as a powerful special interest group that wants to selfishly push for "excessive" and "unnecessary" new rights. These new rights are seen as coming at the expense of the religious freedom or parental rights of those with a Christian worldview. They are also seen as undermining the traditional American values many conservatives believe to be the foundation of a moral society. This logic casts rights as a zero-sum game in which granting protections to one group necessarily comes at the expense of the rights of others. In this way, using special rights discourse creates an inversion process whereby conservatives become the victims of oppression, and gays and lesbians become the oppressors (Schacter 1997; Goldberg-Hiller and Milner 2003).

SPECIAL RIGHTS DISCOURSE IN COURT

Proponents of gay rights responded to the victories of their conservative opponents by shifting this debate to the courtroom. Soon after Amendment 2 was passed, a group of gay and lesbian individuals living in Colorado, along with a handful of cities and counties with antidiscrimination ordinances, filed suit against the law. They argued that Amendment 2 prevented gays and lesbians from using the political process in the same ways as other groups by prohibiting legislative bodies from passing laws that would grant them protected status. They contended that this violated the equal protection of gay and lesbian individuals by denying them the fundamental right to participate equally in the political process. This was a potentially powerful legal argument because laws found to impinge on fundamental rights must be evaluated by the Supreme Court using the stringent "strict scrutiny" standard of review. This standard requires the government to have a "compelling" reason to justify the burdens it is placing on the group in question and to prove that the law is "narrowly tailored" to meet that purpose. In practice very few laws are able to satisfy these exacting standards.

Amendment 2 was defended in court by the state of Colorado with the aid of several religious right organizations that had argued in favor of the law, including CFV.[22] The state argued that the law did not violate a fundamental right and should thus be evaluated by the Court using a "rational basis" standard of review. This standard is typically a mere formality for the government, which need only show that the law in question is "reasonably related" to a "legitimate government interest" in order to pass constitutional muster. The state offered a number of legitimate interests that could justify Amendment 2. Its attorneys argued that the law was meant to protect the religious liberty of those who oppose homosexuality. They also argued that it reserved scarce government resources for use against acts of discrimination directed at the members of a constitutionally recognized "suspect class"—a status not yet granted to gays and lesbians by the Court. In addition to these justifications, members of CFV also offered many of the same arguments made during the campaign regarding the need to prevent gays and lesbians from obtaining "special rights" and a desire to protect against the excessive demands of gay activists (Herman 1997, 151–157).

Amendment 2 was eventually struck down by the Colorado Supreme Court as unconstitutional.[23] The case was then appealed to the US Supreme Court, which upheld the Colorado court's decision by a vote of six to three. The majority opinion issued in this case was written by Justice Anthony Kennedy. It was a brief and somewhat vague decision that provided very little substantive discussion of the central issues of the case. The majority completely avoided the question of whether the law infringed on a fundamental right, instead deciding that Amendment 2 failed to survive even a rational basis standard of review. This was somewhat surprising because laws subjected to rational basis review are rarely found unconstitutional. The defense offered several justifications for the law that would seem to meet this largely perfunctory standard of review. Yet the Court dismissed these concerns, instead finding that Amendment 2 was motivated by a "bare desire to harm a politically unpopular group" and that such a desire "cannot constitute a legitimate government interest" (*Romer v. Evans* 1996, 634).[24]

The implications of this judgment are somewhat mixed. Although the decision was a victory for the cause of gay rights, *Romer* stands out as an anomaly among gay rights cases that have come before the Supreme Court. Most notably, it is the only gay rights case explicitly decided by the Court on equal protection grounds.[25] The majority went out of its way to stress the "unprecedented" nature of Amendment 2 (*Romer v. Evans* 1996, 633) and seemed bent on making a very narrow decision that would not carry much precedential weight. The Court also avoided the thorny question of whether gays and lesbians should be granted suspect class status. This was not surprising—the plaintiffs had not made this argument a central tenet of their case, correctly assuming that past case precedents would make granting such status unlikely. The court's unwillingness to grant gays and lesbians protected status makes a strategy based on the equal protection clause difficult for advocates of gay rights, though, because it means laws that discriminate against them are unlikely to be evaluated using the strict scrutiny standard of review.

Absent suspect class status, gay rights advocates must convince the Court they have been deprived of a fundamental right in order to receive heightened scrutiny. The fact that the Court refused to find that Amendment 2 violated a fundamental right made this strategy questionable as well. Some have argued that the gay rights movement began to focus on same-sex marriage in the 2000s in part because the Court has firmly established a fundamental right to marry (Chauncey 2004; Gerstmann 2008). This may have helped to shift the direction of the gay rights movement away from a class-based approach that argues that gays and lesbians are a disadvantaged minority group to a movement focused on arguing that gays and lesbians are "just like everyone else" and thus deserving of the same fundamental rights. As a result the due process clause has ultimately been much more important for the gay rights movement than the equal protection clause.

Despite these issues, *Romer* remains a landmark decision that continues to shape the cause of gay and lesbian rights today. The case provided gay and lesbian rights activists a clear blueprint for winning future legal battles. It freed them from having to get bogged down in a messy, legalistic debate over which level of scrutiny should be applied and instead allowed them to simply make the case that laws that infringe on gay rights serve no purpose other than a bare desire to harm gays and lesbians. This would prove a winning strategy in cases such as *Lawrence v. Texas* (2003), *United States v. Windsor* (2013), and *Obergefell v. Hodges* (2015). Each of these cases featured a majority decision written by Justice Kennedy, with copious citations from *Romer*.

For antigay activists, *Romer* represented a significant setback. Although the logic of "special rights" has considerable appeal in the popular arena of a ballot measure campaign, when placed under the gaze of judicial scrutiny, such arguments have been found lacking in substance (Gerstmann 1999, 99–127; Andersen 2005, 143–174). Perhaps the most important legal precedent established in this decision was the Court's finding that moral disapproval of gays and lesbians could not constitute a legitimate government purpose. This was a shift away from the decision rendered in *Bowers v. Hardwick* (1986), in which the Court had ruled that moral disapproval was a satisfactory justification for Georgia's antisodomy law. Though the Court took pains to indicate that the *Romer* decision did not overrule *Bowers,* the dissenting opinion written by Justice Antonin Scalia rightly pointed out the contradictory logic of the two decisions.[26] With the Court no longer willing to recognize morality as a legitimate government interest, opponents of gay rights would feel increasing pressure to find secular arguments to justify their positions in court. The rights-based appeals issued by conservatives would prove incapable of meeting this standard. This would become even more apparent during the debate over same-sex marriage, in which the rights discourse of opponents would be found by the Court as not only lacking in substance but also as harboring underlying discriminatory stereotypes—making them a serious liability for opponents of same-sex marriage.

CONCLUSION

This chapter has provided a brief examination of the gay rights movement and the opposition it has inspired. Although far from exhaustive, the analysis offered here does reveal several broad patterns that provide important context necessary for understanding the current debate over same-sex marriage. This historical analysis has shown that debates over gay rights are closely intertwined with issues of identity. The question of whether gays and lesbians deserve equal rights has frequently turned on whether they are considered to be conforming with, or presenting a threat to, prevailing cultural norms and values.[27] How gays and lesbians are perceived—both by themselves and by others—has been a dynamic and often fiercely contested process, with activists on both sides of this issue fighting to advance their particular frames of meaning and undermine opposing conceptions.

This historical analysis also makes it clear that social movements are not monoliths. Ideological differences have plagued activists on both sides of the gay rights debate. In order to show that they are deserving of equal rights, gays and lesbians have had to construct a positive image of themselves. The question of how best to go about doing this continues to be hotly debated within the gay rights movement. Some have sought to build a positive gay identity by championing a powerful image of gays and lesbians as independent individuals willing to challenge the established order by expanding our understanding of human sexuality, questioning traditional gender norms, and embracing alternative family structures (Warner 1999). This more liberation-minded approach emphasizes that gays and lesbians see the world differently and asks us to celebrate the value of these diverse viewpoints. Many within the gay rights movement have disagreed with this approach, however. Instead, they advocate for a gay identity that emphasizes that gays and lesbians are "just like everyone else" (Ghaziani 2011). Those with this more assimilation-minded viewpoint argue that sexual orientation is just one of a number of characteristics a person might have and that we should not define people based on this quality alone. Instead, we should understand gays and lesbians as "normal" citizens seeking not to challenge the established order but to join it.

In contrast, those who oppose gay rights have typically sought to frame gays and lesbians as dangerous others living a deviant lifestyle that threatens to undermine traditional values. Here again, there is disagreement over how to construct this image. Some of the most radical opponents of gay rights see gays and lesbians as sinful and depraved individuals who pose a physical threat to society. They often depict gays and lesbians as threats to children, either because they are perceived as more prone to being pedophiles or because they might seek to convince impressionable young people to join their deviant gay lifestyle (see, for example, Sprigg and Dailey 2004). Others have disagreed with this approach, choosing to focus instead on the threat gays and lesbians might pose to the rights of others. They see rights as a zero-sum game and argue that the rights claims being made by gays and lesbians are excessive because they threaten the free speech, religious liberty, or parental rights of those who disagree with their lifestyle (Goldberg-Hiller and Milner 2003).

These disagreements are motivated in part by sincere ideological differences and in part by more pragmatic concerns. Both pro- and antigay activists fear that the arguments made by the more radical elements of their respective movements will alienate potential allies and undermine their causes. Gay rights activists have responded to these concerns by discouraging more liberation-minded individuals from taking a public role in their campaigns and actively working to present an image of gays and lesbians that is less threatening to the average citizen. Opponents of gay rights have also been motivated by instrumental concerns. They realize that although overtly discriminatory and religious arguments play well with evangelical Christians, such language has a tendency to alienate more moderate voters. By couching their arguments in the secular language of rights, opponents of gay rights are able to extend their appeal beyond this base of supporters.

The historical analysis provided here also suggests that debates over gay rights have been shaped powerfully by the institutional environments in which they occur. Antigay activists seem to have the most success when debating this issue in the popular arena of a ballot measure campaign. Conversely, proponents of gay rights have been more successful when arguing their cause in the elite-centered environments of the state legislature and the courtroom. This pattern has continued to shape the more recent debate over same-sex marriage. Why does this dynamic exist? And what larger lessons can it teach us about the role that rights discourse plays in movements for social change generally? The answer to these and other questions will be taken up more fully in the remaining chapters of this book.

3. Sites of Conflict: How Institutions Shape the Same-Sex Marriage Debate

In Chapter 2 I traced the history of the gay rights movement in the United States and the countermobilization against it. In this chapter I shift my focus to the more recent debate over same-sex marriage, paying particular attention to the actions of its conservative opponents. I begin with a brief overview of the origins of the marriage equality movement and the conservative response it engendered. I then turn to a more detailed examination of the development and organizational structure of the anti-same-sex-marriage movement. I conclude this chapter by conducting an empirical examination of the institutional dynamics of this debate. To do this, I generated an original dataset and conducted a quantitative content analysis of arguments made by conservative opponents of same-sex marriage in three different institutional environments. The results of this content analysis show that conservatives are much more likely to make rights claims outside of the courtroom than they are to do so inside it and are much more likely to have success opposing same-sex marriage when they are able to mobilize their own counter-rights discourse.

These findings suggest that conservative rights discourse is more useful as a tool for mobilizing popular support outside of the courtroom than as a means of resisting legal change directly by winning favorable court decisions. I theorize that this is because institutional norms and constraints present inside the courtroom discourage conservatives from using rights discourse by subjecting these arguments to a level of scrutiny that they do not receive in more popular arenas. This suggests that institutional norms and constraints shape cultural conflicts by causing some types of arguments to be "mobilized out of politics" (Schattschneider 1960; Bachrach and Baratz 1962). This theory and its implications will be explored in more detail in the case studies presented in Chapters 4 and 5.

MARRIAGE EQUALITY AND COUNTERMOBILIZATION

The issue of same-sex marriage first exploded onto the national scene in the United States in 1993. That year the Hawai'i Supreme Court ruled that the state's prohibition on same-sex marriage discriminated against individuals on the basis of gender, a potential violation of Hawai'i's equal rights amendment (*Baehr v. Lewin* 1993). The Hawai'i Supreme Court then remanded the case back to the trial court with instructions that it determine if there was a "compelling state interest" that justified denying same-sex couples the right to marry. The trial court ultimately found that no such interest existed, but Judge Kevin Chang stayed his decision pending further review (*Baehr v. Miike* 1996). The issue became moot two years later when Hawai'i voters passed a constitutional amendment giving the state legislature the exclusive power to define marriage.[1]

The *Baehr* decision took many supporters of gay and lesbian rights by surprise. Although the ruling ultimately failed to legalize same-sex marriage in Hawai'i, favorable lower court decisions often attract media attention and act as catalysts for social movements, even if they are ultimately overturned on appeal (McCann 1994, 48–91). This case did just that, attracting national attention and showing, for the first time, that some state courts could be convinced to extend marriage rights to same-sex couples. Before the *Baehr* decision, same-sex marriage had been a fringe issue; after *Baehr,* marriage equality catapulted to the top of the agenda for many gay and lesbian rights activists.

Baehr was a remarkable decision, but it was not the first time a court had considered the issue of marriage equality. Attempts to legalize same-sex marriage in the United States go back to the 1970s. These early efforts culminated in the Minnesota case of *Baker v. Nelson* (1972). In this case the Minnesota Supreme Court unanimously ruled that there was no fundamental right to same-sex marriage. The case was automatically appealed to the US Supreme Court, but it declined to consider it "for want of a substantial federal question," making the Minnesota Supreme Court's decision binding precedent in federal cases as well.[2] Despite being a clear defeat for the cause of gay rights, this ruling had little impact on the gay and lesbian community at the time. This is because in the 1970s most gays and lesbians saw marriage as a distinctly heterosexual institution replete with sexual and gender norms they had no interest in perpetuating (Chauncey 2004, 87–136). Many activists thought that the public would never approve of same-sex marriage and that pursuing this cause was a waste of time and resources. Instead, they argued, energy should be spent on efforts to overturn prohibitions on sodomy, pass antidiscrimination ordinances, and combat the growing HIV/AIDS epidemic (Clendinen and Nagourney 1999). Over time these attitudes changed, however, and many gays and lesbians began to clamor for both the symbolic and pragmatic benefits that come with marriage (Cott 2000, 216–221; Hull 2006). Although there are still many in the gay community who see the pursuit of marriage equality as problematic,[3] by the mid-2000s a sizable majority had come to view this issue as the most important cause in the contemporary struggle for gay and lesbian rights (Chauncey 2004).

Baehr mobilized supporters of same-sex marriage, but unfortunately for them, it also mobilized their opponents. The reaction to the Hawai'i Supreme Court's ruling was swift. In 1996, as the second *Baehr* trial was being conducted, Congress passed the federal Defense of Marriage Act (DOMA). DOMA defined marriage as a union of one man and one woman at the federal level and declared that states did not have to give full faith and credit to same-sex marriages conducted in other states. The bill passed easily by a margin of 85–14 in the Senate and 342–67 in the House; it was signed into law with little controversy by Democratic president Bill Clinton (Government Accountability Office 1997). Soon after, states began passing their own "mini-DOMAs." Fifteen states passed DOMA laws in 1996, and by 2004, forty states had passed laws that defined marriage as between one man and one woman (Alliance Defense Fund 2008).

The marriage equality movement won its first lasting victories in 2003. That year two landmark gay rights court decisions were handed down: *Lawrence v. Texas* (2003) and *Goodridge v. Department of Public Health* (2003). In *Lawrence*, the US Supreme Court ruled that prohibitions on sodomy violated a constitutional right to privacy. The majority insisted that the case had "nothing to do with same-sex marriage," but Justice Antonin Scalia's scathing dissent warned that the decision could be used as a precedent for finding that gays and lesbians have a fundamental right to marry. In *Goodridge*, the Massachusetts Supreme Court showed that Scalia's concerns were warranted. It ruled that prohibitions on same-sex marriage were an unconstitutional violation of the commonwealth's equal protection clause and cited *Lawrence* as a precedent for its decision. This made Massachusetts the first state to legalize same-sex marriage. Emboldened by these victories, a group of mayors and county clerks began unilaterally issuing marriage licenses to same-sex couples in San

Francisco, California; Portland, Oregon; Sandoval, New Mexico; and New Platz, New York (Mezey 2007, 109–113). In light of these events, conservative opponents of same-sex marriage pushed for the passage of a federal marriage amendment that would enshrine in the US Constitution a definition of marriage as a union of one man and one woman. When a drive to pass such an amendment was defeated in the summer of 2004, many conservative activists turned their attention to the states.[4]

In 2004, the same-sex marriage debate entered a second phase. That year, thirteen states used the ballot measure process to ratify constitutional amendments prohibiting same-sex marriage. These amendments had little immediate impact on the status of same-sex couples living in those states because all but one of them (Oregon) had already passed a statutory prohibition on same-sex marriage. Supporters of these amendments feared that statutory prohibitions were not strong enough, however. They saw a constitutional amendment as the only way to ensure that the definition of marriage would remain "out of the hands of judges" (Bossin 2005, 414). This push to pass ballot measures prohibiting same-sex marriage was overwhelmingly successful for conservatives. Between 1998 and 2012, there were thirty-nine statewide ballot measure campaigns in thirty-five states concerning the issue of same-sex marriage. In thirty-four of those thirty-nine campaigns, voters agreed to define marriage as between one man and one woman (see Figure 3.1); in thirty of those states, voters passed constitutional amendments to that effect. These marriage amendment campaigns varied considerably in scope and intensity. Some marriage amendments were passed easily with minimal effort from supporters.[5] Others were more contentious and much closer. California's 2008 Proposition 8 campaign was the most expensive social policy initiative ever at the time and the second most expensive campaign of the 2008 election cycle, trailing only the presidential contest (Ewers 2008). In that campaign, supporters raised an astonishing $40 million, and opponents raised $45 million. The measure passed by a narrow margin, 52 percent to 48 percent (see Appendix A).

In 2012, the run of conservative victories in ballot measure campaigns came to an end. Voters in North Carolina did ratify a constitutional amendment defining marriage as between one man and one woman, but voters in Minnesota rejected a similar constitutional amendment, and three other states ratified ballot measures that had the effect of legalizing same-sex marriage. These outcomes were a major turning point for proponents of marriage equality, but there is a danger in reading too much into the results of one election cycle.

Figure 3.1. Same-Sex Marriage Ballot Measures by State

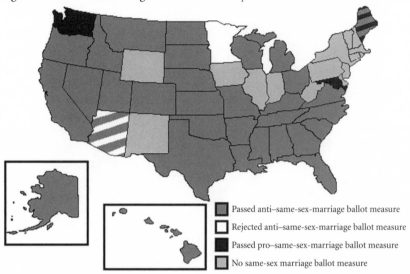

☐ Passed anti–same-sex-marriage ballot measure

☐ Rejected anti–same-sex-marriage ballot measure

■ Passed pro–same-sex-marriage ballot measure

☐ No same-sex marriage ballot measure

These victories all came by narrow margins in states carried easily by Barack Obama. It should also be noted that opponents of same-sex marriage were outspent considerably during these campaigns (see Appendix A).[6] Finally, exit polling data show that voters who saw marriage equality as a rights-based issue were substantially more likely to vote against same-sex marriage in those elections than those who did not (Hatalsky and Trumble 2012). This suggests that using rights discourse to oppose same-sex marriage in ballot measure campaigns continued to be an effective strategy for conservatives, even if they were not ultimately victorious.

The ballot measure process was a crucial tool for conservative opponents of same-sex marriage, but proponents of marriage equality had considerable success in other institutional environments. Early efforts to secure marriage equality focused primarily on litigation in state courts with liberal reputations. This led to victories in Vermont (*Baker v. Vermont* 1999)[7] and Massachusetts. A court decision would make Connecticut the second state to legalize same-sex marriage in 2008 (*Kerrigan v. Commissioner of Public Health* 2008), and Iowa would become the third in 2009 (*Varnum v. Brien* 2009). Ultimately, six states would legalize same-sex marriage through state court decisions (see Figure 3.2).

Legislation was also an effective tool for marriage equality activists. The first successful efforts to legalize same-sex marriage through legislation were

Figure 3.2. Status of Same-Sex Marriage in the United States

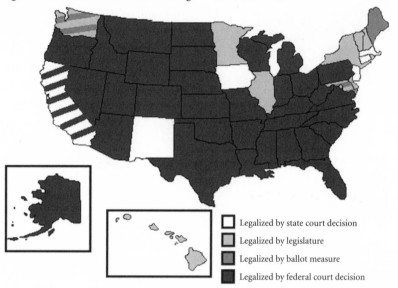

Legalized by state court decision

Legalized by legislature

Legalized by ballot measure

Legalized by federal court decision

sponsored by the Gay and Lesbian Advocates and Defenders. These efforts were part of its "Six by Twelve" campaign, marking the five-year anniversary of the *Goodridge* decision (Gay and Lesbian Advocates and Defenders 2008). The goal of this campaign was to legalize same-sex marriage in each of the six New England states by 2012.[8] The Six by Twelve campaign yielded mixed results. Governors in three states (Maine, New Hampshire, and Vermont) signed legislation legalizing same-sex marriage during a three-month period in 2009. Maine's law was later repealed, however, and heavily Catholic Rhode Island resisted the passage of marriage equality legislation until 2013. Nevertheless, the strategy of pursuing marriage equality through state legislatures would be repeated successfully in eight more states and the District of Columbia (see Figure 3.2).

The final act in the fight for marriage equality began when the US Supreme Court issued a decision striking down Section 3 of DOMA, which had defined marriage as between one man and one woman at the federal level (*United States v. Windsor* 2013). Emboldened by this decision, activists began aggressively pushing for marriage equality in federal courts across the country. Four federal circuit courts would prove receptive to these appeals, issuing decisions in 2014 recognizing that same-sex couples had a fundamental right to marry

(*Baskin v. Bogan* 2014; *Bostic v. Schaefer* 2014; *Kitchen v. Herbert* 2014; *Sevcik v. Sandoval* 2014). These results were appealed to the US Supreme Court, but it declined to hear a marriage equality case initially, perhaps because there was not yet any disagreement among the circuit courts on this issue. However, after the Sixth Circuit Court of Appeals issued a decision finding that there was no fundamental right to same-sex marriage (*Obergefell v. Hodges* 2014), the Supreme Court agreed to review the case. It ultimately overturned the Sixth Circuit Court's ruling, legalizing same-sex marriage nationwide.

ORGANIZATIONAL STRUCTURE OF CONSERVATIVE OPPOSITION TO SAME-SEX MARRIAGE

Most opposition to same-sex marriage was fueled by activists working at the state and local level and orchestrated by national organizations active on conservative social issues. These national organizations first began coordinating their efforts in 2004, when prominent leaders from a number of religious right organizations—including Gary Bauer of the American Values Committee, Richard Land of the Southern Baptists, and James Dobson of Focus on the Family—formed the Arlington Group, a loose coalition of conservative organizations dedicated to working together on the "marriage issue" (Weyrich 2004; O'Connell 2006, 8–12).[9] The Arlington Group was a key force behind the early push to pass marriage amendment ballot measures. Group members formed committees that helped initiate efforts to put marriage amendments on the ballots in eleven of the thirteen states that considered them in 2004 (Weyrich 2004; O'Connell 2006, 23–24), eight of the nine campaigns that took place in 2006 (Moore 2007, 7), and all three of the amendment campaigns in 2008 (Quist 2009). Members of the Arlington Group often lent logistical support to activists during weekly conference calls (O'Connell 2006, 11) and also provided much of the money to fund these campaigns—donations from Arlington Group affiliates frequently made up more than half of the total money raised in support of state marriage amendments (O'Connell 2006; Moore 2007; Quist 2009).

More recently, conservative opposition to same-sex marriage has been led in large part by the National Organization for Marriage (NOM). NOM was founded in 2007 as an organization dedicated to providing "organized opposition to same-sex marriage in state legislatures [and acting] as a national resource for marriage-related initiatives at the state and local level" (National Organization for Marriage 2013). Maggie Gallagher, who cofounded and later served as chair of the board at NOM, was one of the driving forces behind the organization initially. Gallagher is a well-known conservative activist with decades of experience advocating for a wide range of conservative social causes. She was one of the most outspoken critics of same-sex marriage, often appearing on national talk shows and writing articles for conservative publications such as the *National Review* and the *Weekly Standard.* NOM worked to secure the passage of California's Proposition 8 in 2008. It also contributed a considerable amount of money and expertise to the 2009 campaign in Maine and provided financial and logistical support to all five of the anti-same-sex-marriage ballot measures in 2012 (National Institute on Money in State Politics 2013). Additionally, NOM was typically the principal organization fighting against attempts to legalize same-sex marriage through legislation, often lobbying elected officials at the state level or running advertisements that implored voters to voice their opposition to such laws directly.

The most ardent opposition to marriage equality has come from members of the religious right. Churches provided a considerable amount of the funding and logistical support that fueled efforts to oppose same-sex marriage. The Church of Latter-Day Saints drew headlines for its large donations to marriage amendment campaigns (McKinley and Johnson 2008; Shoofs 2008), and Catholic organizations such as the Connecticut-based Knights of Columbus also raised sizable sums in support of the traditional definition of marriage (Kerns 2008). As we will see in Chapters 4 and 5 of this book, organizers of anti-same-sex-marriage ballot measure campaigns frequently relied on church networks to recruit volunteers and consulted church leaders when developing campaign strategy. These tactics are not new; social movements have often used church networks to help build support for their cause. Black churches played an important organizational and ideological role in the African American civil rights movement, for example (Chappell 2004). Unlike during the civil rights movement, however, most religious organizations working on the issue of same-sex marriage were seeking to preserve the status quo, not to challenge it. Although many churches have come out in favor of marriage equality, most major US religious denominations oppose same-sex marriage (Chauncey 2010, 539–558).

One of the religious right organizations most active against same-sex marriage was Colorado-based Focus on the Family. In addition to offering considerable support for marriage amendments through its parent organization, Focus on the Family also has a network of state family policy councils directly affiliated with the national organization. These regional family councils operate semiautonomously. They have local names such as California Family Council and are staffed by activists who live in the state. However, they work in close contact with their parent organization, receive logistical and financial support from Focus on the Family, and consult with national leadership when developing strategy. These groups often took the lead in organizing campaigns to pass marriage amendments in their states. Some of the most publicized and contentious marriage amendment battles, including California's 2008 Proposition 8 campaign, were organized by Focus on the Family affiliates (Quist 2009).

Efforts to oppose same-sex marriage through litigation were led primarily by two conservative legal organizations: Alliance Defending Freedom (ADF)[10] and Liberty Counsel. ADF is a legal organization dedicated to defending religious freedom and advocating for a number of conservative social causes, such as opposition to abortion and same-sex marriage. It is seen by many conservatives as a counter to the more liberal American Civil Liberties Union (Alan and Osten 2005). It was founded in 1994 by a number of prominent Christian leaders, including Dobson. Attorneys representing ADF frequently drafted amicus curiae briefs on behalf of organizations that supported same-sex marriage bans and litigated cases as counsel for an intervening party when government officials refuse to aggressively defend prohibitions on same-sex marriage. Liberty Counsel is a nonprofit law firm focused on advocating for conservative legal issues. It is closely associated with Jerry Falwell's Liberty University, a Christian university located in Lynchburg, Virginia. Like ADF, Liberty Counsel frequently helped draft amicus curiae briefs and occasionally acted as counsel for intervening parties in same-sex marriage court cases.

THE METHODOLOGY OF FRAME ANALYSIS

The foregoing analysis indicates that institutions have had a dramatic impact on the outcome of debates over same-sex marriage. In order to better understand this impact, I created an original dataset containing arguments produced by conservative opponents of same-sex marriage and conducted a content analysis of these selected texts. This content analysis provides insights into how institutions have shaped the way opponents of same-sex marriage frame this issue. Understanding how this issue has been framed is important because this discourse has instrumental impact on the outcome of same-sex marriage debates (Benford and Snow 2000; Cahill 2007; Tadlock, Gordon, and Popp 2007) and constitutive impact on the identities of activists on both sides of this issue (Scheingold 1974; McCann 1994; Engel and Munger 2003; Haltom and McCann 2004; Dudas 2008). The constitutive and instrumental implications of this discourse will be explored in more detail in Chapters 4 and 5 of this book.

Content analysis is a common technique used by scholars to study discursive frameworks. This technique requires that the researcher create several distinct categories and then separate discourse into these categories based on the presence or absence of certain characteristics (Government Accountability Office 1996, 13). This process produces a dataset that can be used to identify recurring patterns of discourse (Weber 1990). The discourse used by anti-same-sex-marriage activists was examined using frame analysis. Frames are thematic "interpretive packages" that help individuals to make sense of the world (Gamson and Modigliani 1989, 2). Scholars from a variety of different disciplines have conducted frame analyses in order to understand how individuals use language as a source of meaning production (Holsti 1969; Krippendorff 1980; Snow and Benford 1988; Gamson and Modigliani 1989; Benford and Snow 2000; Smith 2007). Organizing arguments made by opponents of same-sex marriage in terms of different thematic frameworks allows me to identify patterns of discourse, to study how institutions affect the use of these different discursive frameworks, and to explore the implications of this language.

For the purposes of this study, I identified four distinct master frames that organize conservative discourse on same-sex marriage: populist appeals, rights-based appeals, moral appeals, and constitutional arguments.[11] These frameworks reflect recurring themes in conservative political thought and ideology. Within these master frames I identified a variety of subframes that represent distinct arguments that fit within the overall theme of a particular master frame. These master frames and subframes were identified after a preliminary review of twenty documents included in the sample.

Populist appeals invoke romanticized notions of the superiority of the "common man" and seek to mobilize these individuals to fight against those seen as "subversive elites" (Kazin 1995). Documents were coded as containing elements of populism if they argued that same-sex marriage was being pushed on the average American by elites or that "the people" should be the ones to decide this issue. Within this populist framework I identified two subframes: discourse targeted at judges (including claims of judicial activism) and discourse targeted at other elites (including politicians, members of the media, and academics).

Conservative conceptions of rights often build on long-standing notions of individualism and self-reliance, which have been important components of American identity historically. Assertions of rights based on one's identity as a disadvantaged minority population are often seen as violations of this ethos of self-reliance. They are depicted as selfish attempts to "get something for nothing"—a desire for equal outcomes, not equal opportunities (Schacter 1994; Goldberg-Hiller and Milner 2003; Dudas 2008). Conservatives frequently argue that these "excessive" rights claims come at the expense of the self-reliant individual and threaten the legitimate rights of the majority of hardworking Americans. Documents were found to contain a rights-based appeal if they depicted the rights claims of gays and lesbians as excessive or "special" because they infringed on existing rights. Within this master frame, I identified four different subframes, each concerning a different conservative rights claim: free speech, religious liberty, economic rights, and parental rights.

Appeals to morality are often based on notions of American exceptionalism. Conservatives frequently argue that the United States is morally superior to the rest of the world and that the preservation of traditional values is crucial to maintaining this standing (Madsen 1998). Documents were coded as containing a moral appeal if they argued that same-sex marriage threatened the moral foundation of society. Four subframes were included in this analysis: arguments that the traditional definition of marriage is crucial to the success of the nation because it is the best environment for raising children; arguments that claim allowing same-sex marriage would lead the United States down a slippery slope toward legalizing polygamy, bestiality, or incest; arguments that traditional marriage should be preserved because it was created by God, and the United States is a Christian nation; and arguments that gays and lesbians represent a physical threat to society because they are more likely to be mentally unstable, have diseases such as HIV/AIDS, or be sexual predators and pedophiles.

Arguments based on constitutional analysis are concerned with whether a state or federal constitutional provision requires a court to recognize a right to same-sex marriage. Subframes existing within this framework include the argument that past case precedent requires the court to rule that same-sex marriage is not a fundamental right; that gays and lesbians do not constitute a "suspect class" subject to heightened judicial scrutiny; that prohibitions against same-sex marriage do not discriminate based on gender or sexual orientation; and that the full faith and credit clause does not require states to recognize same-sex marriages conducted in other states.

I selected three different categories of documents for this study: documents used in state ballot measure campaigns, documents used in court cases, and a control group of documents produced by conservative interest groups outside of the context of a particular campaign or court case. Documents were obtained online from organization websites and select databases. Online documents were chosen because the Internet is the primary medium these groups used to interact with citizens. Interest groups and legal organizations that advocate against same-sex marriage all owned and maintained detailed websites. Indeed, one of the first things an organization typically did when embarking on a ballot measure campaign against same-sex marriage was to establish a campaign website. Citizens seeking more information on the campaign were directed to these sites, which typically also included links to documents produced for use in offline media such as television and radio advertisements, letters to public officials, and articles in local newspapers.

The sample used for this study includes 95 documents from ballot measure campaigns, 98 documents from court cases, and 50 documents from interest group websites, for a total of 243 documents. Each document contained multiple arguments, and each of these arguments was coded separately as a distinct observation, for a total sample size of 976 arguments. Ballot measure campaign documents include television advertisements, campaign posters, arguments posted on official campaign websites, and arguments in support of the ballot measures posted in official voter information guides published by the states. In some cases, documents from websites since taken down were accessed using the Internet Archive, an online database that allows individuals to view websites as they looked in previous incarnations. Documents were obtained from fourteen different ballot measure campaigns.[12]

Legal documents include briefs used by defendants and intervening parties in marriage cases and amicus curiae briefs authored by interested parties and organizations in support of same-sex marriage prohibitions. These documents were obtained directly from organization websites or from the

ADF's extensive database of same-sex marriage court documents.[13] Documents were obtained from fourteen state and four federal same-sex marriage court cases.[14] Documents from interest groups include pamphlets and advertisements concerning same-sex marriage, reports and articles produced by conservative think tanks, and documents posted on organization websites. Documents were obtained from ten different conservative interest groups or think tanks.[15]

When coding these documents I read the text or watched the advertisement several times in order to identify the specific arguments made within them. I then identified the different discursive frameworks underlying each individual argument and made a notation on a coding sheet. It should be noted that only one notation was made for each specific discursive framework. For example, if a document contained four versions of the judicial activism subframe, only one notation was made on the coding sheet. This was done because there is no theoretical basis for weighing documents that make repeated use of one discursive framework more heavily than documents that use that framework only once. Coding documents this way also prevents longer documents from weighing more heavily on the results than shorter ones. In order to determine if these categories were coded in an impartial manner, a preliminary sample of forty documents was coded by two different coders, and Cohen's Kappa was used to calculate the level of intercoder reliability.[16] This resulted in a Kappa of .72, indicating a substantial agreement above that expected by chance and suggesting that the discursive frameworks used in this study were sufficiently differentiated.

THE STRANGE CASE OF THE DISAPPEARING RIGHTS CLAIMS

As Figure 3.3 demonstrates, all four of the master frames analyzed in this study featured prominently in conservative discourse on same-sex marriage. The most prevalent framework was morality-based appeals, with 69 percent of all the documents analyzed including some elements of the moral arguments master frame. The second most popular master frame was populism, featured in 54 percent of documents, followed by rights-based appeals, which appeared in 53 percent, and constitutional arguments, which appeared in 36 percent (see Figure 3.3).

Figure 3.3. Percentage of Discourse Using Master Frames

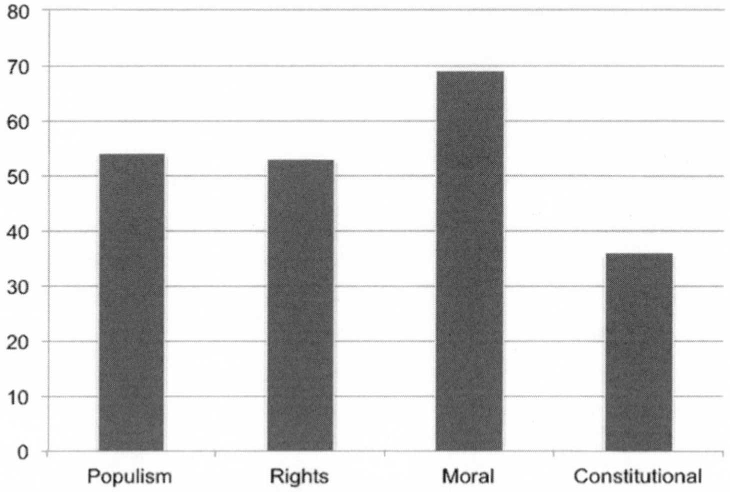

Source: Author, using original dataset.

When institutional environments are taken into account, some patterns begin to emerge. As Figure 3.4 shows, morality-based appeals were a prominent master frame regardless of institutional environment. Populism was also a fairly common framework in all three institutional contexts: 53 percent of ballot measure documents, 68 percent of interest group documents, and 48 percent of courtroom documents included populist discourse (see Figure 3.4). Not surprisingly, constitutional analysis was most common inside the courtroom environment and almost nonexistent outside of it. Only 4 percent of ballot measure documents and only 16 percent of interest group documents featured constitutional analysis, whereas 78 percent of courtroom documents included constitutional arguments (see Figure 3.4).

Perhaps the most interesting result can be seen with regard to the rights-based appeals master frame. Rights-based appeals were the most common discursive framework in both ballot measure campaigns and in the discourse of interest groups. Altogether, 84 percent of documents used in ballot measure campaigns and 72 percent of documents produced by interest groups contained rights-based appeals. Yet, after the debate over same-sex marriage shifted to the courtroom environment, these rights-based appeals became much less common. Only 13 percent of courtroom documents used the rights-based appeals master frame, making it the least prominent framework in that

Figure 3.4. Impact of Institutional Environments on Use of Master Frames

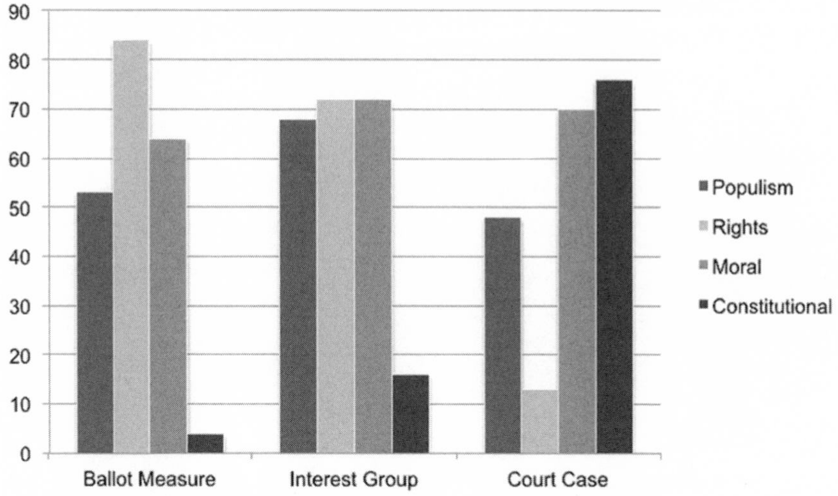

Source: Author, using original dataset.

institutional context (see Figure 3.4). This effect was tested for statistical significance using a two-tailed *t*-test. The courtroom environment was found to have a statistically significant, negative impact on the use of the rights-based appeals master frame. These results were also confirmed by a logit regression model (see Appendix B).

Figure 3.5 shows the use of the two most common subframes within the rights-based appeals master frame: parental rights and religious liberty. The parental rights argument expresses a fear that if same-sex marriage is legalized, children will be taught about it in schools without parental permission. This argument usually features an explicit rights claim. A typical example can be seen in the "No Right for Parents" television advertisement, which ran during Washington's 2012 Referendum 74 campaign. This advertisement featured David and Tonia Parker, conservative activists who also participated in campaigns against same-sex marriage in California, Maine, Maryland, Minnesota, and North Carolina. In this advertisement the Parkers state, "If R74 is approved, same-sex marriage could be taught in local Washington schools, just as it was in Massachusetts. Local Massachusetts schools took away the right of parents to decide how to discuss the issue of gay marriage" (Preserve Marriage Washington 2012). Sometimes this rights claim was made implicitly. For example, an advertisement that ran during Wisconsin's 2006 Question 1 campaign

Figure 3.5. Rights Subframes

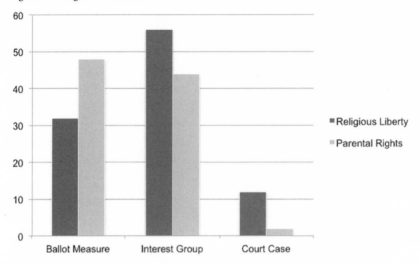

Source: Author, using original dataset.

captured the sentiment of the parental rights subframe without ever actually using the word "rights." It features a group of children looking confused or frightened while talking about same-sex marriage. A little girl with red hair and freckles says, "God created Adam and Eve? That's so old-fashioned." A little boy says, "Grandma, teacher says if grandpa was a girl, it's OK, you can still get married." The same little boy later asks, "If my dad married a man, who would be my mom?" The advertisement concludes with a narrator stating, "If we change the definition of marriage, our children will be taught a new way of thinking. Marriage means a man and a woman; vote yes to keep it that way" (Yes for Marriage 2006).

The religious liberty subframe argues that if same-sex marriage is legalized, those who object to it on religious grounds could be forced to provide services to same-sex couples or prohibited from publicly expressing their disapproval of marriage equality. A typical example of how this argument was made can be seen in the "Broken Promises" television advertisement, which ran during all five of the same-sex marriage ballot measure campaigns in 2012. The version of the advertisement that ran in Maryland states, "Question 6 makes a lot of broken promises about gay marriage. Like it won't affect anyone else, even as small businesses are fined, charities are closed, and people suspended from their jobs. Or it protects religious liberty, even though Question 6 has huge loopholes impacting churches, small businesses, and individuals" (Maryland Marriage Alliance 2012). As the narrator speaks, pictures of people who have suffered negative consequences for expressing opposition to same-sex marriage scroll across the screen.

Ballot measure campaigns featured both of these subframes prominently. The parental rights subframe was most common, with 48 percent of these documents using this framework. The religious liberty subframe was somewhat less prevalent, with only 32 percent of these documents using this framework (see Figure 3.5). The rights-based appeals master frame was rarely used inside the courtroom, but when courtroom documents did use this framework, they tended to use the religious liberty subframe rather than the discourse of parental rights. Only 2 percent of these documents referenced parental rights, whereas 12 percent of courtroom documents included claims of religious liberty (see Figure 3.5). Interest group documents also made frequent use of these subframes. The religious liberty subframe was most common in this environment, with 56 percent of these documents using this framework. The parental rights subframe was used in 44 percent of these documents (see Figure 3.5). According to these findings, interest groups actually had a statistically significant, positive impact on the use of the religious liberty subframe. This might indicate reluctance on the part of conservative opponents of same-sex marriage to embrace religious argumentation in the context of a ballot measure campaign for fear of alienating more secular, moderate voters. Such fears would be less of a restriction on the discourse of the interest groups, which are more likely to be talking to an audience of supporters and less likely to be concerned with convincing undecided voters.

These results raise some interesting questions about how institutions shape rights discourse. The finding that rights claims are *least* likely to be made inside the courtroom is counterintuitive because the legal language of rights would seem to fit well inside a courtroom environment. The remaining chapters of this book are dedicated in large part to explaining this surprising result. It is helpful to preview those arguments a bit here, however. The fact that rights claims were less likely to be made inside the courtroom may indicate that such arguments cannot withstand the considerable scrutiny that they must be subjected to in that environment. Although arguments made in more popular arenas outside of the courtroom are subject to little review, inside the courtroom these arguments must be supported with evidence and must be able to withstand scrutiny both from opposing counsel and from judges.

There are a few potential problems with these conservative rights claims that may limit their value in the courtroom environment. First, even if the Supreme Court recognizes the validity of these rights claims, it is not clear that this should result in it prohibiting same-sex marriage. There is considerable precedent for the Court recognizing the First Amendment rights of religiously motivated individuals (see, for example, *West Virginia State Board of Education v. Barnette* 1943). However, the judicial remedy for a violation of these rights is not to invalidate the offending law but to carve out an exemption for those whose objections are motivated by sincerely held religious beliefs (NeJaime 2009). This fact limits the utility of citing religious liberty as a mechanism for denying marriage rights to same-sex couples. However, now that the Court has recognized that same-sex couples have a fundamental right to marry, many members of the religious right have argued that the state must allow them to opt out of these laws in order to accommodate their religious beliefs (Family Research Council 2014, 14–32; Marriage Anti-Defamation Alliance 2014). The Supreme Court's ruling in *Burwell v. Hobby Lobby* (2014) suggests that it may be receptive to this line of argumentation. It is likely that, as this issue evolves, litigation will become a more fruitful tactic for conservative opponents of same-sex marriage.

Another reason these rights claims may have limited value in the courtroom environment is because they often rest on implicit moral assumptions that, if unpacked, would undermine their credibility. This is particularly true of the claim that parents should have the right to protect their children from being taught about same-sex marriage in school. This logic suggests that children need to be protected from gays and lesbians because same-sex marriage is obscene and gay people are sinful or threatening. These arguments resonate with voters, in part because they tap into a fear that legalizing same-sex marriage would make children more tolerant of gays and lesbians and thus increase the likelihood that they might "choose" to become gay themselves—something that, it is implied, would be an undesirable occurrence. This echoes the logic of earlier campaigns against gay rights led by activists such as John Briggs and Anita Bryant that warned that homosexuals wanted to "recruit," "molest," or "prey on" children (Fejes 2008). The logic of parental rights is difficult to refute in the confines of a ballot measure campaign because, unlike in these earlier campaigns, its discriminatory assumptions are not made explicitly. However, the more stringent scrutiny offered by the courtroom environment provides marriage equality activists the opportunity to expose the discriminatory stereotypes underlying the parental rights argument, limiting its effectiveness.

THE POPULARITY OF POPULIST APPEALS

Figure 3.6 shows how the "judges" and "other elites" subframes of the populism master frame were used in different institutional environments. These findings indicate that judges were a favorite target for conservative opponents of same-sex marriage regardless of institutional context: 39 percent of ballot measure campaign documents, 56 percent of interest group documents, and 48 percent of courtroom documents used judicial appeals (see Figure 3.6). The prevalence of these arguments in ballot measure campaigns is not surprising given the fact that many of these amendments were placed on the ballot by conservatives as a direct response to unfavorable court decisions. It is perhaps a bit surprising, however, to find that these arguments are also so commonplace in the courtroom environment. Courts are elite institutions, and one might assume that a judicial audience would be less receptive to arguments that call into question the scope of their judicial authority. The flexibility of this discursive framework is testament to the considerable resonance of populist appeals.

Judicial appeals were used by conservative opponents of same-sex marriage in all three institutional environments, but the mechanics of how this argument was made were slightly different inside and outside of the courtroom. Documents used in ballot measure campaigns and produced by interest groups emphasized a need to take the same-sex marriage issue "out of the hands of judges," frequently warning of the problems of "judicial activism." A typical example of this appeared in the television advertisement "Why We Need a Marriage Amendment," which ran during Arizona's 2008 Proposition 102 campaign. The advertisement consists of interviews with people on the street answering the question, "Why is a constitutional amendment necessary?" Many express concerns about judicial activism. A young woman says, "I think Prop 102 will protect marriage in Arizona from judges." A man says, "If it's not in the constitution as an amendment, rather than just a law, then some judge can come by and overturn the thing." The advertisement closes with a Latina saying, "It needs to become an amendment so that the people have the last word" (YesForMarriage.com 2008).

Figure 3.6. Populism Subframes

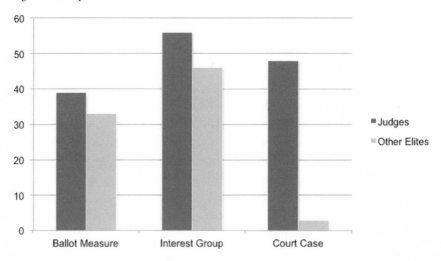

Source: Author, using original dataset.

These statements are notable for their simplicity. Documents used in ballot measure campaigns that made judicial appeals almost never explained the underlying logic behind this argument. They never discuss why the people are a superior decision-making body or why allowing a judge to decide this issue would be undesirable. This was most likely done for practical reasons. It would be difficult to give a full explanation of this logic when operating within the confines of a short television advertisement. Such elucidation is probably unnecessary, though. This is because these arguments fit within a familiar cultural tradition that celebrates the wisdom of the common man and is distrustful of the machinations of elites (Kazin 1995). Judges have been a particularly ripe target for this populist outrage. They are often depicted as intellectual and social elites with value systems woefully out of touch with the desires of most Americans. Worse yet, these "activist" judges are thought to be fueled by a sense of self-righteousness that causes them to disregard the people's authority and impose their own values on average citizens (Bork 1991).

Courtroom documents also frequently featured judicial appeals. In this context, however, such arguments tended to be framed in more legalistic terms, and their underlying logic was explained in greater detail. Conservative opponents of same-sex marriage would often present this argument as a "separation of powers" issue, contending that judges do not have the proper legal authority to define marriage because the US Constitution requires that this issue be decided instead by the people. A typical example of this approach can be seen in an amicus curiae brief submitted by the Marriage Law Project (2002) in the case of *Goodridge v. Department of Public Health* (2003). The brief argued in part:

> The method of constitutional interpretation that is proposed by those seeking the imposition of a reconfigured marriage scheme is one which . . . seeks to impose new content fashioned from modern enlightened opinion. By this method, brand new "rights" with no historic precedent can magically spring from ancient constitutional provisions which, as a historical matter, never have been even wildly imagined to authorize a social revolution like that [the] Plaintiffs seek. This practice is . . . a shameless petition for judicial usurpation of legislative prerogative. (7–8)

Using this logic allows courts to avoid the thorny question of whether same-sex marriage *should* be legal and instead focus on the more value-neutral question of whether they have the authority to make it so. When presented in this way, these arguments can be persuasive. Not surprisingly, such appeals featured prominently in all four of the separate dissenting opinions written in *Obergefell v. Hodges* (2015).

The other elites subframe often appeared in documents produced by conservative opponents of same-sex marriage for use outside of the courtroom. A total of 33 percent of ballot measure documents and 46 percent of interest group documents used this subframe. These other elites were almost never mentioned inside the courtroom, however; only 3 percent of courtroom documents reference them (see Figure 3.6). This may indicate that it is difficult to convert distrust of nonjudicial actors into a viable legal argument.

Advertisements that targeted "other elites" were almost identical to ones focused on judges; in fact, they often mentioned judges as well. One example is the television advertisement "Threat to Marriage," which ran during Minnesota's 2012 Amendment 1 campaign. In the advertisement a woman asks, "Who should decide the definition of marriage? We think it should be the people, not judges or politicians" (Minnesota for Marriage 2012). The advertisement then mentions a pending court case and marriage equality legislation working its way through the Minnesota legislature. It concludes with the same woman arguing, "If they succeed, voters will have lost their say. . . . Vote yes on the Marriage Protection Amendment so that voters always have the final say" (Minnesota for Marriage 2012).

The fact that these other elites also proved vulnerable to populist concerns suggests that these appeals have less to do with an ideological devotion to democratic principles and more to do with an instrumental desire to have one's viewpoint prevail. Some scholars have theorized that unpopular court decisions are uniquely susceptible to causing backlash because of the antidemocratic nature of courts (Rosenberg 1991; Klarman 2006). If this is true, then we should expect legislative officials to be somewhat insulated from populist appeals because, unlike most judges, they are elected by the voters. This should allow them to credibly claim to be representing the people and give them more authority to decide thorny political questions such as these. Yet, conservative opponents of same-sex marriage had little problem extending populist appeals beyond activist judges to include "corrupt politicians" seeking to advance their own political agenda or the agenda of "special interest groups." The fact that legislative officials are not immune from these attacks may give us reason to be somewhat skeptical of some of the principles of backlash theory.

HARNESSING THE EMOTIONAL POWER OF MORAL APPEALS

Figure 3.7 shows the four subframes within the morality-based appeals master frame. The defense of the traditional family subframe was by far the most common argument used within this master frame regardless of institutional context. It appeared in 61 percent of ballot measure campaign documents, 64 percent of interest group documents, and 69 percent of courtroom documents (see Figure 3.7). In some respects, the prevalence of this argument is not surprising. The question of whether gays and lesbians should be allowed to marry is at its core a moral one. It is to be expected that conservative opponents of same-sex marriage would justify their positions by expounding on the moral superiority of the traditional family. Such arguments do not necessarily resonate with everyone, however. It is perhaps a bit surprising to see these moral appeals being used in ballot measure campaigns, in which secular voters might not be responsive to them, or in the courtroom environment, in which legal actors expect laws to have a legitimate *secular* interest that justifies them.

Figure 3.7. Moral Subframes

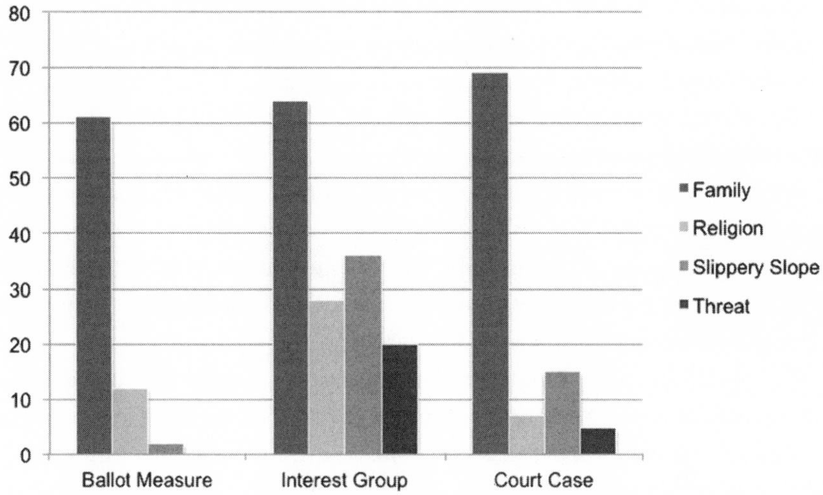

Source: Author, using original dataset.

As was the case with populist appeals, the traditional family framework was presented without much elaboration during ballot measure campaigns. For example, a television advertisement that ran during Oregon's 2004 Measure 36 campaign features a man and a woman lying on a bed playing with a baby. The baby laughs, and a lullaby plays in the background. A narrator says, "The most precious gift of all, a man, a woman, a child, a family. The way marriage should always be. Please, vote yes on Measure 36" (Defense of Marriage Coalition 2004).[17] A similar advertisement, "One Thing," ran in both Arizona and Florida in 2008. The advertisement consists of a series of idyllic depictions of family life. These include scenes of a woman getting ready for a wedding, an African American family having a barbeque, a mother and father playing with a small child at the beach, and a Latina woman and her child making tortillas. As these images scroll across the screen, a narrator says, "Amendment 2 does only one thing. Defining marriage as a union of a man and a woman. That's it. When you vote, say yes to pass life to the next generation. Vote yes to keep marriage one man and one woman" (Florida4Marriage.org 2008).

These advertisements say little of substance. They provide no explanation for why traditional families are valuable or how allowing same-sex marriage would undermine this value. Instead they play heavily on emotions, show-ing sentimental images of family life and presenting an uplifting message seemingly designed to cause the viewers to reflect on the importance of family to their own life. As with populist appeals, this message is already so familiar to voters that it probably does not need to be elucidated for them. There is a subtext here, however, that is a bit more menacing. These advertisements suggest that marriage is important to heterosexual couples because they value family, love, commitment, and raising children. It is implied that gay people disagree with this perspective in some way, that they see marriage as a way to get rights and benefits, not as the foundation for a loving family. This logic fits with a long-standing historical tradition of using "moral panics" to demand action be taken to combat threats such as "sexual deviance" thought to imperil the moral foundation of society (Morone 2003).

The courtroom version of this argument contains similar themes, but here conservative opponents of same-sex marriage had to explain the logic of why the traditional definition of marriage is important, and how allowing gays and lesbians to marry would imperil it, in more detail. They usually did this by arguing that laws prohibiting same-sex marriage were motivated by a legitimate state interest in encouraging "responsible procreation." A typical example of this argument can be seen in an amicus curiae brief submitted by the Family Research Council (FRC), a conservative Christian organization based in Washington, DC, in the case of *Kerrigan v. Commissioner of Public Health* (2008). It argued in part:

> The state's interest in marriage is rooted in addressing the consequences of the biological reality that opposite-sex couples *will procreate*, intentionally or accidentally. This state interest in regulating marriage has been termed "responsible procreation." This concept acknowledges two objectives: (1) steering the inevitable opposite-sex procreation into a stable environment for the good of children and society; and (2) promoting an optimal environment for child-rearing that encourages the biological mother and father to stay together to raise their child. (2005, 23)

The brief goes on to argue that preserving the traditional definition of marriage is central to the preservation of American values, quoting the US Supreme Court's 1888 decision in *Maynard v. Hill*, which states, "Marriage is the foundation of the family and society without which there would be neither civilization nor progress" (Family Research Council 2005, 24).

This brief made a compelling case that marriage is about the responsible rearing of children.[18] However, it failed to provide much support for the idea that same-sex couples are incapable of also adhering to this model. Although the brief offered evidence showing that children do best when raised by "a mother and a father" (Family Research Council 2005, 29–32), those studies are not really relevant because they are based on a comparison between children raised in single-parent households and children raised in two-parent households. There is no credible evidence to suggest that children raised by same-sex couples are any worse off than those raised by similarly situated opposite-sex couples.[19] In fact there are numerous examples of gay couples raising children in stable family environments, in spite of the fact that they had been denied access to the institution of marriage. The Court's decision in *Obergefell* specifically mentioned a desire to lift the stigma imposed on households such as these by allowing gay parents to marry (*Obergefell v. Hodges* 2015, 15).

Whereas the defense of the traditional family subframe was ubiquitous in all three institutional settings, the other morality-based arguments subframes were rarely used in ballot measure campaigns or courtroom documents. Only 2 percent of ballot measure documents used the slippery slope subframe, 12 percent used the religion subframe, and none depicted gays and lesbians as a physical threat (see Figure 3.7). Only 15 percent of courtroom documents used the slippery slope subframe, 7 percent used the religion subframe, and 5 percent described gays and lesbians as a physical threat (see Figure 3.7). These subframes were a relatively large part of the discourse of interest groups, however; 36 percent of interest group documents made the slippery slope argument, 28 percent used religious appeals, and 20 percent depicted gays and lesbians as a physical threat (see Figure 3.7).

A typical example of these types of arguments can be seen in documents produced by the FRC. One of the FRC's primary functions is to lobby politicians and individuals on behalf of conservative causes. As part of this mission, it produces research reports and pamphlets on topics such as homosexuality, religion in public life, and family structure. One such pamphlet, "The Top Ten Harms of Same-Sex Marriage," mixes some fairly common concerns about parental rights, religious liberty, and the importance of the traditional family environment for children with some more overtly discriminatory arguments. For example, the pamphlet contends that gays and lesbians are less likely to remain sexually faithful to their partners:

> Homosexual relationships, including "partnered" relationships, covering a
> span of decades, have shown that sex with multiple partners is tolerated and
> often expected, even when one has a "long-term" partner. . . . If homosexual
> relationships, promiscuity and all, are held up to society as being a fully equal
> part of the social ideal that is called "marriage," then the value of sexual fidelity
> as an expected standard of behavior for married people will further erode—even
> among heterosexuals. (Sprigg 2011, 4)

It also argues that legalizing same-sex marriage will lead to greater demands
for polygamy: "If it violates the equal protection of the laws to deny homosexuals their first choice of marital partner, why would it not do the same to deny
pedophiles, polygamists, or the incestuous the right to marry the person (or
persons) of their choice?" (Sprigg 2011, 7).

Another FRC pamphlet, "Top 10 Myths about Homosexuality," goes even
further. The pamphlet spends a considerable amount of time arguing that homosexuality is a choice and that "reparative therapy" designed to make gay
people heterosexual is ethical and can be successful (Sprigg 2010, 4–17). The
pamphlet also lists a number of problems it associates with homosexuality,
including higher incidences of mental disorders, drug abuse, and sexually
transmitted diseases (Sprigg 2010, 22–29). Perhaps most controversially, the
pamphlet takes on the "myth" that "homosexuals are no more likely to molest
children than heterosexuals." It states:

> If this myth were true, it would support the notion that homosexuals should
> be allowed to work with children as schoolteachers, Boy Scout leaders, and Big
> Brothers or Big Sisters. However, it is not true. The research clearly shows that
> same-sex child sexual abuse (mostly men molesting boys) occurs at rates far
> higher, proportionally, than adult homosexual behavior, and it strongly suggests
> that many of those abusers are homosexual in their adult orientation as well.
> (Sprigg 2010, 34)

These arguments are clearly more extreme than those that typically appeared in ballot measure campaigns and court cases. In order to test how institutional environments affect the use of these more "extreme" arguments, I
constructed a dummy variable that accounted for the use of slippery slope, religious, or physical threat arguments. Documents were coded positively if they
used one or more of these subframes. The effect of institutional environments

on the use of these extreme arguments was tested for statistical significance using a two-tailed *t*-test. Interest groups were found to have a statistically significant, positive effect on the use of these arguments. These findings were also confirmed by a logit regression model (see Appendix C). This finding suggests that these more extreme arguments may have been downplayed for instrumental reasons by conservatives arguing in a court case or ballot measure campaign. These arguments were more common, however, when discussing the issue of same-sex marriage within the confines of an already supportive audience, where there is no need to convince undecided or potentially hostile individuals. These findings confirm the insights of previous scholars who have shown that conservatives tend to couch moral arguments in the language of rights in an attempt to appeal to a wider audience that may be alienated by such appeals (Schacter 1994, 289–290; Herman 1997, 115, 144; Hardisty 1999, 114).

CONCLUSION

This chapter has offered a first glimpse at how different institutional environments shaped the debate over marriage equality in the United States. Throughout this debate activists on both sides of this issue attempted to advance their causes by capitalizing on what they perceived to be favorable institutional environments. For proponents of marriage equality this meant using litigation as a central tactic. From the earliest stages of this debate, the courts have proven most receptive to the argument that same-sex couples have a fundamental right to marry. As this debate progressed and public support for same-sex marriage began to increase, marriage equality activists started looking to advance their cause in the legislative environment as well, with some success. In contrast, conservative opponents of same-sex marriage have typically viewed this issue as one that should be decided by the people, not the courts. They sought to put the question of marriage equality before voters directly using the ballot measure process and built an impressive record of success in this environment, winning thirty-four of thirty-nine campaigns.

The content analysis conducted in this chapter begins to give us some hints as to how these different institutional environments have shaped this debate. This inquiry reveals that conservative opponents of same-sex marriage were much more likely to use rights language when arguing this issue outside of the courtroom and much less likely to make rights claims when inside it. It also shows that although populist appeals and moral arguments were equally as likely to appear in ballot measure campaigns as they were to be used in court cases, the way these arguments were presented was heavily influenced by the institutional contexts in which they were advanced. The questions of why these differences occurred and what the implications of these effects are will be taken up more thoroughly in the remaining chapters of this book, but a few preliminary conclusions can be gleaned from the analysis provided thus far.

In general, arguments presented in ballot measure campaigns must be short and straightforward to be effective. This is done both to contain costs (longer advertisements are more expensive) and because they are targeted at a popular audience that does not have the time or inclination to consider more nuanced contentions. The advertisements used by conservative opponents of marriage equality during these campaigns mostly followed this framework. They rarely exceeded a minute in length. Most consisted primarily of simple, declarative statements about the importance of values such as parental rights, religious liberty, the traditional family, or the need to keep this issue out of the hands of judges.

In contrast, the courtroom environment is a place in which arguments are expected to be presented in much more detail, and positions must be defended with evidence. Moving to a courtroom environment forced conservative opponents of same-sex marriage to articulate the underlying logic of their arguments. In some cases, they were able to do this with few problems. The assumptions motivating populist appeals, for example, were easy to elucidate in a courtroom environment and could be supported with considerable constitutional analysis and historical precedent. Other arguments were a bit more difficult to transition. Although legal briefs presented by conservative opponents of same-sex marriage often offered a detailed discussion of the importance of the traditional family, they had difficulty providing credible evidence supporting the idea that gays and lesbians presented a threat to this model. In the case of rights language, the effect of the courtroom environment was even stronger. These arguments appeared to be so difficult to transition to the courtroom that conservatives typically did not even attempt to do so.

These findings underscore the legitimating power of rights discourse in our society. As Stuart Scheingold's (1974) now famous conception of the "politics of rights" suggests, rights are crucial political resources for movement activists because they have significant cultural resonance. Although one must be careful not to assign too much instrumental importance to this language, not having rights discourse available to them in the courtroom environment seems to have been a hindrance for conservative opponents of marriage equality. The fact that opponents of same-sex marriage succeeded so often when they were able to make rights-based appeals, as they were during statewide ballot measure campaigns, and struggled when they could not, is a testament to the power of this language.

4. No Right to Object?
Opposition to Same-Sex Marriage in the Golden State

Chapter 3 of this book provided a big-picture examination of the way the debate over same-sex marriage has been carried out in the United States. This overview reveals several interesting patterns. It is clear from this analysis that conservatives had success opposing same-sex marriage when they were able to effectively mobilize their own counter-rights discourse and were less successful when they were unable to do so. It is also clear that institutional environments had a dramatic impact on the use and effectiveness of this rights discourse—conservatives used rights discourse heavily when opposing same-sex marriage outside of the courtroom and almost never used this discourse when debating this issue inside the courtroom. These findings raise additional questions: Why are conservative rights claims so effective in the popular arena? Why are they so seldom used in the more elite-centered environment of the courtroom? In this chapter and the next I explore these questions by conducting an in-depth examination of same-sex marriage debates in select states.

This chapter focuses on the same-sex marriage debates in California. I have chosen California for this chapter in part because it has often been a bellwether for cultural conflicts in the United States (Schragg 2008). Thus, studying the way the same-sex marriage debate played out in California can tell us not just about that state but about broader trends in politics generally. The state is also important because it has played a formative role for activists on both sides of the same-sex marriage issue. The New Right conservative movement was forged in California during the 1960s by conservative activists based primarily in the southern part of the state (McGirr 2001). The gay rights movement also emerged during the 1960s in large part as a result of the work of activists in San Francisco and Los Angeles (Armstrong 2002). There are practical reasons for focusing on California as well. Californians spent more than a decade debating same-sex marriage in a wide variety of institutional settings. Focusing on California provides a unique opportunity to analyze how institutional frameworks have affected the way opponents of same-sex marriage thought and talked about their cause while holding other factors such as region, culture, and time frame constant.

I begin this chapter with a brief overview of the political development of California. This historical analysis traces the development of the state's political culture and institutions and examines how this dynamic has affected the current debate over marriage equality. I then conduct an in-depth analysis of the 2008 Proposition 8 campaign. This analysis begins by describing the organizational structure and strategy of the campaign. I then use interpretive textual analysis to explore the constitutive and instrumental implications of arguments used in support of the measure. I conclude the chapter with an analysis of the *Perry v. Schwarzenegger* trial (2010). Here I examine arguments made during the trial and show how institutional norms and constraints present inside the courtroom make it difficult for conservatives to effectively mobilize rights discourse in this environment.

The results of this analysis show that rights discourse has played an important role in same-sex marriage ballot measure campaigns. Framing their arguments using the discourse of rights, and minimizing the use of moral or religious appeals, allows opponents of marriage equality to connect with a more secular audience and helps them build popular support for their cause. In addition to its instrumental implications, this discourse also has constitutive impact on opponents of same-sex marriage. Thinking about their cause using the discourse of rights helps mobilize opposition to marriage equality. It allows these activists to see themselves not as a recalcitrant majority stubbornly opposing the rights of gays and lesbians but as victims of oppression standing up against the excessive and unnecessary rights claims of subversive elites.

After the debate over same-sex marriage moves inside the courtroom, however, these rights claims become much less effective. Opponents of same-sex marriage attempted to downplay the rights-based arguments they had used in the Proposition 8 campaign during the *Perry* trial, but proponents of marriage equality made the Yes on 8 campaign's arguments a centerpiece of their case. They used expert testimony to expose the stereotypes underlying advertisements run by conservatives in support of Proposition 8 and showed that the law was motivated by a discriminatory intent, not a compelling government interest. This strategy proved successful because the court largely agreed with this analysis. This decision was later upheld by the US Supreme Court, legalizing same-sex marriage in California (*Hollingsworth v. Perry* 2013). Thus, the rights-based arguments used by conservatives during the Proposition 8 campaign were not merely ineffective in the courtroom environment, they actually became counterproductive.

POLITICAL DEVELOPMENT OF CALIFORNIA

California's politics have been heavily influenced by the state's individualistic political culture, which tends to reward officials who champion a populist style of politics and are distrustful of elites (Starr 2009). This political culture reflects the state's unique history and geography. When California was annexed by the United States in 1848 at the conclusion of the Mexican-American War, it was a sparsely populated territory at the edge of a distant frontier. This began to change, however, after gold was found at Sutter's Mill, near modern-day Sacramento. This touched off the first of many waves of migration to the state. More than 300,000 "forty-niners" would eventually come to California in search of gold, dramatically boosting the territory's population and fueling a successful drive to become the thirty-first state in 1850 (Starr 1973, 49–68). California would eventually grow into a large western state rich in natural resources but far removed from the political and economic power structures of the Northeast. These features were attractive to many Americans. As the state developed, it would be settled by successive waves of migrants who viewed California as a physical embodiment of the American dream—a land of opportunity where hardworking, self-reliant individuals could build a new life for themselves. These cultural ideals shaped the political institutions of California and, as we shall see, have had a lasting impact on how cultural debates such as the one over same-sex marriage are conducted in the state.

The completion of the transcontinental railroad in 1869 dramatically increased the speed with which people and goods could be distributed between California and the rest of the nation.[1] The railroads boosted the state's development, but they brought new problems to the region as well. Railroad corporations became a dominant force in California's economy, and they used their power to exert enormous influence over the state's politics. The largest and most powerful of these corporations was the Southern Pacific (SP) Railroad. In addition to controlling rail travel in the state, the SP also owned vast tracts of land, steamship companies, irrigation projects, hotels, and commercial properties. The company exerted influence over the state's political officials by rewarding them with free passage on its railcars and steamships, free hotel rooms, large campaign contributions, and special rates for their businesses and friends (Starr 1985, 199–234). The SP also used its influence to direct California's political machines. These machines were able to dominate the state's political process by using their influence to control the party conventions and dictate the nomination of elected officials. By the early 1870s, the SP enjoyed near-complete control over the state's political system. The company hand-picked elected officials it knew would have railroad interests in mind and used its influence to win lucrative government subsidies and defeat attempts to regulate the industry.

During the early twentieth century, popular frustration with the corrupting influence of the railroads bubbled over, fueling the progressive movement in California. In 1907 a group of progressive-minded reformers formed the League of Lincoln-Roosevelt Republican Clubs with the goal of "affecting the constructive destruction of the Southern Pacific Machine" (Starr 1985, 236). These clubs pushed for a number of reforms designed to curb the power of the SP, such as direct primary elections, the secret ballot, and direct control over legislation through initiative, referendum, and recall. Progressive reformers scored a key victory in 1909 when they successfully lobbied the state legislature to pass a law mandating direct primary elections for state office. This allowed them to nominate their own slate of candidates, independent of the political machines and uncorrupted by the railroad interests. In the 1910 election, reformers won sweeping victories by electing the progressive-minded Hiram Johnson to the governorship and giving progressive legislators control of the state legislature. Progressives used this power to pass a host of reforms, including use of the citizens' initiative and referendum and the right to recall elected officials (1911);[2] the ability of candidates to cross-file as representatives for multiple parties at the same time (1913); and the removal of partisan designations from the ballot for all elections to statewide office (1915). These reforms effectively broke the railroad's political machines and severely crippled the strength of political parties in the state. Not all of these reforms would last; partisan designations were later returned to the ballot and cross-filing was repealed in 1959, bringing an element of partisanship back to California politics. Political parties and elites remain fairly weak in California, however, with most major issues decided directly by the people through the ballot measure process (Schragg 1998, 5–24).

The Rise of the New Right

California is not a place many would associate strongly with conservative politics today. The state has not voted for a Republican presidential candidate since narrowly supporting George H. W. Bush in 1988, and its politics have been dominated of late by the Democratic Party. Yet, the modern Republican Party has its roots in California. The New Right political movement's most prominent early leaders, including Barry Goldwater, Ronald Reagan, and to a lesser extent Richard Nixon,[3] were all from the West. These New Right conservatives enjoyed strong support all across the Southwest, but the epicenter of this movement was Southern California, particularly Orange and San Diego Counties (McGirr 2001; Perlstein 2001, 120–141).

Southern California became a haven for conservative politics following the postwar migration to the state. Most of Southern California lay largely undeveloped until after World War II, when local officials used the lure of cheap land and loose restrictions to win lucrative defense contracts from the federal government.[4] Many people were drawn to California by the promise of good jobs in the rapidly growing defense industry, and most of them settled in this region. Working in the defense sector influenced the political views of these new migrants, leading many to develop strong support for interventionist foreign policy and become virulent opponents of communism (McGirr 2001, 51). These issues would become key elements of New Right political ideology.

Because Southern California still contained vast tracts of undeveloped land at the time of the postwar migration, real estate developers were able to construct new communities from the ground up there. These developers constructed the region in a way that reinforced its conservative political culture. Although most large urban areas are typically filled with dense residential zones consisting of multifamily units, in Southern California developers tended to build single-family homes, which reinforced privacy, individual property rights, and home ownership. Transportation networks also reflected a desire for privacy and individual space. Southern California was built specifically to accommodate automobiles. The region developed a large and complex highway system designed to allow people to commute from their suburban homes to work and back again without ever leaving the privacy of their car. This helped foster a heightened sense of individual autonomy and a strong belief in self-reliance that would become hallmarks of New Right conservativism (Starr 2009, 245–266).

New migrants who came to California typically had no preexisting social networks to draw on in the area. This meant they had to construct a sense of community for themselves after they arrived in the state. Conservative organizations filled this void for many. The newcomers joined social organizations such as the John Birch Society, volunteered to help advocate for conservative causes, or became active members of one of the many evangelical churches in the area (McGirr 2001, 39, 48).[5] Churches in particular played an integral role in helping to build organizational support for the burgeoning New Right political movement. Church leaders in the area gladly lent their support to conservative political candidates and causes. This helped conservatives tap into large volunteer networks of committed supporters eager to help elect conservative candidates and to advocate for a number of conservative social causes at the state and national level (Perlstein 2001, 120–140). As we shall see, these same church networks would play a key role in organizing conservative opposition to same-sex marriage in the state as well.

Gay Marriage in the Golden State

Perhaps no state felt the effects of the fight over same-sex marriage more acutely than California. Californians spent more than a decade debating this issue in a variety of different institutional contexts. The state was the site of two marriage equality ballot measures (Proposition 22 in 2000 and Proposition 8 in 2008), two nearly successful attempts to legalize same-sex marriage through the state legislature (AB 849 in 2005 and AB 43 in 2007), and three major marriage equality court cases (*In re Marriage Cases* 2008; *Strauss v. Horton* 2009; and *Hollingsworth v. Perry* 2013). The remaining sections of this chapter explore two of these events (Proposition 8 and the *Perry* trial) in more detail, but it is helpful to first briefly review this larger history to better understand the context in which these events occurred.

The same-sex marriage debate first came to California with Proposition 22 in 2000. This measure was placed on the ballot in California shortly after the Vermont Supreme Court ruled that same-sex couples could not be denied the benefits and protections of marriage (*Baker v. Vermont* 1999). Though same-sex marriage had not been recognized in California, opponents of marriage equality feared their state could be compelled to give "full faith and credit" to same-sex marriages conducted in states such as Vermont. Supporters of Proposition

22 sought to prevent this from happening by adding a statutory provision to the California Family Code explicitly stating that the union of a man and a woman is the only valid or recognizable form of marriage in the state of California. The measure met little resistance and was ultimately passed by a wide margin.

Following the passage of Proposition 22, same-sex marriage receded into the background as a political issue in California for a few years. During this time gay rights activists in the state focused primarily on expanding domestic partnership rights for gay couples, reasoning that the time was not yet right to push for same-sex marriage (Cummings and NeJaime 2010, 1256–1272). Marriage equality exploded back onto the scene again in February of 2004, when San Francisco Mayor Gavin Newsom began unilaterally issuing marriage licenses to same-sex couples.[6] In response, then California attorney general Bill Lockyer and a group of conservative citizens filed petitions seeking to have the California Supreme Court invalidate these marriages. The court ruled that city officials had exceeded their authority in issuing marriage licenses to same-sex couples and nullified the approximately 4,000 same-sex marriages performed in San Francisco prior to their decision (*Lockyer v. City and County of San Francisco* 2004). This decision barred city officials from unilaterally issuing marriage licenses to same-sex couples in the future, but the court emphasized that the substantive question of the constitutionality of California's prohibition on same-sex marriage would have to be decided in a separate case.

While the debate over same-sex marriage was winding its way through the California court system, proponents of marriage equality began trying to push the issue through the state legislature. In July of 2005, Democratic representative Mark Leno, one of the first openly gay men to serve in the California General Assembly, introduced Assembly Bill (AB) 849, a proposal to legalize same-sex marriage in the state.[7] The Senate approved the bill twenty-one to fifteen. It then went to the House, where, after some intense lobbying of Democratic lawmakers who had abstained from voting on an earlier version of the bill, it passed forty-one to thirty-five with four abstaining. This made AB 849 the first bill legalizing same-sex marriage to pass a state legislative body. The victory was short-lived, however, because the state's Republican governor, Arnold Schwarzenegger, vetoed the legislation. Leno reintroduced a similar bill, AB 43, two years later. The bill once again narrowly passed both houses of the state legislature only to be vetoed by the governor.

At the same time the California legislature was considering legislation to legalize same-sex marriage, the fight over marriage equality was also being carried out in the California court system. This issue began winding its way through the courts in 2005, after the San Francisco County Superior Court combined six separate challenges to California's ban on same-sex marriage into one consolidated case (*In re Marriage Cases*). In 2005, superior court justice Richard Kramer ruled in favor of the plaintiffs in the case, invalidating California's marriage restrictions. The case then went before the California Appeals Court, which reversed Kramer's ruling in a two-to-one decision. The California Supreme Court took up the case and rendered its final decision on May 15, 2008. A deeply divided court found by a vote of four to three that California's ban on same-sex marriage violated the equal protection clause of the state's constitution. The decision legalized same-sex marriage in the state immediately and sent conservatives scrambling to overturn it. These efforts culminated in Proposition 8, a ballot measure that sought to amend the state's constitution and define marriage as between one man and one woman.

PROPOSITION 8

Opponents of same-sex marriage began laying the groundwork for the Proposition 8 campaign in 2007, while the California Supreme Court was considering *In re Marriage Cases*. Activists formed the Protect Marriage Coalition—a loose alliance of conservative churches and political organizations—and drafted the ballot measure Limit on Marriage, which would eventually become Proposition 8.[8] They hired Schubert and Flint Public Affairs to manage their campaign and started mobilizing supporters and gathering signatures to qualify the measure for the ballot.[9] Signatures were submitted to the secretary of state for approval one month before the California Supreme Court announced its decision in the case. After the court legalized same-sex marriage, Proposition 8 changed from an initiative that would have merely reinforced the status quo to one that would overturn the court's decision and take newly won marriage rights away from same-sex couples. In order to reflect this change, then attorney general Jerry Brown changed the title of the initiative from Limit on Marriage to Eliminates Rights of Same-Sex Couples to Marry.[10]

The court's decision to legalize same-sex marriage raised the stakes of the Proposition 8 campaign and galvanized the measure's supporters. However, proponents of Proposition 8 faced a difficult task. California is a solidly Democratic state, and many Californians were reluctant to support a measure that would eliminate existing rights. Polling data released in mid-September, just one and a half months before Election Day, showed the measure trailing among likely voters by seventeen points (DiCamillo and Field 2008). To combat this deficit, the Yes on 8 campaign leaders worked to mobilize their enthusiastic base of religious right supporters and also developed a message that would resonate beyond this base and appeal to a broader audience.

Mobilizing the Base

The most ardent opponents of same-sex marriage are typically evangelical Christians. These individuals were predictably outraged by the California Supreme Court's decision to legalize same-sex marriage. The Yes on 8 campaign leaders realized early on that this built-in base of supporters could provide a huge advantage if they could effectively capitalize on their outrage. The campaign leaned heavily on existing church networks to reach out to these individuals.[11] They enlisted religious leaders to serve as precinct captains and area supervisors in charge of recruiting volunteers and organizing supporters, and they used church facilities as meeting places for campaign rallies and events (Schubert and Flint 2009, 45). Establishing a firm foundation of volunteers was key to the success of Proposition 8. It is extremely difficult to run an effective ballot measure campaign without a core group of supporters willing to do the hard work of gathering signatures, canvassing neighborhoods, and running phone banks. This is particularly true in a state as large as California, which has more than 40 million residents, 17 million registered voters, and 20,000 voting precincts.

As we shall see shortly, proponents of Proposition 8 were careful to use secular language when making their case against same-sex marriage to voters in official campaign materials. They frequently used religious language and imagery to justify their positions when appealing to a sympathetic audience in a private setting, however. California church leaders organized three ninety-minute simulcast events during the Yes on 8 campaign designed to rally supporters and attract new volunteers. These events were broadcast live to audiences assembled in churches across California. During these simulcasts, religious leaders and conservative activists spoke passionately in support of Proposition 8. They often used stark language to depict the fight over same-sex marriage as a high-stakes battle between good and evil. One simulcast opened, for example, with a speaker who argued, "Confrontation between light and darkness will happen this November, a battle to save the very sanctity of marriage. To the victor goes the soul of the nation" (Ingle 2008, 89–90). This may seem like hyperbole to some outsiders, but to many proponents of Proposition 8 these fears were real. This apocalyptic language helped to create a powerful sense of purpose for opponents of same-sex marriage, a sense that they were fighting for a cause much bigger than themselves.[12]

Many of these speakers justified their opposition to same-sex marriage by arguing that the Bible condemns homosexuality as sin. They argued that instead of normalizing the "homosexual lifestyle" by legalizing same-sex marriage, efforts should be made to help gays and lesbians change their sexual orientation and overcome their sin. One speaker implored supporters to "cry out to God for the deliverance of the homosexual, for the salvation of their lives, for the love of God to be poured out over their hearts. Where there is no hope, where there is no human remedy, God still has the holy prescription" (Ingle 2008, 90). Each simulcast closed with a story from a "former gay" who had been converted and was now living a Christian lifestyle as a heterosexual person (Chambers 2008, 64–73; Fryrear 2008, 99–103; Schneider 2008, 15–16). This focus shows that the idea that sexual orientation is a choice is fundamental to the worldview of many conservatives. According to this logic, gays and lesbians can legitimately be denied marriage rights because they have chosen to embrace a "deviant" lifestyle. Conservatives believe gays and lesbians can earn marriage rights by renouncing this lifestyle, disciplining their sexual urges, and becoming heterosexual. In their eyes, this fact distinguishes the drive for marriage equality from other "legitimate" civil rights movements that confront discrimination based on immutable characteristics such as race or gender.

Rights discourse also played an important role in rallying opponents of same-sex marriage. Many who spoke at these simulcasts raised concerns that legalizing same-sex marriage would infringe on the religious liberty of those with a Christian worldview. During one of these events, Pastor Frank Pavone described in passionate terms the need to protect religious freedoms:

> Religious freedom really is a core, fundamental human right. Much like life
> itself it defines what it means to be human. . . . If we don't exercise our religious
> freedoms without fear, if we don't sacrifice on behalf of those truths that we say
> we believe, then those freedoms will be taken away from us. We're given religious

liberty in this country, but it's not given to us on a silver platter. We have to fight for it. The cost of this foundational change that has been forced upon society is simply too high. We cannot, we must not allow religious liberty and the ability of Christian people to serve in the public square to be sacrificed on the altar of political correctness. (Pavone 2008, 35–36)

Other speakers raised similar concerns. They provided examples of ministers required to marry same-sex couples (Stanton 2008, 47), churches that risked losing their tax-exempt status because they opposed same-sex marriage (Tyler 2008, 50), a Christian physician sued for refusing to artificially inseminate a lesbian couple (Gallagher 2008, 45–46), and a wedding photographer sued for refusing to perform her services during a same-sex marriage ceremony (Morse 2008, 48–49).

The Yes on 8 campaign's efforts to mobilize this base of supporters were ultimately successful. The campaign was able to use religious organizations to recruit hundreds of thousands of volunteers and raise more than $40 million. These volunteers were instrumental in helping to qualify the amendment for the ballot[13] and in working to pass the measure. According to the campaign's own self-assessment:

> We set ambitious goals: to conduct a statewide Voter ID canvass of every voter; to distribute 1.25 million yard signs and an equal number of bumper strips; to have our volunteers recontact every soft yes and soft no voter; and to have 100,000 volunteers, five per voting precinct, working on Election Day to make sure every identified Yes on 8 voter would vote. All of these goals, and more, were achieved. (Schubert and Flint 2009, 45)

Expanding the Scope of the Conflict

Mobilizing this base of supporters was clearly an important component of the Yes on 8 campaign, but these efforts alone would not be enough to bring about victory in a left-leaning state such as California. To win, the campaign leaders needed to develop a message that would resonate with a majority of California voters, most of whom were not members of the religious right. Efforts to expand the appeal of Proposition 8 beyond this base focused primarily on two seemingly persuadable populations: moderate secular voters who were not receptive to religious appeals but who might find arguments framed using the secular discourse of rights convincing, and racial and ethnic minorities who typically voted Democratic but held socially conservative views regarding the issue of sexual orientation.

The feedback they received from focus groups, surveys, and field polls convinced campaign organizers that they needed to make undecided voters believe that allowing same-sex marriage to stand would have tangible consequences on their lives (Schubert and Flint 2009, 45). To do this, the campaign sought to frame opposition to same-sex marriage as necessary for safeguarding fundamental rights and "protecting children." For this strategy to work, the campaign had to make sure that its supporters stayed on message. To ensure message discipline, members of the Protect Marriage Coalition were required to sign a statement of unity. This statement of unity informed supporters that "independent strategies for public messaging . . . are counterproductive and increase the likelihood of defeat." It required that "public communications by coalition supporters must be approved by the Campaign Manager for Strategic Discipline. . . . Coalition supporters must publicly promote the marriage amendment through the unified face of the ProtectMarriage.com campaign" (Pugno 2008). Requirements such as these allowed the campaign to present a unified strategy in official campaign documents and made it possible for campaign organizers to discipline the unruly elements of their grassroots organization.

The Yes on 8 campaign began airing its initial television advertisement, "Whether You Like It or Not," a month before the election. The focal point of this advertisement is a clip from San Francisco mayor Gavin Newsom's 2008 press conference reacting to the California Supreme Court's *In re Marriage Cases* decision. In the clip, Newsom appears to be taunting opponents of same-sex marriage when he says, "This door's wide open now. It's going to happen, whether you like it or not." The advertisement repeats this sound bite several times in order to make the point that supporters of marriage equality were forcing acceptance of same-sex marriage on Californians against their will (ProtectMarriage.com 2008b). According to Schubert and Flint, "That 7 second sound bite perfectly summarized for California voters why this issue was before them, reminding the voters that four judges had overruled four million voters by imposing same-sex marriage on California" (Schubert and Flint 2009, 46). The advertisement concludes with a statement by Richard Peterson, a law professor at Pepperdine University. In his statement Peterson lists the "consequences" of legalizing same-sex marriage. He states that because acceptance of gay marriage is now "mandatory" in California, "people could be sued over personal beliefs, churches could lose tax-exempt status, and gay marriage could be taught in public schools" (ProtectMarriage.com 2008b).

As Election Day neared, the argument that legalizing same-sex marriage would infringe on the rights of parents to "protect children" from being taught about the subject in school became the defining issue of the Yes on 8 campaign. Supporters of Proposition 8 argued that if same-sex marriage were legalized, teachers would be compelled to teach students about it regardless of the wishes of parents. A typical example of this argument was published by members of the Yes on 8 campaign in the official California voters' guide:

> If the gay marriage ruling is not overturned, TEACHERS COULD[14] BE REQUIRED to teach young children there is *no difference* between gay marriage and traditional marriage. We should not accept a court decision that may result in public schools teaching our kids that gay marriage is okay. That is an issue for parents to discuss with their children according to their own values and beliefs. *It shouldn't be forced on us against our will.* (Prentice, Avila, and McKinney 2008)

As the campaign drew to a close, Yes on 8 released a series of television advertisements that focused specifically on the parental rights argument, including: "It's Already Happened" (ProtectMarriage.com 2008c), "Everything to Do with Schools" (ProtectMarriage.com 2008d), "Finally the Truth" (ProtectMarriage.com 2008f), and "Have You Thought about It?" (ProtectMarriage.com 2008j). Volunteers who talked with undecided voters were encouraged to make these arguments as well. According to Ron Prentice, director of the Yes on 8 campaign, the parental rights issue was the main focus when campaign officials talked to undecided voters. He explained, "If they weren't a solid yes 80 percent of the time, all it took was to tell them that 'did you know that every public school child will be taught this' and they would flip" (Prentice 2008).

In addition to presenting their opposition to same-sex marriage using the secular language of rights, the Yes on 8 campaign leaders also made an instrumental decision to target their message at different racial and ethnic minority groups. This was a fairly standard tactic at the time. Same-sex marriage was often used by conservatives as a wedge issue to peel away reliably Democratic constituencies such as African Americans and seniors (Lucas 2007; Egan and Sherrill 2009; Klarman 2012, 105). Proponents of Proposition 8 recruited minority community leaders to direct outreach efforts for the campaign, often using existing church networks to locate these individuals (Pollo 2008). Religious leaders were particularly instrumental in mobilizing African American voters in support of Proposition 8. The church has traditionally been the primary means of organizing the African American community (Dawson 1994). Most historically black churches in the state were in favor of the measure, and many organized rallies and worked to build support for the campaign (Abrajano 2010, 924).

The campaign also produced advertisements and materials targeted at specific racial and ethnic communities. These materials were printed in more than forty different languages. The messages presented in these documents were not significantly different from the ones presented elsewhere in the campaign, but they were clearly packaged to appeal to specific groups. The goal, according to Yes on 8 leaders, was to put a familiar face on the message of the campaign, to show members of these communities that members of their community also supported Proposition 8 (Schubert and Flint 2009, 46). Direct mail advertisements targeting African American voters, for example, featured a large picture of Barack Obama with a misleading quote from him stating that he was "not in favor of gay marriage" (ProtectMarriage.com 2008g).[15] The advertisement also included quotes regarding same-sex marriage from a number of African American pastors. These quotes typically reflected standard campaign themes, particularly the concern that if same-sex marriage were legalized, children would be taught about it in schools.[16] Advertisements targeted at Latino/as also emphasized standard campaign themes. The Yes on 8 campaign created a specific campaign theme for Latino/as, Family Is Sacred: Protect Children's Education (Cunningham 2008). The campaign also released Spanish-language television advertisements warning that legalizing same-sex marriage would require teachers to teach about homosexuality in schools (ProtectMarriage.com 2008h).

This approach appeared effective. California voters approved Proposition 8 by 52 percent to 48 percent. Exit polling data showed that the education issue was decisive for many voters who supported the measure (Garrison, DiMassa, and Paddock 2008). According to Schubert and Flint, the opposition leaders' "failure to respond to the 'consequences' message (especially the education message) in a timely fashion ultimately led to their downfall" (Schubert and Flint 2009, 46). Efforts to target racial and ethnic minorities also proved successful. Exit polling data suggest that support from these groups was key to the passage of Proposition 8. An initial National Election Pool exit poll showed that African Americans made up 10 percent of the vote in California in 2008 and supported Proposition 8 by a large margin, with 70 percent voting in favor of it. Latino/as accounted for 18 percent of the vote and also supported Proposition 8, although by a much smaller margin, with only 53 percent voting yes. Asian Americans made up 6 percent of voters and were actually slightly more likely to oppose Proposition 8, with 49 percent voting in favor of it. Whites made up 63 percent of the vote and were also slightly more likely to oppose Proposition 8, with 49 percent voting yes (CNN 2008). Some scholars have criticized these numbers, arguing in particular that these polling data overestimate African American support for the measure, which they estimated instead to be between 57 percent and 59 percent (Egan and Sherrill 2009). They also argue that higher rates of religiosity among African Americans, not race, accounted for their increased support for Proposition 8. This is a valid critique, but even these revised estimates indicate that African Americans supported Proposition 8 in greater numbers than did other racial and ethnic groups. Other studies have also found that African Americans supported Proposition 8 in higher numbers than whites, even when controlling for religious beliefs (Abrajano 2010). This suggests that opponents of same-sex marriage did an effective job of reaching out to minority communities during the campaign.

Constructing Culture Warriors

Proponents of Proposition 8 were clearly motivated by an instrumental desire to have their point of view prevail. However, instrumental concerns only tell half the story. In addition to having instrumental impact on the outcome of the campaign, the rights discourse used by proponents of Proposition 8 also had constitutive impact on how they saw themselves in relation to their opponents. Framing their opposition using the language of rights provided considerable legitimacy for opponents of same-sex marriage. Such rights discourse empowers individuals, enabling them to claim an identity for themselves as virtuous US citizens (Passavant 2002; Dudas 2008). Conservatives used this rights discourse to construct an image of themselves as an embattled minority group heroically standing up for their own civil rights rather than as a recalcitrant majority stubbornly opposing the rights of gays and lesbians.

Proponents of marriage equality often invoke the language of equal rights to help build support for their cause. No on 8 campaign materials repeated the mantra that Proposition 8 "eliminates fundamental rights" and described

the measure using words such as "unfair," "divisive," "discriminatory," "intolerant," and "offensive" (NoOnProp8.com 2008a, 2008c, 2008d, 2008e, 2008f). In
order to combat these rights-based appeals, opponents of same-sex marriage
countered by arguing that the purpose of Proposition 8 was not to take rights
away from gays and lesbians but to preserve the rights of everyone else. As one
supporter argued during the campaign:

> The marriage controversy has been contaminated by the language of rights. We
> must remember there are other groups and other people who also have their own
> rights besides gays. We have to think about children, their right to be raised by
> a mother and a father. We have to think about religious groups that believe that
> marriage is an institution established by God who are right now are [sic] having
> their rights violated by the supposed rights of the gay portion of our society.
> (Miranda 2008, 53)

These views were echoed by other supporters as well. At a rally in support
of Proposition 8, Jim Garlow, a pastor at Skyline Church in San Diego, spoke
passionately about the need to protect religious liberty from attack by proponents of same-sex marriage:

> Rights have been crushed under every time same-sex marriage is legal. Some
> pastors have been threatened with jail. Many have been muzzled and silenced.
> Churches have been threatened and intimidated and parents . . . and business
> persons [sic] as well. . . . This is ultimately really not about marriage and
> homosexuality at its core. At its core is they have found a loophole hiding under
> the guise of civil rights by which they can put underfoot and crush underfoot
> the rights of every person who has a Biblical worldview. That is what is at stake.
> (Garlow 2008a, 45–46)

Adopting such a perspective personalizes opposition to same-sex marriage,
transforming it from a fight to protect the somewhat abstract institution of
marriage to a personal defense of one's individual rights. Using the discourse
of rights in this way causes opponents of same-sex marriage to see themselves
as "cultural warriors" fighting to preserve fundamental rights and values
threatened by the "excessive" and "unnecessary" rights claims of gays and lesbians. According to this logic, rights are a zero-sum game in which demands
for new rights necessarily come at the expense of existing ones.

If the debate over same-sex marriage really is a zero-sum contest between competing rights claims, as conservatives argue, then they must justify why their rights should be valued above those of others. Proponents of Proposition 8 frequently did this by using populist language to elevate their rights claims and denigrate those of gays and lesbians. They depicted their fight against same-sex marriage as part of a popular grassroots movement. For example, one official argued during the campaign:

> This is a campaign of the people, by the people, and of the people [*sic*]. We don't call the media when we need help . . . we call our good neighbors. Because we know they will show up. And a dozen years from now when our kids or our grandkids ask us where we were when marriage was on the ballot in California . . . all of us, all the millions of you, will be able to say, "I was there. And I did it for you." (Brown 2008)

In contrast, proponents of marriage equality were described as subversive elites, out of touch with the values of average Californians.[17] The campaign repeatedly framed the *In re Marriage Cases* decision as "judicial activism" and made much of the fact that the California Supreme Court was based in San Francisco, repeatedly emphasizing that same-sex marriage had been "forced on Californians" by four "San Francisco judges" (Anderson, Bolingbroke, and Smith 2008; Gallagher 2008, 45; Prentice, Avila, and McKinney 2008; Protect-Marriage.com 2008b, 2008i, 2008j, 2008k, 2008l, 2008m). In this way proponents of Proposition 8 were able to associate support for marriage equality with the values of culturally liberal urbanites, using place as a way to signify that those who support same-sex marriage were advancing extremist positions out of touch with the values of average Americans (Stein 2002; Rasmussen 2006).

In the past, conservatives have often framed their opposition to minority rights claims by using the language of "special rights" to depict these requests as excessive demands perpetrated by a subversive minority group and its elite allies (Schacter 1994; Goldberg-Hiller and Milner 2003; Dudas 2008). This phenomenon was explored in detail in Chapter 2 of this book. Proponents of Proposition 8 never used the language of special rights, but they embraced this same logic. They argued that attempts to legalize same-sex marriage were unnecessary and excessive because gays and lesbians in California already enjoyed domestic partnership rights. Campaign materials often stated that although "gays have the right to their private lives, *they do not have the right to redefine marriage* for everyone else" (Anderson, Bolingbroke, and Smith 2008; Prentice,

Avila, and McKinney 2008; ProtectMarriage.com 2008j, 2008k, 2008m). This logic creates an inversion process whereby gays and lesbians become the oppressors seeking to infringe on individual rights, and conservatives become the victims of oppression (Goldberg-Hiller and Milner 2003).

Opponents of same-sex marriage cultivated an image of themselves as victims of oppression throughout the Proposition 8 campaign. A number of Yes on 8 campaign advertisements featured the story of Robb and Robin Wirthlin of Massachusetts, who complained that their son had been taught about same-sex marriage against their wishes while attending public school in 2006. The Wirthlins, along with David and Tonia Parker, filed suit in federal court arguing that allowing teachers to teach their children about same-sex marriage was an unconstitutional violation of their religious liberty. The court rejected their claim, however, finding that "exposure to ideas through the required reading of books [does] not constitute a constitutionally significant burden on the plaintiffs' free exercise of religion" (*Parker v. Hurley* 2008, 105). Although the court rejected the Wirthlins' rights claims, this ruling did not dampen their belief that same-sex marriage infringes on their parental rights. In one television advertisement produced by the Yes on 8 campaign, "Everything to Do with Schools," the Wirthlins urged voters to help protect parental rights by voting "yes on 8." In the advertisement, they expressed frustration with the court's decision, stating, "We tried to stop public schools from teaching children about gay marriage, but the courts said we had no right to object or pull him out of class" (ProtectMarriage.com 2008b).

Framing their opposition to same-sex marriage using the discourse of fundamental rights caused the Wirthlins to see themselves as victims of intolerance. In another video produced for the Yes on 8 campaign, they reflected on the incident involving their son:

> No longer is it ok to disagree. . . . If you disagree with a particular lifestyle or behavior you are now wrong, you are now bigoted. It's no longer a difference of opinion; you are wrong. . . . The tolerance that the gay community cries out for is not demonstrated to people who have differing points of view. There is no tolerance. The hate, the disparaging remarks, the hostility that we faced were so astonishing. (ProtectMarriage.com 2008f)

The Wirthlins were not the only ones who felt this way. During the campaign, Yes on 8 released a number of news reports detailing "verbal and physical assaults" made against members of the campaign. One article described how a supporter of Proposition 8 was "assaulted for expressing his opposition to same-sex marriage" and stated, "The attack shows that their opponents are not as tolerant and open-minded as they would like voters to believe. It's outrageous that the No campaign calls themselves the voice of tolerance and moderation and wants people to feel bad for supporting Prop. 8. . . . Clearly the man who attacked Jose is intolerant of those who support traditional marriage" (White and Brown 2008c). Another article listed numerous examples of supporters being verbally assaulted and of campaign materials being vandalized (White and Brown 2008b). These acts were highlighted as examples of the other side's intolerance. In one speech to supporters, Garlow argued, "As you stand for Proposition 8, you will be called a hate monger. You'll have all kinds of names thrown at you. Don't stop loving just because the other side attacks in an unloving fashion. Don't trash them the way they're trashing you. Don't yield to that temptation" (Garlow 2008b, 60–61).

Depicting themselves as the real victims of intolerance helped mobilize opposition to same-sex marriage by enabling proponents of Proposition 8 to see themselves as martyrs for a worthy cause and claim the moral high ground in the debate over same-sex marriage. During one rally in support of Proposition 8, Garlow compared opposition to same-sex marriage to earlier struggles for civil rights in the United States. After one speaker shared his story, Garlow pleaded, "Lord, give them the grace and the influence and the protection of Rosa Parks . . . you've become the Rosa Parks of defending the rights of children in America" (Garlow 2008b, 32–33). Using this rights language in this way allows conservatives to co-opt the mantle of the civil rights movement, a common component of New Right political discourse.[18]

Constructing Deviants

In addition to constructing opponents of same-sex marriage as victims, the rights discourse used by conservatives also constructs an image of gays and lesbians as deviant. The argument that parents should have the right to protect their children from being taught about same-sex marriage in school, for example, rests on an implicit assumption that same-sex marriage is obscene and that gays and lesbians are sinful and threatening. As Chapter 2 of this book makes clear, the argument that gays and lesbians "threaten children" has been a long-standing refrain for antigay activists. Opponents of same-sex marriage largely abandoned the harsh, overtly homophobic, and discriminatory language used by activists such as Anita Bryant to oppose gay rights in the 1970s—but the implicit assumption that gays and lesbians want to corrupt children remains a central concern for conservative activists. The parental rights argument used during the Yes on 8 campaign resonated with voters in part because it was able to tap into a palpable fear that legalizing same-sex marriage would make children more tolerant of gays and lesbians and thus increase the likelihood that they might "choose" to become gay.[19]

One television advertisement used by the Yes on 8 campaign, "It's Already Happened," hints at this fear. In the advertisement, a little girl shows her mother a book she read in school called *The King and the King,* and says, "I learned that a prince can marry a prince and I can marry a princess" (ProtectMarriage.com 2008a). The child puts particular emphasis on the second half of the sentence, "*I can marry a princess,*" suggesting that the real fear is not that children will learn about same-sex marriage in school but that they may actually become gay themselves as a result. The advertisement concludes with the parent flashing her child a worried look and then having a stern conversation with her, the implication being that having a child marry someone of the same gender is an occurrence most parents would want to avoid. Another advertisement, "Have You Thought about It?," makes a similar appeal. The advertisement suggests that legalizing same-sex marriage will harm children, concluding with a little girl innocently looking into the camera and asking, "Have you thought about what same-sex marriage means, to me?" (ProtectMarriage.com 2008e).

This discourse relies on the implicit assumption that gays and lesbians are "dangerous" and "deviant" others whose selfish and excessive rights claims threaten the legitimate rights of the majority of Americans (Schacter 1994; Goldberg-Hiller and Milner 2003; Dudas 2008). Such logic builds on a long-standing conception of citizenship that argues that individuals must prove they deserve equal rights by disciplining what are thought to be deviant sexual urges (Comaroff and Comaroff 1991, 365–404; Merry 2000, 221–257). The same-sex marriage debate has been shaped powerfully by this modern conception of citizenship. Marriage has traditionally been viewed as an institution that imposes discipline upon sexual urges by requiring that two people commit to a long-term, monogamous sexual relationship. Those who oppose same-sex marriage often argue, sometimes implicitly and sometimes explicitly, that gays and lesbians threaten this concept of marriage because they lack the ability to discipline themselves in this way (Sprigg and Dailey 2004; Sprigg

2007). Perhaps even more disturbing is the insinuation that because gays and lesbians lack the ability to control their sexual urges, they pose a threat to children. This taps into a long-standing conception of gays and lesbians as sexual predators who seek to seduce children and recruit them into the gay lifestyle (Fejes 2008). If stated explicitly the moral assumptions that undergird such arguments would appear abhorrent and repulsive to many moderate voters who consider themselves otherwise tolerant people. When masked by the secular discourse of rights, however, these underlying stereotypes go unnoticed, and as a result, the arguments that they support become more palatable.

Countering Conservative Rights Claims

Opponents of Proposition 8 worked to defeat the measure by debunking the Yes on 8 campaign's arguments. Of particular importance to the campaign was dispelling the notion that legalizing same-sex marriage would lead to children being taught about it in schools. A number of political leaders and government officials, most notably the California Teachers Association and California superintendent of public instruction Jack O'Connell, spoke against this claim. During the campaign O'Connell released a statement confirming that the California Education Code does not require teachers to teach about marriage. Section 51933 of the code does state that schools that choose to teach comprehensive sex education must also "teach respect for marriage and committed relationships."[20] However, schools are not required to teach sex education; local school boards have the power to determine whether individual schools choose to offer such programs. Furthermore, Sections 51937 and 51938 of the code explain that schools that choose to teach sex education are required to disclose to parents exactly *what* they are teaching students, and parents have the right to exclude their children from those classes if they desire (California Department of Education 2011).

The No on 8 campaign sought to communicate this information to voters in campaign materials and advertisements. A statement published by the campaign that appeared in the official California voters' guide states:

> Don't be tricked by scare tactics. PROP. 8 DOESN'T HAVE ANYTHING TO DO WITH SCHOOLS. There's NOT ONE WORD IN 8 ABOUT EDUCATION. In fact, local school districts and parents—not the state—develop health education programs for their

schools. NO CHILD CAN BE FORCED, AGAINST THE WILL OF THEIR [*sic*] PARENTS, TO BE TAUGHT ANYTHING about health and family issues. CALIFORNIA LAW PROHIBITS IT. And NOTHING IN STATE LAW REQUIRES THE MENTION OF MARRIAGE IN KINDERGARTEN! It's a smokescreen. (Bell, Salcido, and Eastin 2008)

A similar argument was presented in a television advertisement released by the campaign, "Prop. 8 Has Nothing to Do with Schools." The advertisement featured O'Connell making this statement: "Prop 8 has nothing to do with schools or kids. Our schools aren't required to teach anything about marriage, and using kids to lie about that is shameful" (NoOnProp8.com 2008b).

Proponents of Proposition 8 dismissed these claims. They pointed out that though sex education is not required by law, 96 percent of California public schools teach it, and they argued that those schools would be required to teach same-sex marriage as well. They sought to discredit O'Connell specifically by insinuating that his statement was a reflection of his own political beliefs, not an unbiased reading of the law. A press release put out by the campaign in response to the O'Connell advertisement stated, "There is no foundation for O'Connell's untruthful statements that nothing in California law requires teaching about marriage.... The voters deserve to hear the truth. While O'Connell may personally favor gay marriage, as a public official it is his obligation to tell the truth about California's education laws" (White 2008). Proponents of Proposition 8 often used populist appeals like these to depict those who offered their opinion on the parental rights issue as elite advocates of same-sex marriage providing biased analyses (White 2008; White and Brown 2008a).

A major turning point of the campaign occurred one month before the election, when a group of first-grade students at a San Francisco public school took a field trip to City Hall to witness the wedding of their lesbian teacher. Proponents of Proposition 8 found out about the event after the story was broadcast by local news outlets. They used it as tangible evidence that if Proposition 8 were rejected, same-sex marriage would be taught to children in public schools. It became the focal point of an advertisement, "Finally the Truth," in which a narrator describes how students were taken to the wedding as part of a "teachable moment" while foreboding music plays in the background. The advertisement concludes with the statement, "Children will be taught about gay marriage unless we vote yes on Proposition 8" (ProtectMarriage.com 2008f). This advertisement proved powerful. Schubert and Flint called the event the "most ill-considered publicity stunt ever mounted in an initiative campaign" and remarked, "Now we not only had an example of something that had happened in California (as opposed to might happen) we had video footage to prove it" (Schubert and Flint 2009, 47). However, the advertisement left out a number of important details that undermined the claim that the event was a violation of parental rights. The field trip was actually orchestrated by a parent of the students, not the school, and was a complete surprise to the teacher. Students who attended had to have written permission from their parents. Two families opted not to have their children participate in the field trip; those students spent the day with another first-grade class instead (Tucker 2008). The omission of these details shows that, in the context of a ballot measure campaign, it is easy for information to be presented in a way that distorts voters' understanding of the issue.

Opponents of Proposition 8 did attempt to counter the parental rights claims advanced by the Yes on 8 campaign at a factual level, but the moral logic behind the argument that children must be protected from being taught about same-sex marriage in school went largely uncontested. The No on 8 campaign leaders argued repeatedly that Proposition 8 was discriminatory, but they were constrained by the need to fit these arguments into short sound bites. As a result, they produced advertisements that typically featured a celebrity or political official imploring voters to vote no on Proposition 8 because it was "unfair and wrong" (NoOnProp8.com 2008a, 2008c, 2008d) or to "vote against discrimination" (NoOnProp8.com 2008e). These thirty-second advertisements never attempted to provide the kind of in-depth analysis necessary to fully explain, for example, why arguing that students need to be protected from being taught about same-sex marriage in schools is discriminatory. Attempting to counter the parental rights argument on a factual level was also doomed to fail because these arguments are not based on a dispassionate examination of the issue but instead appeal to a particular notion of morality designed to generate a visceral, emotional response. Instead of disputing this moral logic, though, opponents of Proposition 8 actually gave credence to it by vehemently insisting that same-sex marriage would not be taught in schools—an argument that implies such an occurrence would be a bad thing.

Conceding this moral logic forced advocates of marriage equality to convince voters that the supposed moral harms that stem from exposing children to the issue of same-sex marriage would absolutely not occur, whereas proponents of Proposition 8 had only to raise doubts about this assumption. This is a difficult undertaking in a ballot measure campaign because most voters do not have the time or inclination to expose arguments to the kind of scrutiny required to dispel factual inaccuracies or unmask underlying discriminatory stereotypes. Obtaining a complete understanding of the parental rights issue, for example, requires a fairly nuanced reading of the California Education Code. The complexity of this code is difficult to convey in short campaign advertisements, and the average voter is unlikely to read the statute for herself. This allows members of both campaigns to control voters' understanding of the issue through advertising and results in a disconnect between what elites know to be true about an issue and how it is perceived by the general public (Haltom and McCann 2004). When the debate over same-sex marriage moves to a courtroom environment, however, this rights discourse is subjected to more careful scrutiny and, as a result, becomes a liability for conservatives.

PERRY V. SCHWARZENEGGER (2010)

Proponents of same-sex marriage responded to the passage of Proposition 8 by once again taking the marriage issue to the California Supreme Court.[21] They argued that because Proposition 8 eliminated the rights of a historically disadvantaged minority group, it was an invalid "constitutional revision," not an amendment. The court was ultimately unpersuaded by this argument, however, and allowed the measure to stand (*Strauss v. Horton* 2009).[22] One day after the court announced its decision in *Strauss v. Horton,* the American Foundation for Equal Rights (AFER) announced that it had filed a suit in federal court arguing that Proposition 8 violated the due process and equal protection clauses of the Fourteenth Amendment. Their case, which came to be known initially as *Perry* v. *Schwarzenegger,* made headlines both because it represented the first major federal challenge to a prohibition on same-sex marriage and because the effort was being led by Theodore Olson and David Boies—two well-known attorneys famous for representing opposing sides in the high-profile case *Bush v. Gore* (2000).

The case became more complicated after the state of California took the unusual step of refusing to defend Proposition 8 in court.[23] In light of the state's position, the judge assigned to the case, Vaughn Walker,[24] allowed the sponsors of Proposition 8, the Protect Marriage Coalition, represented by the conservative legal organization Alliance Defense Fund (ADF), to intervene on behalf of the defense.[25] In another somewhat unusual decision, Walker also announced that he wanted to hear the factual issues of this case at trial. Few previous marriage cases at the state or federal level had ever gone to trial. Most had been decided via summary judgment based on testimony provided through affidavits and declarations. Walker argued, however, that because this case was likely headed to the Supreme Court, it was important for the district court to establish a fully developed factual record for future courts to consider (Walker 2009a, 24–25).

Though the same group responsible for engineering the Proposition 8 campaign would also be responsible for defending the law in court, the arguments its members used to frame their opposition to same-sex marriage during the *Perry* trial were considerably different from those used during the ballot measure campaign. Attorneys representing the Protect Marriage Coalition adopted a two-part strategy for defending Proposition 8 in court. First, they used legal analysis and past case precedent to argue that the court should dismiss the plaintiffs' rights claims. Second, they employed expert testimony to show that the state had a legitimate government interest that justified treating same-sex and opposite-sex couples differently with respect to marriage.

Dismissing Rights Claims

The defense began its case by arguing that the court should summarily dismiss the plaintiffs' claim because the US Constitution does not recognize a fundamental right to same-sex marriage. As support for this position the attorneys cited the case of *Baker v. Nelson* (1972), in which the Court declined to review a Minnesota court's finding that there was no fundamental right to same-sex marriage. The defense argued that because the case had come to the Court through mandatory review, rather than the certiorari process, its summary dismissal constituted a decision on the merits and is thus binding precedent that future courts must follow (Alliance Defense Fund 2009a, 13–18; 2009b, 2; 2010, 36).[26] As further support for the argument that same-sex marriage was not a fundamental right, the defense attorneys contended that although there is a long tradition of recognizing opposite-sex marriage in the United States, there is no history or tradition of same-sex marriage in this country (Alliance Defense Fund 2009a, 21–22; 2009b, 2–3; 2010, 32–36; Blankenhorn 2010; Cooper 2010c; Thompson 2010a). They argued, "The striking lack of historical precedent for extending marriage to same-sex couples provides strong evidence that liberty and justice can exist in a regime that does not recognize same-sex marriages" (Alliance Defense Fund 2009a, 22). This suggests that same-sex marriage is not implicit in the concept of ordered liberty and thus not a fundamental constitutional right.

In addition to arguing that there is no fundamental right to same-sex marriage, the defense also argued that this case should be dismissed because the court lacked the authority to decide an issue with such important moral and political implications.[27] In making this argument, the defense relied heavily on the precedent established in the case of *Washington v. Glucksberg* (1997). In this case the Supreme Court unanimously declined to recognize a fundamental right to physician-assisted suicide, arguing instead that such difficult moral dilemmas must be decided by the people through the political process. Charles Cooper, lead attorney for the defense, laid out this argument in his opening statement, providing an impassioned defense of the people's right to decide the proper definition of marriage:

> The political process, not you, not the members of the Ninth Circuit, and not even ... the Justices of the United States Supreme Court are here to reflect the attitudes of the American people. That's what they have ballot booths for, your Honor. ... The question is whether anything in our Constitution insists on [same-sex marriage]. Whether anything in our Constitution takes that issue out of the hands of the people of California and the people of the neighboring states to California and the people of my home state and says, this is what the Constitution demands. You have no say in it. (Cooper 2010a, 70–71)

These populist appeals are similar to the judicial activism arguments made during the Proposition 8 campaign. The fact that these arguments work equally well in both institutional contexts is testament to the adaptability of this discursive framework.

The legal analysis the ADF provided during the *Perry* trial can be persuasive. Using this logic allows the court to avoid the thorny question of whether same-sex marriage *should* be legal and instead focus on the more value-neutral question of whether the court has the authority to make it so. A number of courts have used these arguments as justification for upholding statewide prohibitions on same-sex marriage (see, for example, *Andersen v. King County* 2006; *Hernández v. Robles* 2006; *Lewis v. Harris* 2006; *Conaway v. Deane* 2007). Walker did not ultimately find these arguments convincing, however. He dismissed the defense's motion for summary judgment, stating that much has changed in the forty years since *Baker* was decided and that the court should take another look at the marriage issue (Walker 2009c). He also ruled that gays and lesbians were not seeking the creation of a new fundamental right to same-sex marriage but rather access to the existing fundamental right to marry the people of their choosing, making the debate about the historical definition of marriage irrelevant. Finally, he contended that because marriage is a fundamental right, this issue should be decided by the judiciary rather than through the political process (*Perry v. Schwarzenegger* 2010, 991–993).

Clearly, different courts have viewed these legal questions differently. This is because these are not empirical matters that have a definite right or wrong answer—there are plenty of legal precedents that can be used to support either side of these arguments. Instead, these are subjective questions vulnerable to being colored by a judge's own personal ideological preferences (Segal and Spaeth 1993). If a judge is not persuaded by this legal analysis to dismiss the claim that same-sex couples have a right to marry, then he or she must consider the more substantive question of whether there is a government interest that justifies denying gays and lesbians that right. This is, in large part, an empirical question—one to which opponents of same-sex marriage have had considerable difficulty providing a credible answer.

Justifying Discriminatory Treatment

Laws that discriminate by treating two similarly situated populations un-equally are evaluated by the court using either a rational basis, intermediate, or strict scrutiny standard of review. In order to ensure that they had the best chance of winning their case, the defense attorneys argued that Proposition 8 should be evaluated using the lowest level of scrutiny, the rational basis test. Under this standard Proposition 8 would survive judicial scrutiny provided the defense was able to prove it was "rationally related" to a "legitimate government interest." This is a much easier standard to satisfy than strict scrutiny, which would require the defense to show that Proposition 8 furthered a "compelling government interest," was "narrowly tailored," and used the "least restrictive means" available to further that interest.[28]

The defense argued that the court should consider Proposition 8 using the rational basis test because past case precedent had firmly established that discrimination based on sexual orientation was to be evaluated under rational basis review. The attorneys pointed out that no federal court had ever held that sexual orientation should receive a heightened level of judicial scrutiny before—both *Romer v. Evans* (1996) and *High Tech Gays v. Defense Industrial Security Clearance Office* (1990) were decided under rational basis review (Alliance Defense Fund 2009a, 37). The defense also argued that gays and lesbians should not qualify for heightened judicial protections as a "suspect class" because they are not a politically powerless minority group (Alliance Defense Fund 2009b, 5; 2010, 40; Cooper 2010a; Raum 2010; Thompson 2010b, 2010d). They relied on testimony from political scientist Kenneth Miller, an associate professor at Claremont McKenna College, to provide support for this argument. Miller testified that gays and lesbians have won a number of legal advances in recent years, such as the extension of domestic partnership rights in many states, and that they have a number of powerful political allies in government. This is evidence, he suggested, that they are not a politically powerless minority group in need of heightened judicial protection (Miller 2010).

The substance of the defense's case focused on the argument that the state had a legitimate government interest in prohibiting same-sex marriage because the "traditional family" structure, headed by a mother and a father, provides the best environment for raising children. In his closing arguments Cooper summed up this position, stating:

> A family environment with married opposite-sex parents remains the optimum social structure in which to bear children. . . . The raising of children by same-sex couples, who by definition cannot be the two sole biological parents of a child and cannot provide children with a parental authority figure of each gender, presents an alternative structure for child-rearing that has not yet proved itself, beyond reasonable scientific dispute, to be as optimal as the biologically based marriage norm. (Cooper 2010c, 3068)

The defense relied primarily on the testimony of David Blankenhorn to provide support for this argument. Blankenhorn is the author of two books on marriage: *Fatherless America* (1996) and *The Future of Marriage* (2007). He was also the president of the Institute for American Values, a socially conservative think tank. During the trial, Blankenhorn testified that limiting marriage to one man and one woman provides important societal approval for the traditional family unit. This societal approval creates a powerful "marriage norm," effectively encouraging individuals to create this type of family structure and discouraging the creation of so-called alternative families. Expanding the definition of marriage to include same-sex couples would, he argued, "deinstitutionalize" marriage by treating alternative family structures the same as traditional, opposite-sex ones. This would weaken the power of marriage as an institution designed to create stable two-parent family environments and ultimately lead to more children being raised outside of this structure (Blankenhorn 2010).[29]

Unfortunately for the defense, the testimony provided by these two expert witnesses faltered under judicial scrutiny. During his voir dire it was revealed that Miller had published a number of books and peer-reviewed journal articles on the initiative process and its impact on California politics generally. He had even used Proposition 8 as a case study in one of these publications. The court considered him an expert on those topic areas. However, during the trial he was asked to testify at length about the political power of gays and lesbians, a topic that attorneys for the plaintiffs argued was beyond his range of expertise. During cross-examination it was revealed that Miller was unaware of key moments in the history of the gay rights movement, was unfamiliar with the work of several prominent scholars who write on this topic, and had been assisted considerably by attorneys for the defense in writing his expert report. He also seemed to contradict himself under cross-examination, admitting at one point that Proposition 8 was "discrimination" (though he said it was not "invidious") and that gays and lesbians are still subject to a considerable amount of discrimination and stereotyping (Boies 2010a). His testimony was further refuted by experts called for the plaintiffs who pointed out that gays and lesbians have a long history of being subjected to discriminatory treatment that continues to limit their political power (Chauncey 2010; Segura 2010).

Some aspects of Miller's testimony were clearly questionable, but Blankenhorn's was a disaster for the defense. Blankenhorn claimed to be an expert on marriage, but during his voir dire, the plaintiffs argued that he did not meet the definition of "expert" on this issue because he had no degree in a related field, had never taught a college or university course on the topic, had never published any peer-reviewed work, and had never conducted any empirical research on the subject (Boies 2010b).[30] He struggled to answer basic questions from the plaintiffs during cross-examination and even contradicted much of his own testimony. Though he was allowed to testify at trial, his opinion was ultimately given no consideration by the court because Walker found that he failed to meet the definition of an expert on marriage (*Perry v. Schwarzenegger* 2010, 945–950). Three of the plaintiffs' expert witnesses also refuted Blankenhorn's testimony directly. They testified that he had misrepresented the existing literature and that there was no evidence to suggest that children raised in same-sex households are in any way worse off than those raised by opposite-sex couples (Badgett 2010a; Lamb 2010; Peplau 2010).

The inability to support their positions with adequate testimony from expert witnesses severely hampered the defense attorneys' case during trial. Although the defense attorneys contended that many researchers agreed with them, they chose not to call their own experts to counter much of the plaintiffs' testimony, despite Walker frequently urging them to do so (Walker 2010, 61–62, 1494–1496, 3039–3040, 3042–3043). In his opinion, Walker found that the defense had failed to support most of its assertions with evidence. He stated that the two witnesses the attorneys did call had dubious credentials and contradicted much of their own testimony during cross-examination (*Perry v. Schwarzenegger* 2010, 944–952). In contrast to the defense, the plaintiffs called nine expert witnesses from top academic institutions and four lay witnesses to provide support for their positions. The expertise of these witnesses was never questioned. The defense made no attempt to challenge their qualifications; it even waived its right to voir dire at trial. Attorneys for the defense attempted to refute the plaintiffs' case mostly by pointing out small inconsistencies of logic and by suggesting that the testimony provided by their expert witnesses was motivated by a personal desire to see same-sex marriage legalized (Cooper 2010b; Raum 2010; Thompson 2010a, 2010b, 2010c, 2010d). These arguments had limited impact on the outcome of the case in large part because the plaintiffs' witnesses were not basing their testimony on personal opinion alone but on empirical studies subjected to the rigors of the peer-review process.

In light of the defense's deficiencies and the overwhelming amount of evidence presented by the plaintiffs, Walker concluded that he must reject the arguments provided in support of Proposition 8. He found the argument that gays and lesbians were not a powerless minority group unconvincing (*Perry v. Schwarzenegger* 2010, 997), but the point was moot because he also found that Proposition 8 failed to survive even a rational basis standard of review (*Perry v. Schwarzenegger* 2010, 997–998). Most crucially, he found that an interest in promoting opposite-sex parenting over same-sex parenting is not a sufficient justification for prohibiting same-sex marriage because there is no evidence showing that opposite-sex couples are better parents than same-sex ones and because prohibiting same-sex marriage would not prevent same-sex couples from raising children (*Perry v. Schwarzenegger* 2010, 934–935, 999–1000).

Rights as a Liability

Even more interesting than the defense's argument during the *Perry* trial is what the attorneys chose not to argue. Although the Protect Marriage Coalition had made the parental rights argument the focal point of the Proposition 8 Campaign, it attempted to downplay this argument in court. A desire to protect parental rights certainly has the potential to be a legitimate state interest that could justify prohibiting same-sex marriage. Yet the defense only mentioned this issue once as part of a long list of "potential state interests" provided in its trial brief (Alliance Defense Fund 2009a, 7). In fact, the attorneys worked hard to keep arguments used during the campaign out of the courtroom altogether. They argued that determining the motivations of voters who voted for a ballot measure was an "inappropriate question for judicial inquiry" (Cooper 2010c, 17) and filed for, and eventually received, a protective order restricting the plaintiffs' access to internal campaign documents (Alliance Defense Fund 2009b). This seemed a calculated decision designed to avoid discussing some of the implicit moral assumptions that undergird the parental rights argument. This shift in tactics did not go unnoticed by the plaintiffs, however. In his closing argument, Olson drew attention to it:

> It is revealing, it seems to me, that the deinstitutionalization message is quite different from the thrust of the proponents' Yes on 8 election campaign. That, in the words they put into the hands of all California voters, focused heavily on: Protect our children from somehow learning that gay marriage is okay. . . . That was not a very subtle theme that there is something wrong, sinister, or unusual about gays, that gays and their relationship[s] are not okay, and decidedly not suitable for children, but that children might think it was okay if they learned about gays getting married like normal people. For obvious reasons, the "gays are not okay" message was largely abandoned during the trial in favor of the procreation and deinstitutionalization themes. (Olson 2010, 2964)[31]

Despite the defense's best efforts to shift the debate away from the issue of parental rights and onto the issue of procreation, arguments made during the Proposition 8 campaign ultimately could not be kept out of the court-room. The plaintiffs made the parental rights argument used by the Yes on 8 campaign a focal point of their case. They provided testimony from gays and lesbians living in California during the campaign who stated that the protect children message was deeply offensive to them because it implied that they were predators who posed a threat to children (Katami 2010; Zia 2010).

They also called a number of expert witnesses able to unpack the discrim-inatory stereotypes underlying the parental rights argument used during the campaign. These experts testified that the notion that same-sex marriage should not be taught in public schools using age-appropriate methods creates the impression that being gay is dirty, deviant, and immoral behavior not fit to be discussed around children and perpetuates the idea that gays and lesbians are dangerous (Chauncey 2010; Herek 2010b; Meyer 2010; Segura 2010). Prohib-iting the discussion of same-sex marriage in the classroom stigmatizes gays and lesbians by creating a clear double standard that says children cannot be taught about same-sex marriage but can be exposed to traditional definitions of mar-riage. These are frequently depicted in books and fairy tales read to children of all ages, and rarely raise objections from parents (Chauncey 2010). Experts also testified that advertisements used during the campaign implied that exposure to same-sex marriage would encourage more children to become gay themselves and that parents should fear such an occurrence (Segura 2010). The defense countered by arguing that advertisements used during the campaign that stated a need to "protect children" were not motivated by animosity toward gays and lesbians but instead by a sincere and legitimate desire to allow parents to control their children's moral education (Raum 2010; Thompson 2010b). They never attempted to dispute the moral implications of these arguments, however.

The defense's inability to keep the parental rights argument out of the courtroom shows that courts are not closed institutions that can be studied in isolation but are frequently influenced by activities that take place outside of their walls. Framing opposition to same-sex marriage using the discourse of parental rights was an effective strategy for conservatives during the Yes on 8 campaign in part because it allowed them to expand the scope of the conflict and draw in more moderate, secular voters who might not have voted in favor of Proposition 8 otherwise. Expanding the scope of the conflict can have neg-ative consequences as well, though. After an argument has been advanced, its author loses control of it, resulting in unpredictable and often negative conse-quences for its proponents (Schattschneider 1960, 3).

The parental rights argument might have helped conservatives to pass Proposition 8, but it became a serious liability for them after this debate moved to the courtroom environment. In his opinion Walker stated that, in light of the evidence presented by the plaintiffs, he must conclude that Proposition 8 was not motivated by a legitimate government interest but an illegitimate discriminatory intent. He agreed with many of the conclusions the plaintiffs drew about Yes on 8 campaign specifically, finding:

> The campaign relied heavily on negative stereotypes about gays and lesbians and focused on protecting children from inchoate threats vaguely associated with gays and lesbians. . . . Proposition 8 played on a fear that exposure to homosexuality would turn children into homosexuals and that parents should dread having children who are not heterosexual. . . . Moral disapproval alone is an improper basis on which to deny rights to gay men and lesbians. (*Perry v. Schwarzenegger* 2010, 1003)

Having ruled that Proposition 8 was not motivated by a legitimate government interest but instead by animus toward gays and lesbians, Walker ruled that he had no choice but to invalidate the law.[32]

Combating Unfavorable Court Decisions

Conservatives responded to Walker's decision by quickly filing an appeal with the Ninth Circuit Court of Appeals. That court upheld Walker's ruling that marriage is a fundamental right that cannot be denied individuals because of their sexual orientation, but it limited the scope of the decision to the state of California (*Perry v. Brown* 2012). Conservatives once again appealed the decision, this time to the Supreme Court, which granted review. The Court's decision was somewhat anticlimactic. The justices declined to rule on the substantive issues of the case, choosing instead to find that the Protect Marriage Coalition did not have proper standing to appeal Walker's decision. This result vacated the circuit court's ruling, allowing the original district court decision overturning Proposition 8 to stand and making same-sex marriage legal in California (*Hollingsworth v. Perry* 2013).

Although they had difficulty opposing the decision on legal grounds, conservatives had more success discrediting Walker's ruling in the popular arena. They did this in large part by framing the decision as an instance of judicial activism rather than as an unbiased interpretation of the law. A typical reaction from one conservative observer commenting on the ruling strikes many familiar chords:

> In support of his radical world view [*sic*] he foists upon us, Walker willingly enlisted the aid of a myriad of plaintiffs' Harvard[-] and Yale-educated elitist scholar "expert" witnesses, many of whom themselves are radical homosexual activists with obvious axes to grind. Predictably, Walker failed to even consider whether the personal beliefs or biases of these activist "experts" could undermine their credibility. And while criticizing Proposition 8 proponents' experts for not basing their expert opinions on facts and data, he buys wholesale the opinions of plaintiffs' experts without referencing the actual facts or data which purportedly support their opinions. Not surprisingly, Walker found these experts credible and reliable, while he found none of the testimony of the proponents' experts valid. (Boyles 2010)

Proponents of Proposition 8 attempted to use similar accusations of bias to discredit the plaintiffs' expert witnesses during trial, but these arguments were largely ineffective in that setting because the defense could not produce adequate evidence to support its claims. However, when used outside of the courtroom as a means of dismissing Walker's decision, these arguments were more persuasive. Here conservatives were able to discredit this decision by appealing to a popular public perception that judges have bias without needing to provide evidence to support their claims. These arguments do not require evidence because they are not based on rational calculations. Instead, such appeals tap into a long-standing ideological tradition of populism that leads many to regard expert opinion with suspicion.

Rights discourse also played an important role in helping to build popular opposition to Walker's decision. Although rights claims had limited instrumental value for conservatives in court, they continued to be a powerful tool when used outside of the courtroom. In addition to representing the Protect Marriage Coalition at trial, the ADF also maintained a trial blog that communicated the day's proceedings to a popular audience. On this blog, lawyers for the ADF would frequently frame the day's events using the discourse of rights to foment popular outrage.

One example of this can be seen in the depiction of the testimony of George Chauncey. Chauncey testified for the plaintiffs during the trial, arguing that gays and lesbians were politically powerless (Chauncey 2010). The defense

countered this testimony by arguing that gays and lesbians have many powerful political allies and, as part of this argument, pointed out that a number
of religious groups had opposed Proposition 8 (Thompson 2010b, 496–503).
This led to a seemingly innocuous moment on redirect when Therese Stewart,
an attorney representing the city of San Francisco, pointed out that two of the
largest religious organizations in the United States had released statements opposing rights for gays and lesbians because they believe homosexuality is a sin
(Stewart 2010, 541). This exchange had little impact on the court proceedings,
but outside of the courtroom it took on increased significance. The official
ADF trial blog post for that day focused on this moment. It reads:

> A chilling moment came when San Francisco city attorney Therese Stewart had
> Professor Chauncey read official doctrinal statements from the Southern Baptist
> Convention and the Roman Catholic Church that both generally restated what
> the Bible says about the definition of marriage as one man and one woman.
> Professor Chauncey said those doctrinal statements reflect historic bias against
> those who engage in homosexual behavior. It's not hard to figure out what is so
> frightening about an attempt in federal court to attack and delegitimize the views
> of the two largest Christian denominations in America. This is further proof
> that this case, and the very definition of marriage, is about much more than
> the personal relationships and the inner feelings of people who choose same-
> sex relationships. It is about imposing a different and intolerant "morality" on
> America and eradicating opposing ideas. (Lorence 2010)

This depiction greatly exaggerates the significance of this moment. It uses language much stronger than anything said by the defense during the *Perry* trial
to depict opponents of same-sex marriage as victims of intolerance and posits
that those who support same-sex marriage wish to eradicate religious viewpoints.

Such arguments were never made during the trial, most likely because they
cannot be supported with evidence that can stand up to judicial scrutiny. Although many conservatives would argue that legalizing same-sex marriage is
merely a first step toward outlawing the public expression of any disapproval
of the "gay lifestyle" (Sprigg 2006; Prentice 2010), such arguments are merely
speculative. Overturning Proposition 8 would not prevent religious individuals from expressing their opinion that being gay is sinful; it would simply
refuse to lend the state's support to this viewpoint by enshrining it in the

Constitution. Even if legalizing same-sex marriage were found to infringe on religious liberty, the judicial remedy for this infringement would not be to invalidate the law but to grant opponents of same-sex marriage the right to opt out of it (NeJaime 2009). Most states that have legalized same-sex marriage provide some sort of exemption for those who object to marriage equality on religious grounds.

Another example of the different way events are framed inside and outside of the courtroom can be seen with regard to the testimony and questioning of Hak-Shing William Tam. Tam was a member of the Protect Marriage Coalition in charge of outreach to the Chinese community during the Proposition 8 campaign. He was called to testify as a hostile witness for the plaintiffs during the *Perry* trial. During direct examination, Boies asked Tam about a number of statements he had made on his personal website regarding gays and lesbians, including, "Studies show that homosexuality is linked to pedophilia" (Boies 2010c, 1918), "Homosexuals are 12 times more likely to molest children" (Boies 2010c, 1919), "After legalizing same-sex marriages they want to legalize prostitution" (Boies 2010c, 1925), and "What will be next? On their agenda list is legalizing having sex with children" (Boies 2010c, 1926). The plaintiffs argued that these statements indicated that the Proposition 8 campaign was motivated by animus toward gays and lesbians (Boies 2010c). The defense attorneys reacted to Tam's testimony during the trial by attempting to minimize the power of his statements. They argued that Tam was not a major part of the Protect Marriage Coalition and that these were his own personal views, not those of the Yes on 8 campaign (Moss 2010).

Outside of the courtroom, however, conservatives reacted to Tam's testimony much differently. The official ADF trial blog entry for that day uses stirring language to depict Tam as a noble man standing up for his religious beliefs against the forces of tyranny:

> In a desperate attempt to continue to paint the over 7 million Californians who voted yes on Proposition 8 as bigots, the plaintiffs called to the stand Dr. Hak-Shing Tam, one of the official proponents of Proposition 8. In the courtroom, Dr. Tam represented many of us who are concerned about attempts to redefine marriage in our country. . . . Yet, the plaintiffs today possessed no shame in their efforts to mock Dr. Tam for holding these beliefs. . . . Dr. Tam had his religious and political views placed under a judicial microscope to determine whether they were "correct" in the eyes of the law. . . . The plaintiffs are trying hard to cast as

legally wrong the political and religious beliefs of those who do not agree with them. . . . I couldn't help but think of . . . Sen. Joseph McCarthy during his grilling of several American citizens [in] committee hearings. (Nimocks 2010)

This type of language depicts opponents of same-sex marriage as victims of persecution, even going so far as to connect their plight with that of those persecuted for suspected Communist affiliations during the Red Scare. Although stirring, such language simply does not correlate with the events that happened in the courtroom that day. Tam was not simply expressing disagreement with the gay lifestyle but was perpetuating several harmful discriminatory stereotypes. His statements were so patently offensive that the attorneys for the defense sought to distance themselves from them in court. Even so, Tam's right to make such statements was never in doubt. The only question was whether they represented his personal views or the views of members of the campaign as a whole.

These examples show that the constitutive power of conservative rights discourse persists outside of the courtroom despite the fact that these arguments have been ignored or even repudiated in court. It is interesting that although conservatives are often unable to keep events outside of the courtroom from being used as evidence inside it, they have no problem preventing events that occur inside the courtroom from having much influence in the popular arena. Unfavorable legal decisions have often been thought to undermine social movements by repudiating existing conceptions of the law and killing alternative legal meanings that develop outside of the courtroom (Cover 1983). These findings complicate this understanding. The fact that conservatives have always treated formal legal actors with a great deal of skepticism may inoculate them against unfavorable judicial decisions, allowing them to easily dismiss them as "judicial activism." This enables conservatives to continue to effectively use rights discourse outside of the courtroom even after these arguments have been rejected by formal legal actors.

CONCLUSION

The state of California was one of the most contentious fronts in the fight over marriage equality in the United States. Same-sex marriage was legalized for the final time in California in 2013, but the state did not arrive at that point easily.

Both proponents and opponents of same-sex marriage successfully mobilized their supporters around this issue, causing the state to oscillate between extending marriage rights to same-sex couples and limiting marriage to "one man and one woman" several times during the more than decade-long debate over marriage equality in the state. This debate was shaped dramatically by the state's unique political culture and institutional dynamics. Conservatives were able to capitalize on California's robust ballot measure process to successfully advocate for a traditional definition of marriage. They succeeded during these campaigns by framing their opposition to same-sex marriage using rights discourse to depict gays and lesbians as subversive elites seeking to selfishly deprive average Americans of their fundamental rights. This conception of rights resonated with voters in part because it was able to tap into California's individualistic political culture, which emphasizes self-reliance and is distrustful of elite scheming.

This strategy was used most successfully during the 2008 Proposition 8 campaign. Here conservatives were able to overcome a large early deficit, and win a stunning victory in a left-leaning state, in part by framing their cause using the language of parental rights. This rights language effectively expanded the scope of the conflict, drawing in secular and minority voters not typically part of the conservative base. In addition to its obvious instrumental value, this rights language also has important constitutive implications. Framing the cause using the discourse of parental rights personalized the debate over same-sex marriage, causing conservatives to view themselves as cultural warriors fighting to protect fundamental rights. Proponents of marriage equality had difficulty combating these rights-based appeals when arguing this issue in a popular environment. Though No on 8 campaign leaders attempted to dispute the other side's factual claims, they never addressed the discriminatory moral assumptions underlying this rights discourse. Combating this moral logic requires a careful consideration of the implications of this discourse and an understanding of the historical context of discrimination against gays and lesbians. This puts proponents of marriage equality at a disadvantage because nuance and context are not easily conveyed in the short advertisements used during ballot measure campaigns. However, when the debate over same-sex marriage moved to a courtroom environment, such arguments became much easier to make.

In a popular environment voters often do not have the time or inclination to subject arguments to careful critique. Claims made in a courtroom environment, however, must be supported with evidence that can stand up to judicial scrutiny. The rights discourse opponents of same-sex marriage had used so successfully during the Proposition 8 campaign crumbled under the scrutiny of the courtroom environment and actually became a liability for conservatives during the *Perry* trial. During that trial, attorneys for the plaintiffs made advertisements used by the Yes on 8 campaign a focal point of their case and used testimony from expert witnesses to unpack the discriminatory stereotypes embedded within these rights-based appeals. These underlying discriminatory stereotypes were used as evidence that Proposition 8 was motivated by animus toward gays and lesbians, not a legitimate government interest.

The impact of the debate over same-sex marriage in California resonated far beyond the borders of the Golden State. Many criticized the decision to challenge Proposition 8 in federal court (American Civil Liberties Union et al. 2009), but the strategy proved successful. California was the first state to legalize same-sex marriage via a federal court decision (*Hollingsworth v. Perry* 2013). This success helped inspire activists in a number of other states to also challenge prohibitions on same-sex marriage in federal court, ultimately culminating in the *Obergefell* decision. Similarly, the success of the Yes on 8 campaign became a blueprint for opponents of same-sex marriage to follow in other states as well. Frank Schubert, the principal strategist behind the Yes on 8 campaign, was hired to orchestrate Maine's Question 1 campaign in 2009 and all five of the ballot measure campaigns against same-sex marriage in 2012. Schubert used the same strategy to oppose same-sex marriage in each of these campaigns, often reusing the same advertisements originally made for the Yes on 8 campaign in these other states as well. These tactics proved successful in Maine's 2009 Question 1 campaign and in North Carolina in 2012. However, opponents of same-sex marriage suffered a major setback in November of 2012, losing ballot measure campaigns in Maine, Maryland, Minnesota, and Washington. In the next chapter, I turn my attention to the push for marriage equality in Maine. I examine how opponents of same-sex marriage were able to use the ballot measure process to successfully overturn a law legalizing same-sex marriage in 2009, and I explore why this strategy failed to yield similar results in 2012.

5. "A Place Apart": Opposition to Same-Sex Marriage in Maine

In Chapter 4 of this book, I explored how different institutional environments affected the push for marriage equality by analyzing the same-sex marriage debate in California. This analysis reveals that conservatives were able to use rights discourse to effectively oppose same-sex marriage when debating this issue in ballot measure campaigns but that this language became a liability for them after the debate moved inside the courtroom. California's experience with same-sex marriage was not unique; opponents of marriage equality used these same tactics to prevail during anti-same-sex-marriage ballot measure campaigns in states across the United States. This strategy was much less successful in New England, however. New England was the site of the marriage equality movement's earliest victories, and same-sex marriage was embraced throughout the region much sooner than it was in the rest of the country. Why was the marriage equality movement so much more successful in New England? In this chapter I answer this and other questions by conducting an in-depth analysis of the same-sex marriage debate in Maine.

I begin my analysis by briefly discussing New England's political development and examining how the region's culture and institutional environment shaped how the same-sex marriage debate was carried out there. I argue that New England's political institutions played a major role in causing the region to embrace marriage equality more enthusiastically than the rest of the nation. The political institutions of New England are different from those in other parts of the country. The citizens' initiative process is a staple of politics in many parts of the nation, particularly in the western United States. This process provides opponents of marriage equality the opportunity to use their own counter-rights discourse to foment popular opposition to same-sex marriage and thwart the efforts of marriage equality activists. In contrast, political systems in northeastern states tend to be much more elite-centered. Only two New England states (Maine and Massachusetts)[1] currently allow citizens to place initiatives on the ballot. As a result, New England's politics tend to be dominated by strong party leadership—a holdover from a tradition of machine politics that thrived in the region until the middle of the twentieth century. This dramatically limited conservatives' ability to effectively oppose marriage equality in the region.

After discussing the development of New England's political institutions, I explore how these institutions have shaped the same-sex marriage debate by conducting an in-depth case study of the push for marriage equality in Maine. I begin this exploration by discussing the passage of LD 1020 in 2009, a bill designed to allow same-sex couples to marry in Maine. I show that marriage equality activists succeeded in passing the bill by capitalizing on the fact that Democrats had won significant majorities in Maine's state legislature in 2008. Conservatives had a difficult time opposing these efforts because legislative officials are primarily concerned with winning reelection and garnering favor with members of their own political party. This makes them less receptive to rights discourse than a popular audience might be.

The success of LD 1020 proved short-lived for marriage equality advocates, however. Maine is unique among New England states in that it does have a robust citizens' initiative process. This meant that the debate over same-sex marriage in Maine did not end with the passage of marriage equality legislation, as it did for many other states in the region. Instead, conservatives were able to shift this debate to the more favorable terrain of the ballot measure campaign. Mainers would spend the next three years debating this issue in this more popular arena. In the final sections of this chapter, I analyze how this debate was carried out in both the 2009 and 2012 Question 1 campaigns. I show that conservatives were able to use the same tactics employed during the Proposition 8 campaign in California to mobilize their own counter-rights discourse and successfully repeal LD 1020 in 2009. This shows that ballot measure campaigns provide conservative opponents of same-sex marriage considerable advantages, even when they take place in a region that has been relatively receptive to the idea of extending marriage rights to same-sex couples.

These tactics proved less successful in 2012, however. That year, marriage equality activists put the issue of same-sex marriage back on the ballot, and this time Mainers voted to legalize it. I conclude the chapter by analyzing the differences in these two campaigns.[2] First, I discuss how a variety of changes that occurred during the three-year period between these ballot measures helped contribute to their different outcomes. I then look specifically at how rights discourse was used in both campaigns. Here, I pay particular attention to how marriage equality activists worked to counter conservative rights claims by framing their support for marriage equality using the language of "family," not rights. The success of this approach led many advocates of same-sex marriage to believe that avoiding the use of rights discourse might be an effective strategy when debating this issue in a popular arena (Hatalsky and Trumble 2012). Although minimizing the use of rights discourse might have had some instrumental value for proponents of marriage equality, I argue that this strategy has problematic constitutive implications.

POLITICAL DEVELOPMENT OF NEW ENGLAND

Politics in the New England states are generally more elite-centered and less transparent than in their western counterparts. Writing in 1959, Duane Lockard described the region as one dominated by a strong Republican Party and the vestiges of once-strong political machines that still exerted considerable influence in many of the urban areas of southern New England at that time (Lockard 1959). Although these political machines and the tacit corruption that typified them have largely disappeared from the region today, New England's politics are, in large part, still controlled by a handful of powerful interest groups and party elites. This is because the progressive movement, which spurred disaffection toward this style of politics in many states during the late nineteenth and early twentieth centuries, failed to take root in New England.

As a result, the region continues to be dominated by strong political parties and has a tendency to address political concerns through compromise and negotiations carried out among political elites behind the closed doors of the legislative chamber or the executive's office rather than in the public forum. As we will see shortly, this lack of citizen involvement makes it difficult for opponents of same-sex marriage to use rights discourse effectively. Rights claims are most effective when their considerable emotional appeal can be used to mobilize supporters by creating a sense of common purpose or identity (Scheingold 1974; Zemans 1983; Burstein 1991; McCann 1994; Engel and Munger 2003) or when used to "expand the scope" of a conflict by drawing in previously undecided or unsympathetic audiences (Dudas 2008). They are not well suited to convincing political elites motivated primarily by partisan concerns (Cox and McCubbins 1993) and a desire to win reelection (Downs 1957; Mayhew 1974).

Political decision making in New England was not always so dominated by elites. The early settlers of the region established a town meeting style of government that allowed citizens to play a direct role in political decision making and encouraged active citizen participation in politics (Doyle and Milburn 1981; Bryan 2004). Under the town meeting system, localities function relatively autonomously. Citizens elect members of the community to be selectmen, responsible for managing the day-to-day operations of the town, and once a year citizens meet to decide legislative priorities regarding important local issues such as infrastructure, education, policing, and zoning laws (Mansbridge 1983, 43). The town meeting system was lauded as a paragon of democracy by a number of well-respected admirers, including Ralph Waldo Emerson, Alexis de Tocqueville, and Thomas Jefferson. Although it was probably never as egalitarian as many of these figures depicted it, during its heyday it did provide New Englanders a level of direct involvement in government that does not exist in the region today.

The town meeting system of government began to lose favor as New England transitioned from a largely rural, agrarian economy to a more urban, industrial one during the latter part of the nineteenth century. Increased populations made the town meeting style of government unwieldy, and in many areas, towns began to cede their powers to the state government. Although the town meeting system still persists to some extent in many of the more rural parts of New England, much of its power has been eroded by encroachments from state governments and a movement toward a town manager system that delegates much of the decision-making power to an unelected, nonpartisan, professional town administrator (Doyle and Milburn 1981, 36–37).

The population boom that took place in New England during the nineteenth century was spurred in large part by an influx of immigrants from Southern Europe and Ireland who came to the region to work in its growing industrial sector (Lockard 1959, 3–5). Many in the Northeast regarded these predominantly Catholic immigrants as uneducated and untrustworthy. They feared that these immigrant populations, which by the early twentieth century outnumbered Anglo-Saxon Protestants in many New England cities, might begin to exert too much influence on the politics of the region (Schmidt 1989, 12). These immigrants were kept in check, in large part, by the political machines that would come to dominate the urban areas of New England. Although the power of many political machines was greatly diminished as a result of the progressive movement, New Englanders eschewed the movement's more popular elements, which urged the adoption of reforms such as the citizens' initiative process, out of fear that adopting such measures would empower these immigrant populations. Although the progressive movement did gain a foothold in the Northeast, it was devoid of much of the populist rhetoric more common in the West. Instead, New England's reformers adhered to the more aristocratic notion that politics should be controlled by well-educated individuals from prominent, upper-class families (Hofstadter 1974, 139–140).

Political Culture and Institutions of Maine

The trajectory of Maine's political development does, in many ways, mirror that of the rest of New England. Maine's initial settlers established a town meeting style of government that dominated the state's politics until the late nineteenth century. Mainers maintained a rural lifestyle typified by local political control longer than their more urban neighbors in southern New England. By the early part of the twentieth century, however, Maine's farmers, like others in the region, had begun abandoning the state's rocky soil for the more fertile lands to the west (Palmer, Taylor, and Librizzi 1992, 14–17). In their place, Maine adopted a more industrial-based economy. The timber industry boomed in the state, leading Maine to become a major producer of paper products and a center for shipbuilding, and Maine's abundance of waterways led to the successful development of hydroelectric power. The success of these industries created a demand for laborers met by an influx of Irish and French Canadian immigrants (Palmer, Taylor, and Librizzi 1992, 16–17).

These forces of industrialization, urbanization, and immigration would, as they did in other New England states, eventually lead Maine to develop a more elite-centered model of politics. For much of the twentieth century, politics in Maine were dominated by corporate interest groups representing the state's major industries. Indeed, in his 1959 assessment of the state, Lockard concluded, "In few American states are the reins of government more openly or completely in the hands of a few leaders of economic interest groups. . . . The abundance of timber and water power in Maine has indirectly created Maine's Number One Political Problem: the manipulation of government by the overlord of the companies based on these resources" (79). These forces continued to dominate politics in Maine until the 1960s, when the development of an effective two-party system and a nascent environmental movement began to challenge this corporate hegemony (Palmer, Taylor, and Librizzi 1992, 44–47).

However, as one of the state's many slogans suggests, Maine is also unique, "a place apart" from the rest of New England. Unlike the more heavily settled lands of other New England states, Maine has been regarded as a somewhat distant eastern frontier for most of its history. Maine is relatively isolated. It is the farthest east of any state in the Union and is the only state in the country that shares a border with just one other state (New Hampshire). As in the West, early settlers were lured to the state by the promise of free land to anyone willing to tame Maine's wild countryside (Palmer, Taylor, and Librizzi 1992, 10–12). Despite these enticements, the vast majority of the state remained unsettled well into the twentieth century. This frontier experience led Mainers to develop an independent spirit and a predilection for popular government more in line with the mood of a western state than of its northeastern neighbors. This desire for more local control led Mainers to adopt the thirty-sixth amendment to the state's constitution, which allows citizens to place issues on the ballot directly through the citizens' initiative process. The relative ease with which citizens of Maine can place issues on the ballot today sets the state apart from the rest of the region.

"The People's Veto" Comes to Maine

In 1909, Maine became the first New England state to adopt the citizens' initiative process. Support for this process was fueled in large part by unease over the management of the state's "wild lands." At that time, Maine had more than 10 million acres of unorganized and unsettled lands. This property, which contained valuable timber, was controlled by a small number of powerful individuals and corporations. These groups wielded considerable political clout, and they used this power to negotiate highly favorable tax rates from the state. As a result, citizens living in organized townships were forced to shoulder a disproportionate share of the state's tax burden (Black 1912, 161). Disaffection toward these corporate interests and the politicians and "bosses" under their control spurred the early push for the citizens' initiatives and referenda in the state.

Initial efforts to promote the ballot measure process in Maine were led by Roland T. Patten, a local Republican and later Socialist Party leader (Pelletier 1951). Patten formed the State Referendum League in 1905, dedicated to securing "the people's right to a direct vote on questions of public policy" (Black 1912, 164). The State Referendum League tirelessly lobbied political officials from both parties in Maine and eventually succeeded in getting the state legislature in 1907 to consider a bill that would allow citizens' initiatives and referenda. After a somewhat heated debate, the legislature approved a provision to amend the constitution that would allow citizens to petition to place statutes on the ballot or repeal laws enacted by the legislature before they could take effect using the "people's veto" process but would not allow citizens to initiate constitutional amendments.[3] The amendment was approved by voters by a fairly wide margin the following year.

To the dismay of many of its supporters, the adoption of the ballot measure process did little to undermine the power of the state's business interests. Only seven citizen-initiated statutes were considered by voters between 1909 and 1971, and only two such initiatives passed.[4] The "people's veto" was more commonly used during this time. Twenty-two laws were subjected to the people's veto from 1909 to 1971, and half of those resolutions succeeded (Maine State Law and Legislative Reference Library 2011). More recently, Mainers have shown renewed interest in the power of ballot measures. Between 1971 and 2010, forty-nine initiated statutes and seven "people's vetoes" were considered by Maine voters. As a result, twenty-three initiated statutes were passed, and four laws were repealed (Maine State Law and Legislative Reference Library 2011). As we shall see, the presence of this popular outlet in Maine had a profound effect on the debate over same-sex marriage in the state.

LD 1020

Proponents of marriage equality began laying the groundwork for the legalization of same-sex marriage in Maine in 2005. That year Maine voters rejected a referendum that would have repealed a gay rights law making it illegal to discriminate based on sexual orientation with regard to housing, employment, public accommodations, and credit.[5] Equality Maine, the organization responsible for coordinating opposition to the 2005 referendum, sought to capitalize on the momentum from this victory by mobilizing its supporters and lobbying state legislators to legalize same-sex marriage.[6] These efforts failed to gain much traction, however, until after the 2008 election, when Democrats gained five seats in Maine's House of Representatives and two seats in the Senate. These gains gave the party relatively comfortable majorities of ninety-five to fifty-five in the House and twenty to fifteen in the Senate.[7] Democratic leadership decided the time was right to push for legislation legalizing same-sex marriage. On January 13, 2009, Dennis Damon (D-Trenton), serving his last term in the Senate because of term limits, held a press conference announcing that he would be sponsoring such a bill. LD 1020, An Act to End Discrimination in Civil Marriage and Affirm Religious Liberty was drafted and sent to the Judiciary Committee for consideration.

Mobilizing Opposition to LD 1020

Opponents of marriage equality began organizing in opposition to LD 1020 immediately. As was the case in California, initial opposition to same-sex marriage in Maine was led in large part by local religious organizations. Like the rest of New England, Maine's population is heavily Catholic. More than 29 percent of Mainers identify as Catholic, making it the largest religious denomination in the state, with more than 200,000 devoted followers (Pew Research Center for the People and the Press 2011). Not surprisingly, the Catholic church played a key role in organizing early opposition to same-sex marriage in Maine. Bishop Richard Malone of the Roman Catholic Dioceses of Portland, the most prominent religious leader in the state, denounced the push to extend marriage rights to same-sex couples and announced that the church would be active in opposition to it even before the legislation was drafted. He granted Marc Mutty, director of public policy for the Portland Dioceses, leave from his post so that he could lobby against the passage of LD 1020 full time and later assigned him to chair Stand for Marriage Maine, the primary organization dedicated to repealing the law.[8]

Mutty's appointment represented a break from past campaigns against gay rights in Maine, which were led by Reverend Michael Heath. Heath, an evangelical minister, directed the Christian Civic League of Maine, an affiliate of Focus on the Family dedicated to pursuing a variety of social conservative causes in the state.[9] He had led the opposition to gay rights in Maine since the early 1990s. Heath successfully organized a 1997 campaign to overturn Maine's gay rights law and oversaw the failed attempt to repeal a similar law in 2005. Heath became a lightning rod for criticism, however, after he issued a statement in 2004 asking people to email him "tips, rumors, speculation, and facts" regarding the sexual orientation of Maine's political leaders (as quoted in Nemitz 2009a). He stirred further controversy in 2005 when he made statements comparing the push for gay rights to "Nazi tyranny" and argued that to remain passive in the face of the "desperately evil" crusade for gay rights was to invite the fate of those who failed to stand up to Hitler (as quoted in Nemitz 2009a). This change in leadership seemed to indicate a desire on the part of conservatives to break with the extremism of past campaigns and strike a more moderate tone.

Opponents of same-sex marriage realized early on that it was going to be difficult to prevent LD 1020 from being passed given the large Democratic majorities in the state legislature. As a result, they launched a two-pronged strategy of opposing the bill, while at the same time preparing for a ballot measure campaign to repeal the legislation, should it pass. They encouraged supporters to write letters to their representatives urging them to vote no on LD 1020 and also worked behind the scenes to lobby legislative officials they thought might be susceptible to persuasion. At the same time, conservative leaders held rallies and began building a volunteer network in anticipation of a possible ballot measure campaign.

Letters to the Legislature

Opponents of LD 1020 encouraged their supporters to lobby their representatives in the hopes of convincing legislators that the majority of their constituents were against the bill and warn them that they might risk losing future bids for reelection if they chose to endorse it. Local organizations opposed to LD 1020 recommended that citizens send a "simple statement" to their representatives, such as, "Please protect traditional marriage by voting 'no' on Senator Damon's bill" (Maine Marriage Alliance 2009). Little effort was made to control the content of these letters in any organized way, though. This suggests the campaign believed the volume of complaints legislative officials received was more important than the content of those appeals.

Legislators received thousands of letters and emails from constituents urging them to vote for or against LD 1020. Some of these letters were sent to local newspapers by their authors, or posted on conservative websites, making them available to the general public as well. Religious arguments featured prominently in many of these appeals. One such letter, drafted by a coalition of religious leaders from across Maine, defended "traditional marriage" on religious grounds: "Catholics, Protestants, many Jews, as well as many members of other faith traditions have for centuries maintained that marriage is a sacred bond ordained by God between one man and one woman. . . . Creating by legislative fiat parity between same-sex marriage and the union of one man and one woman in matrimony is contrary to sacred scripture and the long-standing traditions of our shared faiths" (Ackley et al. 2009). This letter offers a familiar conservative religious perspective coupled with a populist appeal that contends that legislative officials should not have the authority to force citizens to accept a decision with such important moral implications by "fiat."

Other letters raised concerns about the bill's impact on religious liberty—combining religious appeals with the language of rights. One such letter was drafted by Professor Douglas Laycock of the Michigan Law School. In it Laycock states that he supports same-sex marriage but is concerned that LD 1020 does not do enough to protect religious freedoms. According to him, the push for marriage equality should not trump concerns over religious liberty:

> The pending bill can be a great advance for human liberty. But careless or overly aggressive drafting could create a whole new set of problems for the religious liberty of those religious believers who cannot conscientiously participate in implementing the new regime. The net effect for human liberty will be no better than a wash if same-sex couples now oppress religious dissenters in the same way that those dissenters, when they had the power to do so, used to oppress same-sex couples. (Laycock 2009)

LD 1020 included protections for religious liberty that allowed members of the clergy who oppose same-sex marriage on religious grounds to speak out against it. It also enabled church officials to refuse to conduct same-sex wedding ceremonies. It did not, however, allow religious individuals who own private businesses to refuse services or to deny benefits to same-sex couples on the grounds of religious liberty. Laycock and others argued that a more sweeping religious liberty exemption that covered all religious "conscientious objectors," including those who are not members of the clergy, should be added to the bill (Berg et al. 2009, 8–10; Laycock 2009).

A Public Hearing

Before LD 1020 could come to a vote in the state legislature, it had to make it through the Judiciary Committee. Prior to making its recommendation to the legislature, the Judiciary Committee scheduled a public hearing on LD 1020 and invited all members of the public who wished to express their support or opposition to the legislation to attend. An estimated 4,000 citizens attended the hearing, held at the Augusta Civic Center, which lasted more than ten hours—nearly 200 gave testimony. Those who spoke against the bill touched on many of the same themes expressed by conservative opponents of same-sex marriage elsewhere. One of the most prominent advocates to speak against the bill during these hearings was Malone. His message emphasized the important role "traditional marriage" plays in our society. He argued that the traditional definition of marriage is the foundation of a moral society and is crucial to the healthy development of children. According to him:

> Our objection to same-sex marriage is not based on a belief that gay and lesbian Mainers are somehow undeserving of civil rights because of their sexual orientation. . . . We speak in opposition to same-sex marriage because we are deeply concerned about the institution of marriage itself. . . . The decline of marriage in many communities has led to steep rises in crime, violence, and the perpetuation of poverty. . . . Studies prove that children who are not raised in traditional heterosexual married households are less likely to be successful at school and [the] workplace, more likely to engage in crime, more likely to have substance abuse problems, and tragically even to commit suicide. (2009)

Arguments like these emphasize the supposed moral consequences of same-sex marriage but avoid an explicitly religious defense of traditional marriage. According to this logic, same-sex marriage is just another in a long parade of horribles thought to undermine the nation's moral foundation, including an increasing divorce rate, increases in the number of children born out of wedlock, and increases in the number of fatherless, single-parent households. These issues are frequently lamented by conservatives as signs of moral decay and are a crucial aspect of New Right political discourse (Blankenhorn 1996; Daniels 2000; Donovan 2011).

Although Malone declined to frame his opposition to same-sex marriage using overtly religious language, many who spoke at the hearing did offer religious justifications for their positions. Father Paul Dumais, chaplain of St. Joseph's College of Maine, for example, contended:

> The sacred text found in Genesis, "therefore a man leaves his father and his mother and cleaves to his wife and they become one flesh," derives from what is inscribed in man himself and not from the conventions of religion, government,

politics, or changing social mores. . . . Marriage between one man and one woman is consistent with the spousal meaning of the body and ordered to the transmission of life. On the contrary homosexual acts are intrinsically disordered as they are contrary to the natural law discovered by the use of reason and clarified by the light of faith. (2009)

The prevalence of this religious discourse is a reminder that many of the most ardent opponents of same-sex marriage are motivated by religious belief. These individuals see the legalization of same-sex marriage as part of a disturbing trend toward the normalization of the "gay lifestyle," which they consider inherently sinful.

Rights-based discourse was not commonly invoked by opponents of same-sex marriage during the public hearing, but a few speakers did raise concerns that legalizing same-sex marriage would have negative implications for religious liberty or parental rights. David Parker, a Lexington, Massachusetts, man who also campaigned actively in favor of Proposition 8 in California, spoke at the public hearing. He argued that legalizing same-sex marriage would result in the "subversion of parental rights" because it would allow students to be taught about it in public schools without parental consent. Parker bemoaned the fact that he was given no right to "opt out" of instruction for his son that acknowledged the existence of same-sex relationships after Massachusetts legalized same-sex marriage in 2003 (Parker 2009).

The arguments made by opponents of LD 1020 during this public hearing provide a good barometer for how conservatives in Maine were thinking about the issue of same-sex marriage at that time. The discourse itself seems to have had little impact on the outcome of the debate, however. The Judiciary Committee took this testimony "under advisement" and, after some deliberation, voted in favor of the legislation eleven to two to one.[10] The committee's vote occurred largely along party lines—only one Republican on the committee, Representative Michael Beaulieu (R-Auburn), voted in favor of the legislation. No Democrats voted against it.

Debating Marriage Equality in the State Legislature

After receiving the endorsement of the Judiciary Committee, LD 1020 was considered by the Senate. Opponents of the bill believed that the Senate represented their best chance to defeat the legislation because the Democrats held a narrower majority in that body. Senators who spoke against LD 1020 when it came up for debate echoed many of the same concerns expressed by citizens and religious officials opposed to the bill. Senator Carol Westin (R-Montville) argued that the traditional definition of marriage is an important "marker" for civilization and warned that allowing same-sex marriage might be a "slippery slope" toward further erosion of this institution (Westin 2009, S-515). Others raised similar concerns that allowing same-sex marriage would undermine the moral foundation of our society (Raye 2009, S-512–S-513). One senator, Jonathan Courtney (R-Springvale), framed his opposition to the bill using the discourse of rights. He listed examples of how legalizing same-sex marriage might have consequences for the rights of those who oppose it:

> When same-sex marriage was legalized in Massachusetts, Catholic Charities in the state were forced to abandon a long-established and successful program for adoption of difficult-to-place children because the State held that it must be willing to place them with same-sex couples. Parents in the state lost the right to remove their children from public school classrooms when the issue was taught. There are numerous cases from other parts of the country and other nations in which it is clear, while churches may not be required to marry same-sex couples, religious liberties are indeed compromised as a consequence of same sex marriage. (2009, S-516)

Despite the efforts of the bill's opponents, the Senate narrowly ratified the legislation by a largely partisan vote of twenty to fifteen. Only one Democrat voted against the bill, and one Republican voted for it.

After the Senate voted to approve the bill, a number of Republican senators launched a last-ditch effort to pass an amendment that would have sent the issue directly to the people for a referendum without a legislative vote. Supporters of this amendment argued that the bill was most likely going to end up before voters anyway (McCormick 2009, S-518–S-519; P. Mills 2009, S-518), and raised concerns that if the bill were passed and then put to a "people's veto," the language might be confusing to voters because a "yes" vote for the veto would constitute a "no" vote against same-sex marriage (Hastings 2009, S-517; Trahan 2009, S-519). Others used populist appeals, arguing that this was an issue best decided by the people, not legislative elites. Senator Peter Mills (R-Skowhegan), for example, argued:

It strikes me that all of the e-mails and letters that I have received, begging me
not to support an initiative or a referendum in this case, have built inside of them
a message of arrogance. A message that says the people of Maine should not be
trusted with this issue. . . . Move this important issue, this important moral issue,
out into the people's sphere, where it properly belongs. (2009, S-518)

Despite these appeals the amendment failed thirteen to twenty-two, and the
bill moved to the House for consideration.

The House debate over LD 1020 included discourse similar to that in
the Senate. Most representatives opposed to the bill gave impassioned pleas
to reject it based on a belief that doing so would uphold the moral foundation of the country (Bickford 2009, H-402; Briggs 2009, H-402; Burns 2009,
H-400–H-401; Celli 2009, H-398–H-399; Chase 2009, H-406–H-407; Curtis,
2009, H-411; Thibodeau 2009, H-404); a few also invoked the discourse of
rights (Burns 2009, H-400–H-401; Curtis 2009, H-411). Representative David
Burns (R-Whiting) offered a speech that touched on many familiar tropes.
According to him,

Marriage between one man and one woman is a basic building block of a strong
society, and we must keep it intact. Madam Speaker, I don't believe that this
is about love and equality. I believe that it is in fact about recognition and the
legitimization of habits and lifestyles of a tiny segment of our society for selfish
and personal needs. . . . We have already passed laws in this state to adequately
protect civil rights and rightfully so. Most of us accept gay and lesbian people
on their own personal merits and enjoy and respect our relationships with them
accordingly. I am no exception to that. What we do distain [*sic*] is the destruction
of the institution of marriage. That's what this bill is all about. . . . Already there
have been attacks on religious freedom in Massachusetts, New Mexico, New
Jersey, California, Georgia, and Canada that I am aware of. Right here, where we
live, there will be more of the same. . . . Where will it stop? I promise you that it'll
not stop here. This will have a far-reaching and negative impact on our children,
parents, education, religion, and our economy. (2009, H-400–H-401)

Here, gays and lesbians are depicted as selfish individuals who demand to
have their "personal needs" recognized, even if doing so has negative consequences for the overall moral health of our society and the existing rights of
the majority of Americans. This conception inverts the debate over same-sex

marriage, making gays and lesbians the oppressors and conservatives the embattled group seeking to defend fundamental rights (Goldberg-Hiller and Milner 2003).

Despite these appeals, the House followed the Senate's lead and ratified the bill eighty-nine to fifty-eight (with four absent). Once again, the vote took place largely along party lines. Only six Republicans voted for the legislation, and twelve Democrats voted against it. Opponents of same-sex marriage had some hope that Democratic Governor Jim Baldacci, who had expressed reservations about same-sex marriage in the past, might veto the legislation. However, he surprised supporters and opponents alike by signing the bill into law just one day after it was approved by the House of Representatives.

The Limits of Rights Discourse in a Legislative Environment

The debate surrounding the passage of LD 1020 reveals much about how rights discourse functions in a legislative environment. Rights-based appeals typically became the dominant framework used to express opposition to same-sex marriage during ballot measure campaigns. When used in the popular arena, this discourse can have constitutive impact on how opponents of same-sex marriage see themselves and their movement and an instrumental impact on the outcome of the debate. Although opponents of LD 1020 used rights discourse, it was not invoked as frequently here as it is during ballot measure campaigns, and both the constitutive and instrumental impacts of this language were diminished by the legislative environment.

Opponents of LD 1020 were just as likely to frame their opposition to same-sex marriage by emphasizing the important moral role the traditional family structure plays in our society, or using religious appeals, as they were to invoke the language of rights. The relatively minor role that rights played in framing opposition to LD 1020 might be indicative of the fact that opposition to same-sex marriage was fairly diffuse at that time. At this early stage of the debate, the anti-same-sex-marriage movement lacked organizational structure. Although leaders such as Malone, Mutty, and Reverend Bob Emrich worked to coordinate efforts to oppose the passage of the bill, most individuals who expressed opposition to LD 1020 acted without direction—choosing to express their opposition to the bill spontaneously by writing a personal letter or email to their representative or by testifying at the public hearing. The individuals most active in opposition to same-sex marriage at that time tended to be those who felt passionately about this issue because of their own personal religious beliefs. It is not surprising, given the power of these personal beliefs, that these individuals would use religious and moral language to frame their opposition instead of the language of rights.

As we shall see shortly, after the debate over same-sex marriage in Maine shifted from the legislative arena to a statewide ballot measure campaign, the opposition began to develop a more robust organizational structure. As they became more centrally organized, opponents of same-sex marriage began to mobilize around a common rights-based identity of themselves as part of an aggrieved group dedicated to defending their fundamental rights from attack. Thinking about their cause in terms of fundamental rights created a sense of purpose that helped to fuel the movement against same-sex marriage. It also expanded the scope of the conflict, drawing in more moderate, secular individuals not motivated by personal religious beliefs but perhaps sympathetic to the arguments made by conservative opponents of same-sex marriage when they were framed using the language of rights.

In addition to not being as prevalent, rights discourse also did not have the same impact on the outcome of the same-sex marriage debate when used in the legislature as it often does during ballot measure campaigns. Partisan concerns and a desire to win reelection have more of an impact on whether legislative and executive officials support same-sex marriage than the discourse of rights does. These concerns are particularly prevalent in New England, where a tradition of strong parties and a legacy of machine politics encourage party discipline. Few legislative officials crossed party lines during the debate over LD 1020, and those who did stated that they did so because they felt that it was what their constituents wanted, not out of a desire to protect fundamental rights. Senator Chris Rector (R-Knox), who voted for LD 1020, explained his vote as follows:

> I've sought input from all and received literally thousands of constituent e-mails, phone calls, letters, postcards, and comments in public places. When asked, I've expressed my desire for as much input from my district as possible so I can effectively serve my role as Senator for that district. . . . In the end the constituent responses I have received are overwhelmingly on one side of this issue, and I believe my first responsibility is to reflect the views of the vast majority of my constituents. (2009, S-516)

Senator Troy Jackson (D-Aroostook), who voted against the bill, had a similar explanation for his vote. According to him, "I voted the way I did, and I have to live with that. As the Senator from Knox, Senator Rector, said, he voted the way his constituents, a majority of them, did, and I voted the way I thought the majority of my constituents did" (2009, S-519). These quotes indicate that legislators take seriously the arguments of their constituents and that it is possible to convince at least some of them to cross party lines when considering the issue of same-sex marriage. However, it is not the content of the arguments offered by constituents that seems to matter but the volume of opinions on one side of the issue that is most likely to convince a legislative official.

In fact, most of the arguments made by legislative officials during the debate over LD 1020 seemed to be meant more as a means of explaining their actions to voters than as attempts to convince other legislators to vote a certain way. Representative Doug Thomas (R-Ripley) rather bluntly expressed this sentiment when he said, "I don't expect to change anyone's mind, so this is going to be short. . . . But when future generations look back and wonder what happened to the great State of Maine, I want there to be no doubt where the Representative from Ripley stood. I stand against this proposal" (2009, H-396). Representative Mark Eves (D-North Berwick) expressed a similar desire to have his views written into the historical record when he said, "When history is read, I want to be on the record as supporting civil rights so that my grandchildren and great-grandchildren can know for certain that I was on the right side of history" (2009, H-403). Legislative officials in Maine were aware that same-sex marriage is an incredibly salient issue that many of their constituents have strong feelings about and one for which they would most likely have to answer during their reelection campaigns. Representative Mike Thibodeau (R-Winterport) expressed this point when he rather ominously reminded House members, "You know, each one of us will go back home to our communities, and they'll know how we feel about this issue" (2009, H-404).

THE 2009 QUESTION 1 CAMPAIGN

Opponents of same-sex marriage began working to repeal LD 1020 just days after the legislation was signed into law. A coalition of conservative activists formed Stand for Marriage Maine, an organization charged with directing the repeal efforts, and began working to put the law before voters using Maine's people's veto process. Stand for Marriage Maine gathered the necessary 55,000 signatures to qualify "People's Veto Question 1" for the 2009 ballot in just four weeks.[11] The campaign to pass the measure was modeled after the successful 2008 Proposition 8 campaign in California. Because Maine's population is more than 95 percent white (U.S. Census Bureau 2015), appealing to racial and ethnic minorities was not a priority for the Question 1 campaign. Everything else about the campaign was the same, though. As in California, conservatives in Maine relied on a strong base of supporters from the religious right. They used conservative Christian organizations and evangelical church networks to recruit campaign volunteers and raise money. They also hired Schubert and Flint Public Affairs, the same California-based public relations firm that had successfully engineered the passage of Proposition 8, to craft the campaign's message.

These tactics proved successful. Proponents of Question 1 were able to use existing church networks to mobilize a vast array of volunteers to work on the campaign and were able to raise $3.3 million to fund their efforts. Most of this money came from conservative religious individuals and organizations.[12] The Yes on 8 campaign's message seemed to resonate with Mainers as well. Public opinion polls taken a month before Election Day showed Question 1 trailing by a fairly large margin, with 52 percent opposed and 43 percent in favor (Wickenheiser 2009), but proponents of Question 1 were able to overcome this early deficit—Mainers ultimately voted in favor of repealing LD 1020 by a margin of 53 percent to 47 percent.

Protecting Parental Rights: Framing Support for Question 1

As was the case during the Proposition 8 campaign, proponents of Question 1 framed their opposition to same-sex marriage primarily using the discourse of rights. The campaign's first television advertisement, "Consequences," repeated many of the same arguments used by the Yes on 8 campaign in California. The advertisement features Boston College law professor Scott Fitzgibbon listing the "consequences" of legalizing same-sex marriage while ominous music plays in the background. In it Fitzgibbon states, "Unless Question 1 passes there will be real consequences for Mainers. Legal experts predict a flood of lawsuits against individuals, small businesses, and religious groups. Church organizations could lose their tax exemption. Homosexual marriage, taught in public schools whether parents like it or not" (Stand for Marriage Maine 2009a). This advertisement signaled the campaign's desire to shift away from the explicitly religious and moral justifications commonly used by members of the religious right to frame their opposition to marriage equality during the debate over LD 1020. Instead the campaign chose to frame same-sex marriage as a threat to individual rights. Fitzgibbon's appearance in the advertisement lends credibility to these claims and also puts a secular face on the campaign.[13] The music and tone of the commercial played on the audience's emotions, subtly communicating to voters that they should fear the legalization of same-sex marriage.

As the campaign progressed, proponents of Question 1 began to focus more narrowly on the issue of parental rights. The Yes on 1 campaign's second television advertisement, "Everything to Do with Schools," was an exact copy of one used in defense of Proposition 8. It features Robb and Robin Worthlin, who objected to the fact that their child's second-grade teacher had read a book to the class, *The King and the King,* that they argue teaches that "boys can marry other boys." In the advertisement they invoke the language of parental rights, stating, "We tried to stop public schools from teaching about gay marriage but the courts said we had no right to object or pull him out of class" (Stand for Marriage Maine 2009b). The campaign's third television advertisement, "Safe Schools," struck a similar tone. In it Don Mendel, a public school counselor in Palmyra, Maine, argues that "gay activist" teachers are trying to persuade young children to believe that same-sex marriage is acceptable "before they are old enough to have been convinced there is another way of looking at life." The advertisement concludes with Mendel stating, "Vote Yes on Question 1 to prevent homosexual marriage from being pushed on Maine students" (Stand for Marriage Maine 2009c). The argument that same-sex marriage was being "pushed on Maine students" was also highlighted in another advertisement, "It's Already Happening." Here the campaign argued, "Gay activists throughout the nation are pushing homosexual marriage across New England. . . . They want gay-friendly books in daycare facilities and to appoint gay advocates in every school building" (Stand for Marriage Maine 2009e). Similar arguments were made elsewhere in the campaign as well (Stand for Marriage Maine 2009d, 2009f, 2009g, 2009h, 2009i, 2009j, 2009k).

These advertisements suggested that efforts to legalize same-sex marriage are part of a larger plan to "indoctrinate" children against the wishes of their parents into believing that being gay is normal. Arguments such as these rest on an assumption (sometimes stated explicitly, sometimes implicitly) that parents should have the right to object to such instruction. These rights-based appeals seem to resonate better with a majority of voters than explicitly religious or moral arguments. Legal claims are often seen as more legitimate than other types of arguments in part because the law is typically viewed as an arena of reason in which decisions are based on objective factors, not influenced by moral or emotional concerns (Fitzpatrick 1992; Darian-Smith 2010). These legal arguments are not devoid of moral appeal, however. The logic of protecting parents' rights also resonates with voters because it is able to subtly tap into a long-standing fear that legalizing same-sex marriage could cause children to become more tolerant of gays and lesbians, increasing the likelihood that they might choose to become gay themselves.

Silence and Punish: Rights and the Construction of Identity

In addition to having considerable instrumental value, the rights discourse used by the Yes on 1 campaign also had important constitutive impact on the identity of conservative opponents of same-sex marriage and on gays and lesbians. Members of the religious right often frame opposition to same-sex marriage using explicitly moral and religious discourse. Many who spoke in opposition to LD 1020 when it was being considered by the state legislature cast conservatives as cultural warriors defending the institution of marriage, and the traditional values it is thought to embody, from attack by subversive forces (Dumais 2009; Raye 2009, S-512–S-513; Westin 2009, S-515). This image is fairly powerful for ardent opponents of same-sex marriage, but concepts such as institutions and values are relatively abstract, and their importance might not be so obvious to those outside of this base. When opposition to same-sex marriage is framed using the discourse of rights, however, its "consequences" become much more tangible and immediate. Rights discourse personalizes opposition to same-sex marriage, transforming it from an issue that might pose a vague threat to an abstract institution to one that poses a direct threat to the rights of any individual who does not fully support it. In this way, rights language helps conservatives create an identity of themselves as members of an aggrieved group defending their fundamental rights from attack by selfish elites.[14]

Conservatives cast themselves as victims of discrimination throughout the Question 1 campaign. They frequently complained they were the targets of harassment, intimidation, and threats of physical violence. Supporters of Question 1 often reported that signs and other campaign materials were being stolen or vandalized by their opposition (Mutty 2009a) and that campaign workers were being harassed and threatened (Cover 2009a). These incidents were used as evidence that conservatives were the true victims of intolerance and discrimination, not gays and lesbians. According to Mutty, director of the Stand for Marriage Maine campaign, acts of theft and vandalism indicated that "those who preach tolerance do not practice it" (2009a). In an interview with a columnist for the *Portland Press Herald,* Mutty elaborated, saying that as a result of these acts of harassment and intimidation, "we feel like the minority that's being discriminated against. We are being treated like pariahs everywhere we go" (as quoted in Nemitz 2009b). In reality, these acts of vandalism were, by proponents of Question 1's own admission, isolated incidents, the acts of "fringe groups," not the "organized opposition" (Nemitz 2009b).[15] Despite this reality, the perception of conservatives as victims persisted.

Many proponents of Question 1 believed that advocates of marriage equality sought to "silence" and "punish" those who expressed opposition to same-sex marriage (Mutty 2009b). One incident involving Mendel was seen as evidence of this desire to punish. After Mendel appeared in a Yes on 1 television advertisement, someone logged an anonymous complaint with the Maine Department of Professional and Financial Regulation asking that he be stripped of his license to practice social work in the state. Although the department never acted on this complaint, members of the Yes on 1 campaign used the incident to stoke fears that opponents of same-sex marriage could be punished for their political views. According to Mutty:

> It is ironic that those who claim tolerance as their highest value prove themselves to be so intolerant that they would go so far as to threaten a father's career and put his family's future at risk. This latest attack highlights the true agenda of those who demand that marriage be redefined. . . . This threat to Don and his family's livelihood is proof that those who demand marriage be redefined seek to punish and silence those who disagree. (2009b)

The incident was made into a radio advertisement produced by the Question 1 campaign. The advertisement told Mendel's story and argued that if same-sex marriage were legalized it would be "pushed on Maine students," and those who disagreed would be "silenced" (Stand for Marriage Maine 2009l).

In addition to constructing an image of themselves as victims, proponents of Question 1 used rights discourse that constructed an image of gays and lesbians as deviant. The parental rights argument, for example, resonated with voters in part because it included an implicit assumption that gays and lesbians lead a deviant and destructive lifestyle, and that children must be protected from exposure to that lifestyle. Campaign materials posted on the Stand for Marriage Maine website hinted at these concerns. One piece argued that voting to repeal LD 1020 "protects our children from being taught in public schools that 'same-sex marriage' is the same as traditional marriage as happens in Massachusetts, where children as young as the second grade are being taught that they can grow up to marry either a boy or a girl, and either option is the same, while parents cannot opt their children out of such 'instruction'" (Stand for Marriage Maine 2009j). This shows that claims of parental rights are about more than just allowing parents to control what information their children are exposed to; these claims are also built on an assumption that exposing children to the issue of same-sex marriage is problematic because it lessens the stigma attached to those who identify as gay or lesbian. Lessening this stigma is understood to be a problem because it could lead more children to think it is acceptable for them to choose to become gay as well. It is implied that parents should dread such an occurrence. If stated explicitly, such moral assumptions may appear abhorrent and repulsive to more moderate voters who consider themselves to be otherwise tolerant people. When masked by the secular discourse of rights, however, these moral implications are free to operate at a subconscious level, feeding on latent stereotypes and helping to foment opposition to same-sex marriage. In this way, rights discourse becomes a means of transforming arguments based on moral concerns into something acceptable to a more secular audience.

When Two Rights Make a Wrong:
Challenging Conservative Rights Claims

Opponents of Question 1 attempted to counter the claims of the Yes on 1 campaign by employing legal experts and government officials to debunk its arguments and advance their own rights-based appeals. Efforts to debunk the claims of the Yes on 1 campaign focused in particular on the argument that legalizing same-sex marriage would result in it being taught to students in public schools. A number of local government officials, most notably Maine's attorney general, Janet Mills, spoke against these claims. A report issued by Mills during the campaign dismissed the connection between same-sex marriage and education. In it, Mills stated definitively that because the school curriculum in Maine is set at the local, not the state, level, legalizing same-sex marriage would have no impact on public schools and would not, in any way, compel teachers to teach about the topic (J. Mills 2009). In the event some localities did decide to make the subject of same-sex marriage part of their school curricula, Mills pointed out that state law already included protections for parents who wished to "opt out" of such instruction for religious reasons.[16] A memo issued by a number of past and present elected officials in Maine drew similar conclusions (Mitchell et al. 2009).

The memos produced by Mills and others were intended to inform Mainers about the state's education laws and assure them that the claims being made by proponents of Question 1 were inaccurate. Though these memos were factually correct statements supported with ample statutory evidence, they failed to effectively counter the rights claims advanced by conservatives, in large part because they failed to connect with a popular audience. Memos issued by government officials often attract the attention of academics, political leaders, and members of the media, but most average citizens do not have the time or inclination to read them. Although these memos were discussed in a few local newspaper articles written for a more popular audience, these short articles merely included a few quotes from the memos juxtaposed with rebuttal arguments offered by the opposition (Cover 2009b, 2009c). They did not include much of the analysis or evidence offered by these experts to support their opinions. This format makes these arguments look more like simple differences of opinion than factual statements and results in a disconnect between what elites know to be true about an issue and how it is perceived by the general public (Haltom and McCann 2004).

Mutty himself later admitted to, and even expressed regret over, the Yes on 1 campaign's use of "hyperbole." In one interview released after the campaign had concluded, Mutty said, "We use a lot of hyperbole, and I think that's always dangerous. . . . You know, we say things like 'Teachers will be forced to (teach same-sex marriage in schools)!' Well, that's not a completely accurate statement, and we all know it isn't, you know?" (as quoted in Nemitz 2011). During the campaign, however, proponents of Question 1 dismissed Mills's memo as "a shameless political ploy by supporters of homosexual marriage" (Cover 2009c). This reflects a general strategy adopted by proponents of Question 1 of using populist arguments to depict the government officials who offered their opinion on the parental rights issue as elite advocates of same-sex marriage offering "biased" analyses. Mutty's official response to Mills's memo during the campaign stated that it "has not even a shred of pretense of independence or objectivity. . . . It's a shame that Maine's top lawyer is using her good office for such a transparent political stunt" (Mutty 2009c). Although proponents of Question 1 were quick to paint these officials as biased, they never attempted to refute the claims offered by them. Instead, they chose to simply repeat their own argument that same-sex marriage had been taught in other states and that nothing in Maine's laws precluded teachers from teaching the topic in Maine as well (Mutty 2009c).

Though opponents of Question 1 attempted to counter the parental rights claims advanced by the Yes on 1 campaign at a factual level, their moral logic behind the argument that children must be protected from being taught about same-sex marriage in school went largely uncontested. Conceding this moral logic forced advocates of marriage equality to convince voters that the supposed moral harms that stem from exposing children to the issue of same-sex marriage would absolutely not occur, whereas proponents of Question 1 had only to raise doubts about this assumption. In fact, Jesse Connolly, campaign manager for the No on 1 campaign, later admitted that this dynamic had favored the Yes on 1 campaign. According to him, "Their bar was set really low. . . . All they had to do was raise some doubts, and they did" (as quoted in Miller 2009). Attempting to counter the parental rights argument on a factual level was also doomed to fail because these arguments are not based on a dispassionate examination of the issue but instead rely on an implicit moral appeal designed to generate a visceral, emotional response. Instead of disputing this moral logic, opponents of Question 1 actually gave credence to it by vehemently insisting same-sex marriage would not be taught in public schools— an argument that implies that such an occurrence would be a bad thing. One advertisement produced by the No on 1 campaign did attempt to question these moral assumptions by asking why we should fear instruction that simply introduces students to the existence of diverse family arrangements (Equality Maine 2009b), but this was not a focal point of the campaign.

Though proponents of marriage equality did not attempt to dispute the moral assumptions advanced by the Yes on 1 campaign, they did offer voters alternative moral and rights-based appeals. They emphasized that Maine is a state that values equality and acceptance for all citizens and that intolerance is not representative of "Maine values" (Equality Maine 2009c, 2009d, 2009e). Proponents of same-sex marriage emphasized that LD 1020 was about "equality." The campaign organization was named Equality Maine, and most of its advertisements featured Mainers expressing support for same-sex marriage for reasons of equality, fairness, or individual rights. One such advertisement, "All Families," hit on this theme. It consisted of testimonials from a variety of different Mainers, including a farmer, a firefighter, and a lobsterman. These people expressed support for same-sex marriage using the logic of individual rights. They argued, for example, "Everyone should be allowed to live the way they want to live," "it's not anybody's business to interfere with personal decisions," and "you may disagree, but people have a right to live how they want to live" (Equality Maine 2009f). Another advertisement, "Clear," expressed similar support for individual rights. In it a narrator argues, "We can choose to treat some Maine families differently . . . to deny them basic protections like health care, or making sure their children are cared for when a parent dies . . . or, we can choose equality and make Maine a place where all families . . . have the same protections" (Equality Maine 2009g).

Advocates of marriage equality emphasized that same-sex marriage was in line with Maine's values. In contrast, they depicted the Yes on 1 campaign as being run by "outsiders" seeking to deceive Mainers in order to advance their own political agenda. This argument alludes to the fact that the National Organization for Marriage (NOM), an organization based in Washington, DC, provided substantial funding and organizational support to the Question 1 campaign and that the campaign's advertising was created by California-based Schubert and Flint Public Affairs.[17] This "outsiders" theme was emphasized in a series of advertisements designed by opponents of Question 1 to dispute the connection between same-sex marriage and education. In one such advertisement, a narrator states, "Outsiders are trying to harm our kids and make them feel ashamed by making false claims about what's taught in Maine classrooms that are baseless, not true" (Equality Maine 2009a). Other advertisements made similar arguments (Equality Maine 2009a, 2009c). Maine is a fairly isolated and often insular community with a deep suspicion of those "from away," as they are often called by locals. Proponents of marriage equality clearly sought to capitalize on this dynamic by designing advertisements that put a local face on the campaign's rights-based appeals.

Although this rights-based strategy works well for proponents of same-sex marriage when arguing this issue in an elite environment, such as a courtroom, it seems to be less effective in a popular arena. This might be because framing support for same-sex marriage using the language of rights feeds into the narrative offered by conservative opponents of same-sex marriage, who typically argue that gays and lesbians are making "excessive" rights claims that come at the expense of the rights of the majority. In 2012, proponents of same-sex marriage moved away from this rights-based strategy and instead framed their support for same-sex marriage using the language of family. They believed this approach would prove successful in part because it would cause voters to stop thinking of this issue as a debate between competing rights claims.

THE 2012 QUESTION 1 CAMPAIGN

Losing the 2009 Question 1 campaign, after coming so close to legalizing same-sex marriage in the state, was a blow to the morale of Mainers who supported marriage equality. They could take some solace, however, from the fact that, in contrast to Proposition 8 in California, Question 1 was not a constitutional amendment. This meant that marriage equality activists could continue to pursue a number of strategies to legalize same-sex marriage in Maine, including pushing for new marriage equality legislation. A legislative strategy seemed most promising to activists initially, but the results of the 2010 elections in Maine changed that. A number of conservative organizations worked to make the 2010 elections a referendum on lawmakers who voted for LD 1020. Most of the Republican candidates who ran for local office in Maine in 2010 expressed opposition to same-sex marriage, and voters appeared to respond favorably to these appeals—Republicans took control of the governorship and both chambers of the state legislature.[18] Given these results, marriage equality activists began focusing instead on a strategy of legalizing same-sex marriage in Maine through the ballot measure process—something never attempted before in any state.

Once More unto the Breach: Mobilizing Support
for Marriage Equality

Putting same-sex marriage back before voters was a risky strategy for proponents of marriage equality. Past experience suggested that this environment inherently favored conservatives. Although public opinion polls showed that support for marriage equality was increasing in Maine, public opinion polling has been notoriously unreliable on this issue. This might be because many voters are uncomfortable telling pollsters that they do not support same-sex marriage. If anything, the triumph of Republicans in the 2010 elections in Maine suggested that the electorate was getting more, not less, conservative in the state. Proponents of marriage equality believed this approach could be successful, though. They targeted the 2012 election for a marriage equality ballot measure, betting that in three years they could change enough voters' minds to get a different outcome than in 2009. They also felt that, because 2012 was a presidential election year, it would yield a larger turnout and a younger, more liberal electorate, which would be more favorable to their cause.[19]

Efforts to pass a marriage equality ballot measure in Maine were directed by a coalition called Mainers United for Marriage. This coalition included a number of local organizations, most prominently Equality Maine, the same group charged with defeating Question 1 in 2009. Equality Maine was able to use the sizable volunteer network it had established during the 2009 campaign to get an early start on laying the groundwork for a 2012 effort. It put these volunteers to work canvassing neighborhoods and engaging in face-to-face conversations about same-sex marriage with "persuadable" Mainers. According to Equality Maine, proponents of same-sex marriage had more than 200,000 such conversations with residents between 2009 and Election Day in 2012 (Canfield 2012a). This represents a significant chunk of the electorate in Maine—slightly more than 700,000 Mainers would vote in the 2012 election.

These face-to-face conversations were a crucial component of Equality Maine's efforts to change the minds of voters who opposed same-sex marriage in 2009. As discussed previously, conservative rights discourse is particularly powerful when used in the context of a ballot measure campaign because it is difficult to challenge these claims using short campaign advertisements. Engaging citizens in one-on-one conversations might allow proponents of marriage equality to go beyond the thirty-second sound bites that dominate campaign advertising and to begin to unpack some of the discriminatory stereotypes underlying the rights discourse used by conservative opponents of same-sex marriage. Having these conversations also allowed marriage equality activists to begin to reframe this issue for voters as about family, not rights—a crucial component of the strategy used by proponents of same-sex marriage in 2012 (Canfield 2012a). The success of this approach suggests that proponents

of marriage equality can overcome some of the limitations of the ballot measure process by engaging citizens in a much longer and more in-depth conversation. This strategy was made possible, however, by the fact that Maine has a
relatively small electorate and that activists there had three years to prepare for
this ballot measure campaign. This strategy might not be feasible in states with
larger electorates or in instances in which activists do not have as much time to
lay the groundwork for a campaign.

The Conservative Response: Lather, Rinse, and Repeat

Opponents of same-sex marriage attempted to counter the efforts of marriage
equality activists using the same strategies that had worked so well for them
in 2009—using existing church networks to mobilize supporters and using
rights-based appeals to convince undecided voters. These efforts were complicated, however, when Bishop Richard Malone of the Roman Catholic Dioceses
of Portland announced that the state's largest and most influential religious
institution would not participate directly in the 2012 campaign. This was a significant setback for opponents of same-sex marriage because the Portland Diocese had been a key member of Stand for Marriage Maine, the organization
behind the successful 2009 campaign. The diocese had donated more than
$500,000 to Yes on 1, had lent its staffers to help organize the repeal effort, and
had encouraged its parishioners to actively support the campaign. Though the
church ended up on the winning side of the 2009 campaign, it paid a price for
this victory. A large number of Catholics in Maine believe strongly in marriage
equality, and many felt alienated by the church's decision to involve itself in the
campaign. The diocese also suffered a financial decline in the aftermath of the
campaign, forcing it to close schools and churches and making it difficult for
it to make a significant financial contribution to a second effort.

Because the Portland Diocese chose not to involve itself in the 2012 campaign, opposition to same-sex marriage was led instead by Reverend Bob Emrich. A prominent evangelical religious leader in Maine and a veteran of the
first Question 1 campaign, Emrich was named chair of the Protect Marriage
Coalition, the organization charged with leading the opposition to Question
1 in 2012. He worked to raise money and build a network of volunteers for
the campaign by mobilizing his base of supporters among members of the
religious right. The No on 1 campaign was ultimately able to raise around $2.6

million to fund its efforts (about $1 million less than it had raised in 2009), with a little more than $1 million coming from NOM and the rest donated by local religious organizations and individuals.[20] This amount was dwarfed by the Yes on 1 campaign, however, which raised $8.5 million (see Appendix A).

While Emrich worked to mobilize local activists opposed to same-sex marriage, national organizations such as NOM focused on developing the campaign's messaging and advertisements. These efforts were led by Frank Schubert, the chief architect of the campaign to pass Proposition 8 in 2008 and Question 1 in 2009. Following the successful 2009 Question 1 campaign, Schubert began working on the issue of same-sex marriage full time. He left his public affairs firm, Schubert and Flint Public Affairs, which had specialized in corporate issues—representing big tobacco, timber, and pharmaceutical companies before getting involved in Proposition 8—to form a new firm, Mission: Public Affairs, devoted to conservative social causes. He accepted a position as a chief strategist for NOM and was put in charge of devising the messaging and advertisements used by conservatives in all five of the same-sex marriage ballot measure campaigns in 2012.

The No on 1 campaign's advertisements repeated many of the same rights-based appeals used during the 2009 campaign. The issue of parental rights was once again at the forefront of the campaign. One advertisement, "Parkers," hit on many familiar themes. The advertisement features David and Tonia Parker, a Massachusetts couple who had played a prominent role in previous same-sex marriage ballot measure campaigns. The advertisement begins by warning viewers, "If gay marriage happens here, schools could teach that boys can marry boys" (Protect Marriage Maine 2012a). It then features the Parkers recounting how their son was taught about same-sex relationships in public school after same-sex marriage was legalized in Massachusetts. The Parkers framed their opposition to same-sex marriage using the language of parental rights, arguing that the "courts ruled parents had no right to take their children out of class or to even be informed when this instruction was going to take place" (Protect Marriage Maine 2012a). This statement is a reference to the fact that the Parkers had lost a court case in which they argued that they had a fundamental parental right to opt their child out of instruction that discussed the topic of same-sex marriage (*Parker v. Hurley* 2008).

Other advertisements also focused on the idea that legalizing same-sex marriage would violate the rights of those who oppose it. One such advertisement once again featured Don Mendel, the guidance counselor who became the subject of controversy in 2009 when someone filed a complaint asking that he have his license to practice social work revoked after he appeared in a Yes on 1 campaign advertisement. Although the complaint was never acted upon, the incident clearly troubled Mendel. In a 2012 advertisement, he reflected on the event, stating, "They tried to get me fired . . . claiming that supporting marriage as between one man and one woman was discriminatory" (Protect Marriage Maine 2012b). The advertisement concluded by stating that should same-sex marriage become legal, those who disagreed would be "fired, sued, fined, and punished" (Protect Marriage Maine 2012b). Other advertisements made similar appeals. "I Was Fired" featured a Canadian sportscaster who claimed to have been fired for tweeting his support for traditional marriage (Protect Marriage Maine 2012c). Another featured a Vermont couple sued for refusing to allow a lesbian couple to celebrate a wedding reception at their inn. The inn owners argued that they should be allowed to deny the couple service because they opposed same-sex marriage for religious reasons (Protect Marriage Maine 2012d).

These advertisements all construct a similar image of conservatives as victims of oppression whose rights are threatened by efforts to legalize same-sex marriage and depict gays and lesbians as selfishly advancing excessive and unnecessary rights claims. One advertisement used by the No on 1 campaign captures this sentiment well, stating, "Marriage is more than what adults want for themselves. . . . Every Mainer has a right to love whom they choose, but nobody has a right to redefine marriage" (Protect Marriage Maine 2012e). This logic resonates with voters and has proven powerful for conservative opponents of same-sex marriage in the past. Although many of the claims made in these advertisements were disputed during the campaign (Nemitz 2011), the idea that legalizing same-sex marriage threatens the rights of the majority of Americans has been difficult to challenge in this context.

Focusing on the Family

The task of devising a campaign message that could successfully counter these conservative rights claims was led by two national gay rights organizations, the Human Rights Campaign and Freedom to Marry. These groups began conducting public opinion polls and interviewing focus groups as part of a concerted effort to develop a more effective campaign message soon after the unsuccessful Question 1 campaign in 2009. Their research led them to believe there was a disconnect between what many heterosexual people thought marriage meant to them and what they thought it meant to gays and lesbians. Most of the people polled indicated that they thought their marriage was about "love and commitment," but they believed gays and lesbians wanted to marry for "selfish reasons," such as "access to rights and benefits" (Hatalsky and Trumble 2012, 5–8). In order to combat this belief they began working to craft a new message for the electoral campaign aimed at getting voters to think of same-sex marriage not as a desire for rights but as about family. As part of this shift, the Yes on 1 campaign issued a new slogan for 2012: "Marriage for *All* Families." This was a change from 2009, when the No on 1 campaign's slogan was "Protect Maine Equality." Although the implications of both messages are the same—everyone should have equal access to marriage—replacing the word "equality" with "family" subtly shifts the focus away from a more rights-based approach to one that emphasizes that gays and lesbians desire to marry for reasons of love and commitment.

The Yes on 1 campaign issued a slew of advertisements that reinforced this shift in strategies. Most of these advertisements followed the same basic structure. They featured members of a heterosexual couple talking about their family and describing why marriage has been important to their lives. The couple then explained that gay couples want the same things and should be able to enjoy these same experiences. Oftentimes the couples in these advertisements would talk emotionally about a gay friend or family member who they argue should be able to marry "just like everyone else." One such advertisement featured Pat and Dan Lawson, a middle-aged, heterosexual couple married for thirty years. In the advertisement they talked about their marriage and their twin sons, one of whom is gay. Dan admitted that they were initially troubled by the news that their son was gay but decided "you're going to love your child no matter what" (Mainers United for Marriage 2012a).[21] Toward the end of the advertisement, Dan talked about what marriage means to him and why he thought it should be available to his son, arguing, "Marriage is a commitment that comes from your heart. If that person wasn't there, you're not going to be complete. . . . If my son finds someone that he is in love with and wants to create a bond that will last a lifetime, that's marriage in my mind" (Mainers United for Marriage 2012a). Another advertisement opened with four generations of the Gardner family gathered around the dinner table talking about the importance of marriage and family to them. The advertisement concluded with Harlan Gardner, the family patriarch, talking about his granddaughter Katy, who is gay. He said, "We want for her what we have . . . what has been so good for Dorothy and I [*sic*], is too good not to share with the people that we love" (Mainers United for Marriage 2012b). Other advertisements crafted by the campaign followed a similar formula (Mainers United for Marriage 2012c, 2012d, 2012e, 2012f, 2012g).

These advertisements had powerful emotional appeal. They communicated an uplifting message about the importance of marriage and invited the viewers to think about the role family has played in their own lives. This focus on family was designed to help change voters' perceptions of gays and lesbians. The hope was that framing the desire for same-sex marriage in this way would cause voters to see gays and lesbians not as an aggressive minority group demanding "special rights" but as people who want to marry for the same reasons everyone else does. This approach is interesting because appeals to marriage and family have long been a key component of the conservative response to same-sex marriage, which typically emphasizes the need to protect the traditional definition of the family. Instead of challenging this message at a factual level, here proponents of marriage equality sought to use these same emotional appeals to their own advantage.

This shift in strategy also influenced how proponents of marriage equality responded to the claims of their conservative opponents. Instead of arguing that opponents of same-sex marriage were attempting to mislead or manipulate voters, as had been done in previous campaigns, Yes on 1 ran advertisements designed to quell the fears raised by conservatives without deviating from the overall campaign message of family. One such advertisement designed to combat the argument that legalizing same-sex marriage infringes on parents' right to control their children's education featured Rob Stanton and Amy Bongard. The advertisement opened with Rob and Amy sitting with their children around the kitchen table. They talked about how they discussed the issues of same-sex marriage with their children and communicated their family's values to them. Toward the end of the advertisement, Amy, a public school teacher in Maine, stated, "What we do at a school is no substitute for what happens at home, that's where family values come in, that's where core values come in. No law is going to change the core values that we teach our kids here at home" (Mainers United for Marriage 2012h). This advertisement seems to be designed to alleviate concerns that schools might seek to usurp the role of the parents by "indoctrinating" students into believing same-sex marriage is acceptable. Instead of denying that children will be exposed to the concept of same-sex relationships, the advertisement conceded that children will be confronted with this issue at some point in their lives. However, it argued that parents who communicated their values to their children at home should not fear these interactions. This might be a more effective approach than denying that students will be taught about same-sex marriage in schools, a claim that can be difficult to prove to skeptical voters and that seems to concede that introducing children to this subject would be problematic.

Other advertisements also sought to reassure voters that the "consequences" raised by the No on 1 campaign would not occur and communicate the campaign's message about the importance of family. In one such advertisement, Amy Wilton identified herself as a Christian and also a wedding photographer. She talked about her marriage and her family and then reassured voters that legalizing same-sex marriage would not result in more lawsuits against people like her because "discrimination is already illegal" (Mainers United for Marriage 2012i). Another advertisement featured Pastor Michael Gray and his wife, Robyn. In it they sat side by side holding hands while they explained that Question 1 included protections for religious liberty and mentioned specifically that churches would not have to marry same-sex couples if doing so conflicted with their religious beliefs (Mainers United for Marriage 2012j).

This strategy seems to have been effective—proponents of marriage equality won in Maine 53 percent to 47 percent, a six-point increase in support from 2009. It is impossible to know how much of an impact the shift away from a rights-based strategy had on the outcome of this election. As I noted at the beginning of this section, there were a number of differences between the 2009 and 2012 Question 1 campaigns that could have affected these results. However, exit polling data collected in the five states that considered same-sex marriage ballot measures in 2012 suggested that the strategic decision to shift the campaign's message away from rights and onto family was an important component of this success. Some of the most detailed exit polling data from the 2012 election were collected in the state of Washington. These polls found that only 26 percent of voters who believed same-sex couples wanted to marry primarily so they could have "rights and benefits" voted in favor of same-sex marriage, whereas 85 percent of voters who said gay couples wanted to marry for reasons of "love and commitment" supported marriage equality (Hatalsky and Trumble 2012, 6). This is just one data point, but it suggests that these campaigns succeeded at least in part because they were able to shift the debate away from a focus on rights and convince undecided voters that same-sex couples wanted to get married for the same reasons that they did. This might indicate that proponents of marriage equality are more likely to succeed in the context of a ballot measure campaign if voters see this issue less as a competition between competing rights claims and more as about a desire for love, commitment, and family.

Speak for Yourself: The Constitutive Costs of Victory

The results of the 2012 elections showed, for the first time, that proponents of marriage equality could have success in a ballot measure campaign. This success was not without cost for gays and lesbians, however. Although framing same-sex marriage using the discourse of family instead of rights might have had instrumental value to the campaign, it has some problematic constitutive implications. Proponents of same-sex marriage sought to appeal to undecided heterosexual voters by crafting an image of gays and lesbians that appeared non-threatening to them. However, this image does not always align with how gays and lesbians see themselves, and it often reinforces problematic stereotypes.

Conservative opponents of same-sex marriage typically argue that gays and lesbians are aggressively advancing "selfish" and "unnecessary" rights claims. The campaign sought to avoid this perception by framing same-sex marriage as a desire for family, not rights. Although this approach was successful, it lends credence to the idea that gay rights are excessive and suggests that it would be unacceptable for gays and lesbians to push for same-sex marriage out of a desire for rights and benefits. This sets a troubling precedent that says minority groups should avoid making rights claims when arguing their cause in a popular environment or risk being seen as making excessive demands. This is problematic because many scholars have argued that rights claiming empowers members of oppressed minority groups by allowing them to actively construct an identity of themselves as full and equal citizens entitled to the same rights and protections everyone else is (McCann 1994; Passavant 2002; Engel and Munger 2003). Although avoiding the use of rights discourse during ballot measure campaigns might have instrumental appeal, it denies minority groups access to the constitutive benefits of this discourse.

In addition to minimizing the use of rights discourse, the Yes on 1 campaign also sought to minimize voters' exposure to gays and lesbians. This was in line with a long-standing strategy on the part of gay rights activists that seeks to limit the visibility of gays and lesbians in order to avoid alienating heterosexual voters during ballot measure campaigns (Stone 2012). Almost all of the advertisements used by the Yes on 1 campaign featured heterosexuals talking about their gay and lesbian friends and family. The gay family members discussed almost never actually appeared in these advertisements, however.[22] In the rare cases in which gays did appear in campaign advertisements, they largely remained silent—only one of the thirteen television advertisements produced by the Yes on 1 campaign included a gay person with a speaking role.[23]

The decision to minimize the appearance of gays and lesbians in campaign advertisements is curious given that the Yes on 1 campaign was focused on arguing that same-sex couples should be allowed to marry because they are "just like everyone else." It would seem that the best way to make this argument would be to show that life in gay households is the same as it is in heterosexual ones. Such an approach would help to combat stereotypes of gays and lesbians as deviant and could build greater acceptance for them. Yet only one advertisement issued by the campaign focused on gay families. Interestingly, however, even this advertisement kept gays and lesbians in the background. The advertisement featured Brian Arsenault, the son of two lesbian parents. In it, Arsenault talked about how he was a "normal kid" growing up. He mentioned that he received good grades in high school and played a lot of sports as a child. He said that his moms were always "there for him" (Mainers United for Marriage 2012k). Arsenault's moms never appeared in the advertisement, though. Although the advertisement was ostensibly about gay families, it seemed less concerned with presenting a positive image of gay households to voters and more interested in assuaging fears that children raised by same-sex couples will be harmed by this experience. Arsenault was careful to describe his upbringing as "normal" and emphasized that he himself is straight. He concluded the advertisement by stating, "When I do meet a girl, and fall in love, and settle down, and get married, I want the relationship between me and my wife to be the same as it is between my moms" (Mainers United for Marriage 2012k). This seems designed, at least in part, to address a common conservative fear that raising children in gay households will increase the likelihood of them being gay (see, for example, Sprigg and Dailey 2004, 95–120).

The decision to keep gays and lesbians in the background of the campaign is problematic because it reinforces an image of them as deviant by implying that they have something to hide. It also contradicts the advice of most scholarly studies, which show that encouraging contact with minority groups is actually the best way to reduce prejudice against them (Allport 1954). Many supporters of gay rights have pushed for same-sex marriage as a way to gain greater societal acceptance for gays and lesbians (Chauncey 2004). The fact that proponents of marriage equality have had to minimize the appearance of gays and lesbians in order to win popular support for their cause suggests, however, that many heterosexuals remain uncomfortable with them. Although polling data indicate that Americans are becoming more tolerant of the concept of same-sex marriage, widespread acceptance of gays and lesbians could remain elusive.

Framing same-sex marriage as about family, not rights, is also problematic because many gays and lesbians do not consider themselves "just like everyone else" and do not desire to form traditional family units (Stein 2013). Queer theorists, for example, have long argued that marriage is a "heteronormative" institution representing values that are the antithesis of the calls for sexual liberation that emerged as the driving force behind the gay rights movement in the early 1970s (Warner 1999). They contend that the push for marriage equality threatens to divide gays and lesbians into those deemed acceptable because they choose to marry and form traditional nuclear family units and the "deviant" gays who defy those roles (Warner 1999; Polikoff 2003; Murray 2012). The fact that widespread support for marriage equality has come only after gays and lesbians put increased emphasis on the importance of traditional family values lends credence to this perspective. Some supporters of marriage equality have even gone so far as to explicitly endorse this idea, offering same-sex marriage as an antidote for a sexually deviant gay lifestyle. For example, in his 2004 book, journalist Jonathan Rauch, who is himself gay, argues that marriage is "good for gays" because it "civilizes" them, encourages them to abandon their reckless sexual behavior, and helps them to "mature" (64–68, 75–80). The fact that the Yes on 1 campaign could only win by ignoring these elements of the gay community and presenting an image of gays and lesbians acceptable to the heterosexual majority is troubling. It indicates that rights are not assets given to everyone equally. Instead, rights should be understood as contingent resources given only to those who prove they deserve them by exhibiting behavior acceptable to the majority population. By framing support for same-sex marriage as it did, the Yes on 1 campaign served to reinforce this logic.

CONCLUSION

This chapter has focused on understanding why conservatives had more difficulty opposing same-sex marriage in New England than they did in other
parts of the country. The marriage equality movement took hold earlier and
had more success in that region. This is in large part because the institutional
environment in most New England states favors a decision-making process
controlled by political elites. The citizens' initiative process, a staple of politics in many parts of the nation, was never embraced with the same fervor
in New England. This makes it difficult for opponents of marriage equality
to use rights discourse to foment popular opposition and defeat efforts to legalize same-sex marriage. Maine is an exception in this regard; it is the only
New England state with a robust citizens' initiative process, and the battle over
marriage equality was more contentious there as a result.

The legislative environment has been particularly fertile ground for marriage equality advocates in New England. Four of the six states in this region
legalized same-sex marriage through the legislative process.[24] Marriage equality advocates succeeded in this environment primarily by capitalizing on
Democratic majorities in state government. In Maine, for example, they were
able to use this partisan advantage to legalize same-sex marriage in the state,
passing LD 1020 with a vote largely along party lines. Conservatives have a
difficult time opposing these efforts because legislative officials are primarily
concerned with winning reelection and currying favor with members of their
own political party. This makes them less receptive to rights discourse than a
popular audience would be. Those political officials who did cross party lines
on this issue tended to do so not because they wanted to support fundamental
rights but in response to constituent demand.

In most New England states, the legislature or the courts had the final say
in the same-sex marriage debate. This was not the case in Maine, however.
Conservatives took advantage of the fact that Maine allows citizens to easily
put initiatives on the ballot by placing Question 1 before voters in 2009. During
this campaign, conservatives framed their opposition to same-sex marriage
using the language of rights. They employed the same strategy used during the
Proposition 8 campaign in California, making the argument that legalizing
same-sex marriage would infringe on parents' right to control their children's
education the focal point of the campaign. Proponents of marriage equality
attempted to counter the parents' rights argument by using statements from

experts to debunk these conservative claims and by mobilizing their own rights discourse in support of same-sex marriage, but these tactics failed to convince voters.

In 2012, marriage equality activists made a final push to extend marriage rights to same-sex couples in Maine, this time by putting a ballot measure before voters that sought to legalize same-sex marriage. Proponents of marriage equality spent three years laying the groundwork for this campaign by going door to door and engaging Mainers in one-on-one conversations about marriage equality. They also sought to move the debate away from a discussion of rights, choosing to run campaign advertisements that framed support for same-sex marriage as about a desire for family, love, and commitment. Conservative opponents of same-sex marriage attempted to reuse the same approach that had helped them win in 2009. These efforts were dealt a serious setback, however, when the Catholic Diocese of Portland, the largest and most influential religious organization in the state, announced that it would not be actively participating in the campaign. These factors, combined with a general increase in public support for marriage equality between 2009 and 2012, helped proponents of same-sex marriage secure the passage of Question 1 in 2012.

Marriage equality activists demonstrated that they could have success in a popular environment during the 2012 elections. However, this success was not without cost for gays and lesbians. To succeed in a popular environment, proponents of same-sex marriage felt they must abandon the language of rights and adopt an image of gays and lesbians less threatening to heterosexuals. Such compromises raise legitimate questions about whether legalizing same-sex marriage will lead to greater acceptance for gays and lesbians. In the final chapter of this book, I consider the legacy of the marriage equality movement in the United States and discuss the broader implications of using the ballot measure process to decide questions of fundamental rights.

6. Taking (or Leaving) the Initiative Process

This book has explored how conservative opponents of same-sex marriage used rights discourse to construct an identity of themselves as victims of oppression and construct gays and lesbians as dangerous and deviant "others." My analysis has focused in particular on how this process of identity construction has played out differently in different institutional environments. I have found that conservative rights discourse has been much more prevalent, and much more effective, outside of the courtroom than in it. This suggests that institutional norms and constraints structured this debate, allowing claims advanced by conservative opponents of same-sex marriage to thrive outside of the courtroom despite the fact that these conceptions were typically rejected or ignored by formal legal actors. These findings complicate conventional understandings of legal mobilization, which tend to preference the activities of formal legal actors working inside a legal setting over those that take place outside of the courtroom walls. They also confound popular understandings of rights as a "liberating" force in society, showing that groups seeking to preserve status-quo power structures are just as likely and able to use rights discourse as those who challenge them.

These findings have important implications for those wishing to understand the role that rights discourse plays in the debate over same-sex marriage. However, they have relevance for those who want to understand other issues as well. In this concluding chapter, I expand the scope of this study beyond same-sex marriage and discuss its larger implications. In doing so, my analysis will necessarily be a bit more speculative than that provided in the rest of this book. Here I consider how the same institutional dynamics that shape the use of rights discourse during the debate over same-sex marriage have also shaped other debates about fundamental rights. I then reflect on the normative implications of deciding such important issues in the popular arena of a ballot measure campaign.

LESSONS FROM THE MARRIAGE EQUALITY DEBATE

This book used the debate over marriage equality as an extended case study, conducting comparative analysis of arguments used by opponents of same-sex marriage in different institutional environments. This approach offered an opportunity to empirically test what have often been necessarily theoretical ideas about how different institutional environments might affect the efficacy of social movements. The results yield a number of key insights that can help us understand how institutional norms and constraints shape debates over fundamental rights generally. Before turning to a discussion of these larger implications, however, I will first provide a brief overview of the key findings of this book and then consider how the marriage equality debate will look post-*Obergefell*.

Institutions Shape the Use and Effectiveness of Rights Discourse

Institutions play a central role in the debate over same-sex marriage in the United States. In Chapter 3 of this book, I explored this dynamic in some detail. I showed that marriage equality activists had the most success when arguing their cause in the more elite-centered environments of the state legislature or the courtroom, whereas their conservative opponents fared much better in the popular environment of the ballot measure campaign. The results of this study suggest that these differences in performance are explained in large part by the different institutional norms and constraints present in these diverse institutional environments. I showed that opponents of same-sex marriage were most likely to frame their cause using the discourse of rights when debating this issue in the popular arena of a ballot measure campaign but were least likely to do so when arguing against same-sex marriage inside the courtroom. These results are somewhat surprising given that the language of rights would seem to be well suited for a legal environment.

This suggests that social movement activists have less control over how debates about fundamental rights unfold than is popularly understood because institutions have a direct, and often counterintuitive, impact on the way they think and talk about their cause. This lack of agency is made worse by the fact that activists typically have little choice over where these debates take place. There are some instances in which members of social movements have an opportunity to "venue shop" for the most favorable institutional setting (Ley 2014); however, scholars who study movement-countermovement dynamics have pointed out that activists generally enter a particular institutional environment not by choice but in response to pressure from their opponents (Wilson 2013). This is particularly true in the United States, where our system of federalism and separation of powers creates diffuse power structures and provides ample opportunity for groups to prolong conflicts by shifting the institutional terrain of the debate (Werum and Winders 2001; Smith 2008). In debates over same-sex marriage in particular, activists tended to enter the courtroom less because they believed in the mythic power of courts to bring about social change than as a response to external events beyond their control (Cummings and NeJaime 2010). This is particularly true of conservative opponents of same-sex marriage, who typically entered the courtroom only after being dragged there by proponents of marriage equality.

Chapters 4 and 5 of this book were focused in part on understanding why these different institutional environments had such a dramatic impact on the debate over marriage equality. Both of these chapters provide detailed case studies explaining how opponents of same-sex marriage framed their arguments in ballot measure campaigns—an environment that seems to have favored them. The argument that legalizing same-sex marriage would infringe on parents' right to control their children's moral education was central to the 2008 Proposition 8 campaign in California as well as both the 2009 and 2012 Question 1 campaigns in Maine (Garrison, DiMassa, and Paddock 2008; Schubert and Flint 2009). This argument resonated with many voters by putting a new spin on an old strategy of framing efforts to expand gay rights as a "threat to children." In Chapter 2 of this book, I discussed how activists such as Anita Bryant used this strategy during the 1970s to oppose gay rights ordinances, arguing that such laws would help gays and lesbians "recruit children" into their sinful and deviant lifestyle (Clendenin and Nagourney 1999, 291–311; Fejes 2008). This discourse resonated with many ardent opponents of gay rights, but its overtly discriminatory language had limited appeal for more moderate voters. As a result, antigay activists began adopting a more rights-based strategy during the 1990s (Herman 1997).

Although opponents of same-sex marriage have largely abandoned the harsh, overtly homophobic, and discriminatory language used by activists such as Bryant in the past, the implicit assumption that gays and lesbians want to corrupt children remains a central concern. Indeed, the argument that parents should have the right to protect their children from being taught about same-sex marriage in school rests on an implicit assumption that this topic is obscene and that gays and lesbians are sinful and threatening. These arguments resonated with voters in part because they were able to tap into a palpable fear that legalizing same-sex marriage would make children more tolerant of gays and lesbians and thus increase the likelihood that they might choose to become gay (Chauncey 2010; Segura 2010). This reflects a long-standing conception of gays and lesbians as sexual predators who seek to seduce children and recruit them into the gay lifestyle (Fejes 2008). If stated explicitly, the moral assumptions that undergird such arguments would appear abhorrent and repulsive to many moderate voters who consider themselves to be otherwise tolerant people. When masked by the secular discourse of rights, however, these underlying stereotypes go unnoticed, and as a result, the arguments that they support become more palatable.

Proponents of same-sex marriage struggled to expose the moral underpinnings of the parental rights arguments used by conservatives during ballot measure campaigns because of the institutional norms and constraints present in that environment. During the Proposition 8 and Question 1 campaigns, marriage equality activists sought to debunk the parental rights argument by using statements from experts to reassure voters that legalizing same-sex marriage "had nothing to do with children" and would not result in them being taught about the topic in schools (NoOnProp8.com 2008b; J. Mills 2009). These appeals failed to have the intended effect, however. Opponents of same-sex marriage dismissed these statements as the biased opinion of elites pursuing a political agenda (White 2008; White and Brown 2008a; Mutty 2009c). This response worked well because the education codes of these states are complex, and the memos crafted by these experts are not written for a popular audience. Most voters do not have the time or inclination to sift through this evidence themselves and will instead make decisions based primarily on the information provided to them in campaign advertisements. This results in a disconnect between what voters think about an issue and what experts know to be true (Haltom and McCann 2004).

The courtroom dynamic is completely different, however. As Chapter 3 shows, conservatives typically avoided framing their cause using the language of rights when debating same-sex marriage in this environment. This deprived them of the considerable instrumental and constitutive appeal of this discourse. The case study conducted in Chapter 4 suggests that conservatives choose to avoid making rights-based appeals when arguing this issue in court out of fear that such language can become a liability for them in this setting. This is because success inside the courtroom requires petitioners to present arguments that adhere to legal standards, are supported with evidence, and are able to withstand considerable scrutiny from dispassionate actors. Illogical or erroneous arguments, as well as those based on discriminatory stereotypes or personal moral beliefs, will have difficulty surviving under this type of careful examination.

When Proposition 8 was subjected to a legal challenge in the case of *Perry v. Schwarzenegger* (2010), proponents of marriage equality made the parental rights arguments used by conservatives during the campaign the centerpiece of their case. They used expert testimony to unpack the implicit assumptions that undergirded these conservative rights claims. These experts showed that the parental rights argument perpetuated the idea that gays and lesbians were deviants who "threatened children," fed fears that allowing same-sex marriage might lead more children to adopt a "homosexual lifestyle," and implied that having a gay or lesbian child is something parents should dread (Chauncey 2010; Herek 2010b; Meyer 2010; Segura 2010). This strategy proved successful. The court found that Proposition 8 did not further any legitimate government interest but was instead based solely on illegitimate animus toward gays and lesbians (*Perry v. Schwarzenegger* 2010, 1003).

In Chapter 5, I showed that proponents of same-sex marriage were also able to limit the effectiveness of the parental rights argument in the legislative environment but for different reasons. Legislative officials are primarily motivated by partisan concerns and a desire to win reelection (Downs 1957; Mayhew 1974; Cox and McCubbins 1993). This might make them less receptive to rights discourse than actors in other institutional environments. During the debate over LD 1020, which sought to legalize same-sex marriage in Maine, opponents of marriage equality used a variety of arguments, including rights-based appeals, in an attempt to convince state legislators to reject the legislation. Yet the bill passed because the Democratic Party controlled Maine's state legislature and governorship at the time. Roll-call votes taken on LD 1020 broke down largely along partisan lines. The few legislative officials who did decide to cross party lines explained that they did so not out of any desire to protect individual rights but because they felt it was what the members of their districts wanted (Jackson 2009, S-519; Rector 2009, S-516). Thus, it is not the content of the argument that seems to matter most in a legislative environment but the volume of support shown for any one position.

Rights Can Be Tools of Retrenchment

Rights are often popularly understood to be tools that the politically powerless can use to challenge status-quo power structures. Although a number of scholars have contested this overly simplistic conception (Goldberg-Hiller and Milner 2003; Haltom and McCann 2004; Dudas 2008; Wilson 2013), most scholarship exploring the relationship between law and social movements has nevertheless been primarily concerned with how rights can be used to bring about social change. This book's focus on conservative activists provides some necessary perspective on how rights discourse can also be used as a tool of retrenchment.

Rights carry considerable legitimacy in American politics (Glendon 1993). Conservative activists have often capitalized on this fact by using rights discourse to "expand the scope of the conflict," drawing in moderate voters who might not support their cause otherwise (Dudas 2008). The results of this study suggest, however, that the instrumental power of rights discourse can be undermined if it is used in conjunction with overtly discriminatory language. In Chapter 2 of this book I discussed how conservative activists such as John Briggs and Lon Mabon attempted to pass antigay ballot measures by framing their cause using a mix of rights-based appeals and overtly discriminatory arguments. Although this approach seemed to resonate with ardent opponents of gay rights, these campaigns failed to garner support from a majority of voters. These failures helped spur a shift among many antigay activists, who began adopting a strategy of opposing gay rights through the ballot measure process by framing their cause using exclusively rights-based appeals (Herman 1997).

The results of this study suggest that opponents of same-sex marriage understood this dynamic well. In Chapter 3, I showed that conservative opponents of same-sex marriage largely avoided more "extreme" arguments based on personal religious beliefs or discriminatory stereotypes when arguing against marriage equality in the courtroom or during ballot measure campaigns. This was not an accident. In Chapter 4, I showed that the organizers of California's Proposition 8 took measures to control the message disseminated by campaign members. Those who took part in the Yes on 8 campaign were forced to sign statements of unity that prohibited them from making arguments that deviated from the official campaign message (Pugno 2008). They were also instructed to avoid making arguments when acting in an official campaign capacity that used religious appeals or relied on explicit depictions of gays and lesbians as sinful or deviant (Pollo 2008).

Religious arguments and discriminatory stereotypes were still frequently advanced by conservatives when discussing same-sex marriage with a supportive audience, however. In Chapter 3 I showed that documents produced by conservative interest groups outside of the context of a political campaign or court case frequently framed opposition to same-sex marriage using "extreme arguments" and discriminatory appeals. Similarly, church leaders who took an active but unofficial role in the Yes on 8 campaign organized a series of rallies in favor of the measure. During these events, opponents of same-sex marriage frequently framed their opposition using religious arguments that depicted gays and lesbians as sinful or deviant (Chambers 2008, 64–73; Fryrear 2008, 99–103; Ingle 2008, 89–90; Schneider 2008, 15–16). These arguments proved powerful for ardent opponents of same-sex marriage, many of whom are motivated by deep-seated religious beliefs. This shows that religious language and discriminatory appeals remain important as a mechanism for mobilizing the conservative base.

In addition to the instrumental benefits, thinking and talking about their cause using the discourse of rights also allowed conservatives to construct an identity of themselves as victims of oppression standing up against the excessive and unnecessary rights claims of gays and lesbians. In both Chapters 4 and 5 of this book I showed how adopting such a perspective personalizes opposition to same-sex marriage, transforming it from a fight to protect the somewhat abstract institution of marriage to a personal defense of one's individual rights. Using the discourse of rights in this way energized opponents of marriage equality and lent legitimacy to their cause. It enabled them to see themselves not as a recalcitrant majority stubbornly opposing the rights of others but as "cultural warriors" fighting to preserve fundamental rights and values.

In Chapter 4 I showed that the constitutive power of conservative rights discourse persists outside of the courtroom despite the fact that these arguments have typically been ignored or even rejected by the courts. It is interesting that although conservatives are often unable to keep events outside of the courtroom from being used as evidence inside it, they have no problem preventing events that occur inside the courtroom from having much influence in the popular arena. Unfavorable legal decisions have often been thought to undermine social movements by repudiating existing conceptions of the law and killing alternative legal meanings that develop outside of the courtroom (Cover 1983). The findings of this book complicate this understanding, however. The fact that conservatives have always treated formal legal actors with a great deal of skepticism might inoculate them against unfavorable judicial decisions, allowing them to easily dismiss these rulings as "judicial activism." This enables conservatives to continue to effectively use rights discourse outside of the courtroom even after these arguments have been rejected by formal legal actors.

Rights Are Contingent Resources

Some scholars have argued that rights claiming helps groups typically seen as "outsiders" assert that they belong and are thus entitled to be treated as full and equal citizens (Karst 1991; Passavant 2002; Engel and Munger 2003). Somewhat paradoxically, however, the results of this study suggest that rights discourse might have worked against marriage equality activists' efforts to depict gays and lesbians as deserving of equal rights when used in the popular arena. This might be because rights are not assets given to everyone equally without conditions. Instead, they should be understood as contingent resources, reserved only for those able to effectively demonstrate that they are responsible, disciplined individuals (Goldberg 2007).

When arguing this issue in a popular environment, opponents of same-sex marriage have often depicted this debate as a contest between competing rights claims. According to this logic, rights are a zero-sum game in which demands for new rights necessarily come at the expense of existing ones (Schacter 1994; Goldberg-Hiller and Milner 2003; Dudas 2008). Opponents of same-sex marriage sought to elevate their own rights claims above those of gays and lesbians by using populist appeals to depict their fight against same-sex marriage as part of a grassroots movement supported by the majority of citizens (Brown 2008). In contrast, they described proponents of marriage equality as subversive elites, out of touch with the values of average Americans. During the Proposition 8 campaign, for example, opponents of same-sex marriage repeatedly emphasized that marriage equality had been "forced on Californians" by four San Francisco judges (ProtectMarriage.com 2008b, 2008i, 2008j, 2008k, 2008l, 2008m). This allowed them to associate support for same-sex marriage with the values of large urban areas, using place as a way to signify that those who support marriage equality represent extreme positions that threaten the rights of average citizens (Stein 2002; Rasmussen 2006).

Chapters 4 and 5 of this book show how difficult it was for marriage equality activists to challenge this logic. In the 2008 Proposition 8 and 2009 Question 1 campaigns, proponents of same-sex marriage attempted to counter these arguments in part by advancing their own rights-based appeals (NoOnProp8

.com 2008a, 2008c, 2008d, 2008e, 2008f; Equality Maine 2009f, 2009g). This strategy only served to reinforce the conservative conception of this issue as a clash of competing rights claims, however, and was ultimately unsuccessful.

During the 2012 Question 1 campaign, marriage equality activists tried a different tack. Here, they actively avoided using the discourse of rights, instead framing their support for same-sex marriage using the language of "family" (Mainers United for Marriage 2012a, 2012b, 2012c, 2012d, 2012e, 2012f, 2012g). The hope was that focusing on family would help to change voters' perceptions of gays and lesbians. It would cause crucial swing voters to see them not as an aggressive minority group demanding "special rights" but as people who want to marry for the same reasons as everyone else. Although it is impossible to know for certain how much of an impact this shift in strategies had on the outcome of the campaign, exit polling data indicate that those voters who saw this debate as about "family, love, and commitment" were much more likely to support same-sex marriage, whereas those who saw it as a debate about "rights and benefits" were much more likely to vote against it (Hatalsky and Trumble 2012). This suggests that these campaigns might have succeeded, at least in part, because they were able to shift the debate away from a focus on rights.

So, What Happens Now?

The Supreme Court's finding that same-sex couples have a fundamental right to marry the person of their choosing (*Obergefell v. Hodges* 2015) has had a tremendous impact on the lives of gays and lesbians living throughout the United States. As many scholars have noted, marriage provides significant practical advantages to same-sex couples and their children (Badgett 2010b; Lamb 2010; Meyer 2010; Peplau 2010). Same-sex marriage also has important symbolic implications. In a recent public opinion poll, 36 percent of respondents indicated that they had become "more accepting" of gays and lesbians "over the past few years" (Gallup 2014). This shows that tolerance for gays and lesbians increased considerably during the period in which marriage equality dominated the political agenda of the gay rights movement.

The legal debate over whether gays and lesbians have a fundamental right to marry might be over, but many questions surrounding this issue still remain. The gay rights movement has won some remarkable victories recently, but these victories have come primarily by way of winning access to relatively conservative institutions such as marriage and the military.[1] This might be because those who choose to get married or join the military are typically thought of as responsible citizens who embody core American values. This is somewhat problematic because not all gays and lesbians fit this image. Many gay individuals do not marry or form families either by choice or circumstances, whereas others might desire to marry but do not wish to conform to the traditional nuclear family model (Warner 1999). Attitudes toward marriage are also heavily influenced by socioeconomic factors. Marriage rates have declined considerably in the United States, and it has increasingly become an institution favored primarily by middle-class and college-educated individuals (Fry 2014). This suggests that same-sex marriage might end up primarily benefiting the middle class and might have little tangible impact on the lives of poor and working-class gays and lesbians, for whom marriage is less of a priority (Stein 2013). The gay rights movement achieved its victories in large part by ignoring these less acceptable elements of the gay community. This shows that gaining widespread support for same-sex marriage comes at a cost. It threatens to divide gays and lesbians into those deemed acceptable because they choose to marry and form traditional nuclear family units—as heterosexuals do—and the "deviant" gays who defy those roles (Polikoff 2003; Franke 2006; Murray 2012).

This dilemma echoes the one that faced proponents of African American civil rights in the aftermath of the civil rights movement. Scholars such as Kimberlé Crenshaw (1988) have noted that rights discourse has played a complicated role in the debate over racial equality. The civil rights movement resulted in the rejection of overtly racist laws, but it failed to address much of the structural inequality that exists in this country. This is in large part because conservatives have been able to mobilize their own counter-rights language to effectively resist efforts to address these larger structural issues (Crenshaw 1988, 1336–1349; Hall 2005; López 2006, 143–162). Although the importance of removing overtly racist laws should not be overlooked, for many this has been a mostly symbolic achievement. The legacy of the civil rights movement is problematic for African Americans. It has no doubt had a dramatic impact on the lives of middle-class blacks who have access to quality education and better jobs as a result. However, for many African Americans who remain trapped by generational poverty, attend critically underfunded public schools, or have been incarcerated as a result of a war on drugs disproportionately focused on racial minorities, the civil rights movement has not resulted in real equality

(Beckett 1997; Hancock 2004; Alexander 2010). It is possible that the push for same-sex marriage could leave the gay and lesbian rights movement with a similarly ambivalent legacy.

Conservative opponents of same-sex marriage face a different set of issues. Many members of the religious right have responded to the Court's decision to extend marriage rights to same-sex couples by arguing that these laws conflict with their sincerely held religious beliefs and that the First Amendment should protect their right to opt out of them (Sprigg 2006; Family Research Council 2014, 14–32; Marriage Anti-Defamation Alliance 2014). This shift in tactics might lead conservatives to rely more heavily on a litigation-based strategy than they have in the past. The courts might be a more attractive option for conservatives at this stage of the conflict over same-sex marriage because they are on more solid legal ground when arguing for a free speech exemption. The legal remedy for violations of religious liberty or parental rights has always been to make accommodations for those who object to the activity in question, not to prohibit it altogether (NeJaime 2009). This approach holds much potential for conservative activists. The First Amendment has proven to be a powerful tool for conservatives advocating for religious liberty (Brown 2002) and has been used extensively by those opposed to abortion (Wilson 2013). The Supreme Court's ruling in *Burwell v. Hobby Lobby* (2014) suggests the Court might be receptive to this line of argumentation.

EXPLORING THE INSTITUTIONAL DYNAMICS OF THE "CULTURE WARS"

This book has focused specifically on conservative opposition to same-sex marriage, but these findings can help inform our understanding of other cultural debates as well. In this section of my conclusion, I expand the scope of this project to consider how institutional environments have shaped a number of important cultural conflicts in ways similar to the debate over same-sex marriage. As was the case with marriage equality, these cultural conflicts have typically been sparked by progressive social movements pursuing social change through litigation. Many of today's culture war debates have their roots in the "rights revolution" of the 1960s and 1970s. During this time the Warren and Burger Courts issued a number of decisions expanding the rights of oppressed groups such as African Americans, women, and criminal defendants

(Epp 1998). These decisions generated resentment among many conservatives and helped inspire the New Right conservative movement (Crawford 1980; Diamond 1995; Teles 2008).

Initially, conservatives attempted to roll back these newly won rights by working primarily through the courts. They formed conservative legal organizations, provided training and resources to lawyers interested in pursuing conservative causes, and worked to appoint judges sympathetic to conservative points of view (Stefancic and Delgado 1996; Brown 2002; Hacker 2005; Southworth 2008; Teles 2008). These efforts yielded results. They had a direct impact on the composition of the Supreme Court, causing it to shift ideologically to the right beginning in the 1980s. Despite the Court's rightward shift, however, reversing landmark decisions rendered during the rights revolution proved difficult for conservatives. Although the Rehnquist and Roberts Courts tempered many of these decisions, they have so far stopped short of completely overturning them. In fact, they have often reaffirmed—and in some cases even extended—rights granted by these more progressive courts (Keck 2004, 4).

Much scholarship has focused on how courts have affected cultural conflicts (see, for example, Brown 2002; Carpenter 2012; Wilson 2013; Ellis 2014), but litigation has rarely played a decisive role in these debates. Instead, the diffuse nature of power in the political system and the Court's tendency to issue somewhat flexible decisions have allowed these cultural conflicts to continue to flourish outside of the courtroom (Werum and Winders 2001; Smith 2008). Although the Court has not overturned many landmark civil rights decisions issued during the 1960s and 1970s, it has frequently allowed states and localities to place restrictions on them if they so choose.[2] This leaves many cultural issues to be decided in the popular arena, often through the initiative or referendum process. It also makes it likely that future cultural conflicts will continue to thrive outside of the courtroom regardless of the ideological makeup of the Supreme Court.

Ballot Measure Campaigns and Cultural Debates

The ballot measure process has played a central role in many of the cultural debates that have emerged in the United States over the past fifty years. A number of states adopted the initiative and referendum process during the early twentieth century, but these tools had fallen into disuse by the 1940s.[3] This process was rediscovered, however, during the "ballot measure revolution" of the 1970s (Schmidt 1989, vii–x, 21–23). This rediscovery was aided in part by the rise of the New Right conservative movement, which has often used the ballot measure process as a means of advancing its agendas (Crawford 1980, 322–331).[4] Conservative opponents of African American civil rights, for example, frequently used ballot measures in an attempt to roll back minority rights won through court decisions and the actions of state legislatures. Eleven ballot measures regarding housing and accommodations policies and seven ballot measures regarding school desegregation plans found their way onto state or local ballots during the 1960s and 1970s. These ballot measures were designed to repeal existing civil rights protections or preempt the passage of new ones. Nine of the eleven ballot measures regarding housing and accommodations and five of the seven regarding school desegregation passed (Gamble 1997, 253).

As with the debate over same-sex marriage, conservatives who advocated in support of these ballot measures typically framed their arguments using rights-based appeals. For example, in 1964 Californians considered Proposition 14, a measure that sought to repeal the Rumford Fair Housing Act (1963), which prohibited homeowners from refusing to sell or rent their property to anyone for reasons of race, color, religion, national origin, or ancestry. Supporters of the measure described the fair housing act as "tyranny" and argued that "your 'Yes' vote on this constitutional amendment will guarantee the right of all home or apartment owners to choose buyers and renters of their properties as they wish, without interference by state or local government" (Wilson, Schrade, and Snell 1964, 18–19). These arguments proved effective; voters overwhelmingly approved the measure 65 percent to 35 percent (Cronin 1989, 94). The victory was short-lived, however. The Supreme Court eventually struck down the law as a violation of the Fourteenth Amendment's equal protection clause (*Reitman v. Mulkey* 1967).

A similar rights-based strategy was used by supporters of California's Proposition 21 in 1972. Proposition 21, commonly known as the Wakefield Anti-Busing Measure after its sponsor, Assemblyman Floyd Wakefield, sought to prohibit the use of busing as a remedy for ethnic or racial imbalances in public schools. Supporters of Proposition 21 argued that "a yes vote on this measure will preserve your right as a parent to have your children attend schools in the neighborhood where you choose to live. . . . We believe that all parents are entitled to freedom of choice in choosing the school environment for their most precious possessions, their children" (Wakefield, Brown, and Peterson 1972,

56–57). The ballot measure passed overwhelmingly 63 percent to 37 percent but was later found unconstitutional (*Peña v. Superior Court* 1975).

More recent cultural debates have also taken place in the popular arena of the ballot measure campaign. One issue that has received considerable attention in this environment is women's reproductive rights. Some states have, for example, considered ballot measures mandating parental notification for minors who wish to terminate their pregnancy.[5] These campaigns have typically involved competing rights claims, with conservatives arguing that parental notification laws are "not an attack on abortion" but are "needed to preserve parental rights" (see, for example, Fagan 2009) and liberals arguing that the laws infringe on a woman's right to choose to terminate her pregnancy. More recently, antiabortion advocates have sought to repeal abortion rights by passing "personhood amendments" that define a fertilized human egg as a "person" entitled to the same constitutional rights as any US citizen (Personhood USA 2014). This strategy allows conservatives to argue that opposition to abortion is motivated by a desire to protect the rights of the unborn, not to take rights away from women. It has not yielded much success for conservatives as of yet, however. Colorado voters rejected such an amendment in 2010 and again in 2014, Mississippi voted down a similar measure in 2011, and North Dakota voters rejected one in 2014.

A similar institutional dynamic has also shaped debates over affirmative action. Ward Connerly, a conservative activist and outspoken opponent of this policy, has organized efforts to prohibit affirmative action through ballot measures in a number of states (Kirwan Institute for the Study of Race and Ethnicity 2008). His first success came in 1996, when California voters approved Proposition 209, which prohibited the use of affirmative action by any public employer or university in the state (Miller 1999). Following this success, Connerly has worked to put similar initiatives on the ballot in a number of other states as well. Voters in five states have since approved laws modeled after the California initiative.[6] In 2014, the Supreme Court upheld a ban on affirmative action approved by voters in Michigan, finding that such laws do not violate the equal protection clause (*Schuette v. Coalition to Defend Affirmative Action* 2014).

Connerly and his supporters see this struggle as an attempt to protect rights, not to limit them. The organization he cofounded as a means of combating affirmative action is called the American Civil Rights Institute (ACRI), and he refers to his ballot measures as "civil rights initiatives." During these campaigns, opponents of affirmative action have relied heavily on rights discourse as a tool to sway voters. Proponents of California Proposition 209, for example, attempted to make the ballot measure appear more palatable to average voters by avoiding any explicit mention of affirmative action, choosing instead to label it the California Civil Rights Initiative. The text of the measure avoided specifics; it championed the value of racial equality and framed Proposition 209 as the true embodiment of the spirit of the civil rights movement. It read, "The state shall not discriminate against, or grant preferential treatment to, any individual or group on the basis of race, sex, color, ethnicity, or national origin in the operation of public employment, public education, or public contracting" (California Ballot Pamphlet 1996). As a result of this somewhat vague and misleading wording, many who voted for the measure mistakenly thought they were in fact supporting affirmative action (Kirwan Institute for the Study of Race and Ethnicity 2008).

During the campaign, supporters of Proposition 209 sought to co-opt the mantle of the civil rights movement. An argument in favor of the measure that appeared in the official California voters' guide for that year argued in part,

> We passed civil rights laws to prohibit discrimination. But special interests hijacked the Civil Rights Movement. Instead of equality, governments imposed quotas, preferences, and set-asides. . . . The only honest and effective way to address inequality of opportunity is by making sure that *all* California children are provided with the tools to compete in our society. And then let them succeed on a fair, color-blind, race-blind, gender-blind basis. (Wilson, Connerly, and Lewis 1996)

Campaign advertisements that ran in support of the proposition struck a similar tone. One advertisement linked the ballot measure to the civil rights movement by including clips from Martin Luther King Jr.'s 1963 speech at the Lincoln Memorial. The advertisement ends by quoting King's famous lines, "They will not be judged by the color of their skin but by the content of their character. I have a dream today!" (Miller 1999, 30).

Distorting Democracy

As the foregoing analysis has shown, New Right conservatives have consistently had success advancing their cause in popular environments, whereas the left has typically had more success advocating for social change in elite-centered institutions. This partisan dynamic has influenced the way many people have approached the question of who should decide issues of fundamental rights. Those on the right often construct romanticized notions of the common man as a repository of wisdom and a defender of core values (Kazin 1995). They argue that democracy is based on the idea that the people should make decisions and that the most democratic way to decide difficult moral questions is to take those issues directly to the public (Schmidt 1989, 25–40). Courts, on the other hand, are seen as antidemocratic institutions unaccountable to popular will (Bickle 1962). Conservatives often decry unfavorable court decisions as "judicial activism" or the work of "subversive elites" representing values antithetical to the ones held by average Americans (Meese 1985; Scalia 1997; Boyles 2010).

Those on the left tend to have a different perspective. Many believe that the majority has inherent biases against members of oppressed minority groups and that allowing a majority to vote directly on issues of minority rights will typically result in discriminatory laws (Bell 1978; Cronin 1989, 90–124; Gamble 1997; Miller 2001). Given this, liberals often reject a strictly "majoritarian" definition of democracy (Cronin 1989, 7–37). Instead, they favor a more "Madisonian" model that seeks to prevent majorities from tyrannizing minorities by filtering majority will through representative institutions. According to this logic, protecting members of vulnerable or unpopular minority groups requires that we place some rights outside of the purview of potentially hostile and discriminatory majorities. Judges are often seen as the guardians of these fundamental rights precisely because they are insulated from the influences of popular will.

The results of this study suggest that both of these perspectives are somewhat flawed. This is because institutions do not simply reflect the beliefs of actors working within them; institutional norms and constraints shape how these actors perceive the issues being discussed. Focusing too much on the actors working within these different institutional contexts distorts our view of how cultural debates take place. The evidence presented in this book suggests that the courtroom might be the best environment in which to consider questions of fundamental rights but not because judges possess a superior capacity for reason and logic or because average Americans are ignorant or bigoted. Rather, it is because the courtroom environment encourages actors to carefully consider these questions. Thus, it is not *who* decides questions of fundamental rights but *how* they undertake their decision-making process that should concern us most.

The analysis of the same-sex marriage debates provided in this book gives us reason to doubt that ballot measure campaigns are the best environment for making decisions about fundamental rights. Arguments made to a popular audience during a ballot measure campaign will, in most cases, be subjected to little scrutiny. During these campaigns, voters are bombarded with campaign advertisements that offer short sound bites and slogans. The goal here is not to inform the voter, or facilitate an in-depth discussion, but to capture the attention of a frequently distracted and disinterested audience. Most voters will spend little, if any, time examining the implicit assumptions of these arguments, thus allowing them to go unchallenged. This suggests that the ballot measure process is about much more than "letting the majority decide"; initiative and referendum campaigns do not just reflect the preferences of citizens—they distort them.

Defenders of the ballot measure process often argue that it provides an accurate reflection of majority will, but there is reason to be skeptical of this claim. If the overwhelming success of ballot measure campaigns prohibiting same-sex marriage could be easily dismissed as the product of a population motivated by discriminatory views toward gays and lesbians, then conservatives would not need to make rights-based arguments at all. They could simply play on existing fears that gays and lesbians are sinful and deviant individuals who want to "harm children" and recruit them to a "homosexual lifestyle." Early campaigns against gay rights, such as the one in support of California's Briggs Initiative in 1978, used such a strategy, and they failed. This suggests that these stereotypes are not supported by a majority of Americans.

However, rights can often be used to obfuscate discriminatory stereotypes and transform arguments that would be rejected by most if made explicitly into something acceptable to a majority of Americans. When discriminatory stereotypes, such as the argument that gays and lesbians "threaten children," are reframed as issues of parental rights or religious liberty, the negative assumptions that underlie these arguments become less obvious and more palatable. It is much easier to use rights in this way in the context of a ballot measure campaign than it is in other institutional environments because these campaigns are not conducive to the kind of in-depth, dispassionate analysis required to expose these implicit stereotypes.

This does not mean that the average voter is incapable of unmasking these stereotypes. Many scholars have shown that citizens make different decisions when placed in institutional environments that require them to subject arguments to extensive scrutiny. William Haltom and Michael McCann showed, for example, that popular narratives about excessive litigation, what they refer to as "tort tales," repeatedly transmitted to citizens by media outlets, have incredible persuasive power. However, when citizens serve as jurors and are provided more context about a particular tort case, they are able to unpack the popular logic of the "tort tale" and make dispassionate decisions based on a careful examination of the facts of the individual case (Haltom and McCann 2004, 299). Similarly, proponents of deliberative democracy have long argued that voters make different decisions when they engage in extended discussions of political issues (Fishkin 1991; Gutmann and Thompson 2002, 165). Scholars such as James Fishkin, for example, have used "deliberative opinion polls" to show that preferences often change under these circumstances (Luskin, Fishkin, and Jowell 2002). This suggests that decisions made by citizens who have not engaged in discussion and analysis might not accurately reflect majority will.

The problem, then, is not that ballot measure campaigns allow individuals to make decisions based on discriminatory stereotypes but that in the context of a ballot measure campaign there is no incentive to identify and critically engage with these implicit assumptions. One of the benefits of the courtroom environment is that it fosters just this sort of discussion. Judges are not more capable of using reason than the average American, nor are they immune to ignorance or bias. The institutional norms and constraints present inside the courtroom, however, encourage judicial actors to engage in a sober, dispassionate analysis of the issues. Furthermore, judges are required to publicly justify their decisions by appealing to a particular notion of the "public good," not just their own personal beliefs or prejudices (Rawls 1997, 108–114). This means that courts are more likely to critically examine the logic of rights-based appeals and are less likely to be influenced by discriminatory stereotypes—making them ideally suited to deciding questions of fundamental rights.

Appendix A:
Same-Sex Marriage Ballot Measures

State	Date	Type of Law	Amount of Money Raised Anti	Amount of Money Raised Pro	Result Anti	Result Pro
Alaska	1998	Constitutional Amendment	$597,000*	$108,000*	68%	32%
Hawai'i	1998	Constitutional Amendment	——	——	69%	29%
Nebraska	2000	Constitutional Amendment	$740,000*	$200,000*	70%	30%
California	2000	Statute	$8,422,913	$4,829,543	61%	39%
Nevada**	2000	Constitutional Amendment	——	——	70%	30%
Nevada**	2002	Constitutional Amendment	——	——	67%	33%
Arkansas	2004	Constitutional Amendment	$334,731	$2,952	75%	25%
Georgia	2004	Constitutional Amendment	$92,765	$0	76%	24%
Kentucky	2004	Constitutional Amendment	$201,132	$522,864	75%	25%
Louisiana	2004	Constitutional Amendment	$43,117	$23,547	78%	22%
Michigan	2004	Constitutional Amendment	$1,930,429	$854,212	59%	41%
Mississippi	2004	Constitutional Amendment	$7,215	$0	86%	14%
Missouri	2004	Constitutional Amendment	$29,612	$488,189	71%	29%
Montana	2004	Constitutional Amendment	$10,870	$51,498	67%	33%
North Dakota	2004	Constitutional Amendment	$0	$8,974	73%	27%
Ohio	2004	Constitutional Amendment	$1,202,761	$942,421	62%	38%
Oklahoma	2004	Constitutional Amendment	$21,644	$11,616	76%	24%
Oregon	2004	Constitutional Amendment	$2,434,454	$2,933,998	57%	43%
Utah	2004	Constitutional Amendment	$506,922	$780,740	66%	34%
Kansas	2005	Constitutional Amendment	$154,182	$105,129	70%	30%
Texas	2005	Constitutional Amendment	$495,059	$780,669	76%	24%
Alabama	2006	Constitutional Amendment	$0	$0	81%	19%
Arizona	2006	Constitutional Amendment	$1,039,093	$1,899,948	48%	52%
Colorado	2006	Constitutional Amendment	$1,369,754	$5,459,145	56%	44%
Idaho	2006	Constitutional Amendment	$27,104	$106,378	63%	37%
South Carolina	2006	Constitutional Amendment	$108,545	$370,427	78%	22%
South Dakota	2006	Constitutional Amendment	$123,166	$171,578	52%	48%
Tennessee	2006	Constitutional Amendment	$299,279	$158,814	81%	19%
Virginia	2006	Constitutional Amendment	$413,490	$1,545,257	57%	43%
Wisconsin	2006	Constitutional Amendment	$647,491	$4,313,365	59%	41%
Arizona	2008	Constitutional Amendment	$7,764,115	$823,041	56%	44%

California	2008	Constitutional Amendment	$40,455,774	$45,624,979	52%	48%
Florida	2008	Constitutional Amendment	$1,607,574	$4,327,703	62%	38%
Maine	2009	Statute	$3,367,018	$5,678,579	53%	47%
North Carolina	2012	Constitutional Amendment	$1,595,543	$3,100,000*	61%	39%
Washington	2012	Statute***	$2,700,000*	$15,000,000*	46%	54%
Maryland	2012	Statute***	$2,500,000*	$7,600,000*	48%	52%
Minnesota	2012	Constitutional Amendment	$13,400,000*	$16,400,000*	47%	53%
Maine	2012	Statute***	$2,600,000*	$8,500,000*	46%	52%
		Total	$97,242,752	$133,723,566		

*Approximate

**Nevada requires that a constitutional amendment be approved in two consecutive ballot measures before it can be ratified.

***In 2012, voters in Washington, Maryland, and Maine were asked whether they wanted to allow gays and lesbians to marry. A "yes" vote for the referendum had the effect of allowing same-sex marriage in the state; a "no" vote would have prohibited it.

Source: Compiled by author using publicly available data from the National Institute on Money in State Politics.

Appendix B:
Individualism Master Frame Logit Regression

Variable	Coefficient	Odds Ratio
Court Case	−1.84**	0.1587
	(0.7397)	(0.1174)
Referendum Campaign	1.79*	5.9681
	(1.06269)	(6.3436)
Northeast	−0.92	0.3985
	(0.7555)	(0.301)
South	−0.84	0.4276
	(1.1683)	(0.4996)
West	−1.58*	0.2063
	(0.8354)	(0.1723)
Local Organization	−0.0899	0.9139
	(0.5799)	(0.53)
Constant	0.9445***	
	(0.3149)	

*p > .1

**p > .05

***p > .01 n = 215 r^2 = .3165

This model tests the effect that the courtroom and referendum environments have on the use of the individualism master frame while controlling for region and for documents produced by local versus national organizations. The results indicate that the courtroom environment has a negative effect on the use of the individualism master frame that is significant at the .05 level. Referendum campaigns have a positive effect on the use of the individualism master frame that is significant at the .1 level. In a logit model, odds ratios can tell us more about the size of the effect than the coefficients: odds ratios less than 1 indicate a negative effect; odds ratios greater than 1 indicate that the variable has a positive effect. In this case, the odds ratios show that discourse is .1587 times as likely to use the individualism master frame if it takes place in a courtroom, and discourse is 5.968 times as likely to use the individualism master frame if it takes place in a referendum campaign.

Appendix C:
Religion, Threat, or Slippery Slope Subframe Logit Regression

Variable	Coefficient	Odds Ratio
Interest Group	2.6**	13.495
	(1.0895)	(14.7024)
Northeast	1.32	3.7276
	(1.0958)	(4.0849)
South	2.09	8.1208
	(1.2796)	(10.39105)
West	1.7	5.4758
	(1.0861)	(5.9474)
Local Organization	−0.98**	0.3743
	(0.4009)	(0.1501)
Constant	−2.19**	
	(1.0505)	

*$p > .1$

**$p > .05$

***$p > .01$ n = 215 r^2 = .1184

This model combines the three "most extreme" subframes within the American exceptionalism master frame—slippery slope, religious appeals, and depictions of gays and lesbians as a physical threat—into a single "dummy variable." Documents were coded as 1, indicating the presence of this "extreme" variable, if they used one or more of these subframes. These data were then used to create a logit model testing the effect interest groups had on the use of these extreme arguments while controlling for region and documents produced by local versus national organizations. The results of this regression indicate that interest groups have a positive effect on the use of these extreme arguments that is significant at the .05 level. Odds ratios indicate that discourse is 13.459 times as likely to include extreme arguments if it is produced by these interest groups outside of the context of a referendum campaign or court case.

Notes

1. The terms "initiative" and "referendum" are often used interchangeably, though they represent different things. In the United States, an initiative is typically a new law or constitutional amendment placed on the ballot either by citizen petition or by legislative referral. A referendum is a proposal to repeal a law previously passed by a legislative body. These distinctions are not particularly important for the purposes of this book, however. I will typically use the term "ballot measure" to refer both to initiatives and to referenda generally.

2. Since 1998 there have been thirty-nine statewide ballot measures involving the issue of same-sex marriage. In thirty-four of those instances, voters elected to define marriage as between "one man and one woman" (this trend will be discussed in more detail in Chapter 3).

3. Six states have enacted ballot measures limiting the use of affirmative action: California (in 1996), Washington (in 1998), Michigan (in 2006), Nebraska (in 2008), Arizona (in 2010), and Oklahoma (in 2012). In 2008 Colorado voters rejected a ballot measure that would have prohibited affirmative action in the state.

4. Four states have instituted parental notification laws as a result of ballot measures: Colorado (in 1998), Florida (in 2000), Alaska (in 2010), and Montana (in 2012). Oregon voters rejected a proposed parental notification law in 2006, and California voters have rejected proposed parental notification laws three times (in 2005, 2006, and 2008). More recently, antiabortion advocates have sought to repeal abortion rights by passing "personhood amendments," which define a fertilized human egg as a "person" entitled to the same constitutional rights as any US citizen. Voters in three states have considered such amendments and rejected them: Colorado (in 2010 and in 2014), Mississippi (in 2011), and North Dakota (in 2014).

5. California passed Proposition 187 in 1994, which made undocumented immigrants ineligible for state benefits (the law was later found unconstitutional and was never implemented). In 2006 Arizona voters ratified ballot measures restricting undocumented immigrants' eligibility for bail when accused of criminal charges (Proposition 100), ability to receive punitive damages in civil suits (Proposition 102), and access to state services for education (Proposition 300). In 2012 Maryland voters approved a "Dream Act" ballot measure allowing undocumented immigrants to attend state colleges. Additionally, three states have prohibited bilingual education through ballot measure: California (in 1998), Arizona (in 2000), and Massachusetts

(in 2002). Voters in both Colorado (in 2002) and Oregon (in 2008) have rejected such measures.

6. Medical marijuana advocates have successfully passed ballot measures legalizing the medical use of marijuana in twelve states: California (in 1996), Alaska (in 1998), Nevada (in 1998 and 2000), Oregon (in 1998), Washington (in 1998), Maine (in 1999), Colorado (in 2000), Montana (in 2004), Michigan (in 2008), Arizona (in 2010), and Massachusetts (in 2012). Voters in four states and the District of Columbia (in 2014) have legalized recreational marijuana use via citizens' initiative: Colorado (in 2012), Washington (in 2012), Alaska (in 2014), and Oregon (in 2014). California voters rejected a similar initiative in 2010.

7. I use the terms "conservative" and "liberal" to refer to groups at opposite ends of the left-right political spectrum commonly used to describe the range of modern political ideologies. Although these broad categories obscure much nuance in individual political belief, they can give us a somewhat crude understanding of the worldview of those on opposite ends of the political spectrum generally. In the United States, those on the "right" typically point to a lack of personal responsibility and a decline in the importance of "traditional morality" as the source of societal problems. They believe these issues are best resolved by embracing a limited role for government that allows economic markets to function unhindered and encourages a return to traditional moral values. Those on the "left" tend to emphasize the role socioeconomic factors play in creating societal problems. They support a larger role for government in addressing these problems and embrace a more secular worldview that includes tolerance for diverse viewpoints and lifestyles.

8. This project is focused on conservative opposition to same-sex marriage, much of which comes from the religious right. I use the words "conservative opponents" throughout this book in order to distinguish this position from liberal opposition to same-sex marriage, which is motivated by a very different set of concerns. This choice is not meant to suggest that only conservatives oppose same-sex marriage or that all conservatives do so.

9. This emphasis on institutions has been particularly impactful for scholarship on law and courts because it represents a challenge to the prevailing behavioral models of judicial decision making. These models have largely ignored the role institutional norms and constraints play in shaping judicial behavior, arguing instead that judges make decisions based primarily on their own personal ideological preferences (see, for example, Segal and Spaeth 1993). Many scholars operating from a historical institutionalist perspective have responded to these studies by showing, for example, that judges are often constrained by the need to base their decisions on legal reasoning (Kahn 1999; Whittington 2000, 619; Baum 2006). Scholars of political development have similarly sought to complicate conventional explanations for shifting legal

doctrine that emphasize the importance of changes to the ideological makeup of the Supreme Court (Novkov 2008; Brandwein 2011).

10. Unless otherwise indicated, quotes used in this manuscript are transcribed exactly as they originally appeared. All emphasis is in the original text.

11. Three different procedures allow citizens to vote directly on constitutional or statutory issues: citizens' initiatives (proposals to enact a new law or constitutional amendment placed on the ballot by citizen petition), referenda (proposals to repeal a law enacted by the state legislature placed on the ballot by citizen petition), and legislative propositions (proposals placed on the ballot by the state legislature). Every state except Delaware allows its legislature to place constitutional amendments on the ballot (Delaware allows only the legislature to place statutes on the ballot). Eighteen states allow citizens to place constitutional amendments on the ballot directly: Arizona, Arkansas, California, Colorado, Florida, Illinois, Massachusetts, Michigan, Mississippi, Missouri, Montana, Nebraska, Nevada, North Dakota, Ohio, Oklahoma, Oregon, and South Dakota (Initiative and Referendum Institute 2010). Twenty-four states allow citizens to place statutes on the ballot directly. This includes all states that allow citizen-initiated constitutional amendments as well as Alaska, Idaho, Maine, Utah, Washington, and Wyoming (Initiative and Referendum Institute 2010).

12. Many scholars have, for example, attempted to understand whether litigation is the most effective means of bringing about social change. Perhaps the most famous of these is Gerald Rosenberg in *Hollow Hope* (1991), in which he argues that courts lack the power to enforce their decisions and are thus poor agents of change. Worse yet, Rosenberg argues that legal decisions often generate backlash that actually works against efforts to bring about change. A number of scholars have challenged Rosenberg's arguments, finding that his theories about backlash do not stand up to empirical scrutiny (Keck 2009) or that he drastically underestimates the way favorable court decisions help to mobilize activists and bring about social change indirectly (Feeley 1992; Simon 1992; McCann 1996). Still others have argued that although court decisions might generate backlash, this can actually be beneficial for movement activists because it often exposes the most extreme elements of the opposition to the general public, alienating moderates and helping build greater long-term support for the activists' cause (Klarman 2006).

13. Even those works that do consider how law affects the world outside of the courtroom still often preference the role judges and lawyers play in this process. Scholars have argued that, for example, formal legal actors disseminate legal norms that "radiate" beyond the walls of the courtroom (Galanter 1983; Brigham 1987, 216). In this way, even disputes resolved outside of court take place in the "shadow of the law" and are thus structured by norms of legal behavior established by formal legal actors (Mnookin and Kornhauser 1979, 968).

14. Although Schattschneider does argue that the party that draws in the most supporters will usually be successful, he also indicates that this strategy can be a double-edged sword for activists because they tend to lose control of the terms of the debate as the sphere of conflict widens (1960, 2–3).

15. This is not meant to suggest conservatives are being insincere when using rights-based arguments. In fact, many scholars who have studied the motivations of lawyers who take up conservative cultural causes have found that these individuals are powerfully driven by a sincere belief in the worthiness of their causes (Brown 2002; Hacker 2005; den Dulk 2006, 2008; Southworth 2008).

16. In Western societies rights have always been reserved for responsible, disciplined individuals. The modern understanding of citizenship was developed over time by contrasting those perceived worthy of the title of citizen with a host of others deemed unworthy (Passavant 2002; Darian-Smith 2010). In the United States, Indians and African slaves were the prototypical others. They were regarded as inferior because they were thought to lack the ability to reason and the discipline necessary to behave as responsible citizens. The Indians' perceived unwillingness to work hard and make productive use of their land made them seem inferior to the white settlers, thought to exhibit the values of rugged individualism and self-reliance (Rogin 1975; Slotkin 1992). The African slaves' perceived intellectual inferiority and inability to control their animal instincts were thought to necessitate their servitude to their white masters (Fitzhugh 1960; Rogin 1996, 23–27).

17. The New Right emerged during the 1960s out of frustration with an establishment Republican Party that many conservative Americans saw as unable, or unwilling, to effectively challenge the Democratic New Deal Coalition. Members of what was at the time a radical movement called themselves the "New Right" as a way of separating themselves from what they saw as the elitist, intellectual, and far too moderate "Old Right" (Crawford 1980, 7).

CHAPTER 2. CITIZENS OR DEVIANTS?
RIGHTS AND THE CONSTRUCTION
OF GAY IDENTITIES

1. Most of the gays and lesbians who participated in these early gay subcultures still kept their sexuality private, however. They chose to remain closeted about their sexual orientation during their daily lives, only expressing it openly when participating in this gay subculture during nights and weekends.

2. Despite these restrictions, many characters such as the "sissy," an effeminate male, or the "butch," a masculine female, found their way into films at this time. The sexuality of these characters was never openly discussed, but the audience most likely

understood them to be gay or lesbian. These characters were often used to communicate popular stereotypes of gays and lesbians as deviants (Russo 1987; Fejes 2008, 11–52).

3. One of the most popular treatments was a type of "aversion therapy" in which gay individuals were shown various erotic gay images and then given electrical shocks if they exhibited signs of sexual arousal (Haldeman 1994).

4. In 1975 the American Psychiatric Association removed homosexuality from its list of mental disorders. This change was led in part by people such as Evelyn Hooker, who pointed out major flaws in existing studies linking homosexuality to mental disorders. Such studies did not typically use randomized samples or contain control groups. They were instead based on interviews with gays and lesbians seeking psychiatric treatment or jailed under various sexual psychopath laws. Studies performed using gays and lesbians who did not seek therapy and were not in jail showed that they were no different from heterosexuals (Herek 2010a).

5. This conception was further legitimated by the work of scholars such as Alfred Kinsey, whose groundbreaking studies of human sexuality challenged essentialist understandings of individual sexual orientation. Kinsey argued that individual sexuality, instead of being either "gay" or "straight," could be better understood as falling somewhere on a spectrum (1948, 1953).

6. For a more nuanced discussion of the Stonewall riots and their impact on gay activists in New York at the time, see Kissack 1995.

7. This internal debate continues to plague the push for marriage equality today and has led some to argue that advances for gay rights will come at the expense of those gays and lesbians who do not conform to a heteronormative ideal (Polikoff 2003; Franke 2006; Murray 2012). This debate will be explored in more detail in Chapters 5 and 6 of this book.

8. Ironically, the one political act Bryant had done prior to this campaign was to record a radio advertisement for and donate $1,000 to the city council campaign of Ruth Shack, wife of her agent, Dick Shack. After being elected, Ruth Shack agreed to sponsor Miami's antidiscrimination ordinance and later became one of its most outspoken proponents (Clendinen and Nagourney 1999, 296).

9. The Catholic church had the most comprehensive policy against homosexuality at this time. It views homosexual acts as "sinful" but does not see homosexuals as sinners as long as they do not act on these desires. Southern Baptists, one of the largest evangelical Christian denominations, did not adopt a formal resolution condemning homosexuality as sin until 1976 (Fejes 2008, 73).

10. The initiative did garner attention, but John Briggs failed to gain traction as a candidate for governor. He dropped out of the race a few weeks into the Republican primary, after consistently polling fifth in a five-candidate field (Clendinen and Nagourney 1999, 378).

11. Milk famously tweaked the "recruitment" argument offered by antigay activists, frequently beginning his speeches with "My name is Harvey Milk—and I want to recruit you . . . for the fight to preserve democracy from the John Briggs [*sic*] and Anita Bryants who are trying to constitutionalize bigotry" (as quoted in Clendinen and Nagourney 1999, 382).

12. This outrage culminated in a successful national boycott of Florida orange juice, which caused the Florida Citrus Commission to decline to renew Bryant's contract in 1979. Fallout from her campaign also harmed her music and entertainment career, leaving her bankrupt.

13. The measure represented one of the few victories for antigay activists in the 1980s but was later overturned by the Oregon Court of Appeals in *Merrick v. Board of Higher Education* (1989).

14. The following year the OCA sponsored a slate of local antigay initiatives in small cities and rural counties across Oregon. Although most of these measures passed, their impact was negligible because they took place in conservative strongholds with no visible gay communities.

15. In response to these concerns, the campaign did send to 750,000 Christian households a newsletter that mixed special rights discourse with more familiar moral and religious arguments (Herman 1997, 147).

16. Voters in Maine ultimately approved of the antidiscrimination legislation following a third referendum that took place in 2005.

17. Though the logic motivating special rights discourse continues to resonate today, as we shall see, the actual language of "special rights" has been notably absent from most opposition to same-sex marriage. This might be a reflection of the fact that proponents of gay rights have themselves shifted tactics, moving away from a strategy of advancing rights claims based on group identity in favor of an approach that asks that they be allowed to access the same fundamental right to marry as everyone else (Gerstmann 2008).

18. Collecting comprehensive demographic data on gays and lesbians is difficult because many of these individuals are closeted. However, a number of scholars have disputed the claim that gays and lesbians are members of an economically privileged class. One study found that 15.3 percent of heterosexual men and 21.1 percent of heterosexual women were living at or below the federal poverty line. In contrast, 20.5 percent of gay men and 22.7 percent of lesbians, 25.9 percent of bisexual men, and 29.4 percent of bisexual women were living at or below the federal poverty line (Badgett, Durso, and Schneebaum 2013, 8–9). Another study found that an estimated 40 percent of homeless youth identify as LGBT (Durso and Gates 2012). Children of LGBT parents are particularly vulnerable to economic distress. One study found that LGBT individuals raising children in single-parent families are three times as likely to be living near the poverty line as their heterosexual counterparts, and LGBT couples raising children in

two-parent households are twice as likely to be living in poverty as partnered opposite-sex couples (Gates 2013).

19. As Herman (1997) points out, this conception of gays and lesbians as an inordinately powerful minority group is reminiscent of the anti-Semitic belief in a "Jewish conspiracy" and likely derived from these earlier concerns (125–126).

20. Although the results of studies focusing on the question of whether homosexuality is purely genetic have been inconclusive, most agree that sexual orientation is the result of a complex mix of genetic and environmental factors beyond the individual's control (Frankowski 2004, 1828). Further complicating this issue is the fact that a number of theorists have objected altogether to essentialist conceptions of sexuality that create distinct categories of "gay" and "straight" (Halley 1994; Herman 1994; Kinsey 1948, 1953).

21. As we shall see in Chapter 4 of this book, this tactic would play a crucial role in many campaigns against same-sex marriage as well. This was particularly notable during the Proposition 8 campaign in California, in which opponents of same-sex marriage targeted their appeals at racial and ethnic minority groups to considerable effect (Abrajano 2010).

22. In an ironic twist, Governor Roy Romer, who had criticized the law and campaigned against its passage, became the named defendant in the case.

23. The case actually ended up winding its way through the Colorado court system twice. The first time, the courts focused on the question of whether Amendment 2 violated a fundamental right to equal political participation. The Colorado Supreme Court ultimately agreed that it did in a two-to-one decision. It then remanded the case back to the trial court with instructions that it take up the question of whether there was a compelling government interest that could justify the burdens imposed by the law. After an exhaustive inquiry, Judge Jeffrey Bayless dismissed the government's justifications for the law, finding that there was no compelling reason for the burdens it imposed. He also dismissed the plaintiffs' claim that gays and lesbians should be considered a suspect class, finding that they were too politically powerful to be considered eligible for such protections (Gerstmann 1999, 80–84). Both aspects of this decision were later upheld by the Colorado Supreme Court.

24. The Supreme Court spent very little time considering the merits of the different justifications for the law offered by the state attorneys. The majority dismissed these arguments, finding that the "breadth of the Amendment is so far removed from these particular justifications that we find it impossible to credit them" (*Romer v. Evans* 1996, 635). This line of argumentation is somewhat curious given that the rational basis standard does not require that laws be "narrowly tailored" to meet their proposed government interests. It suggests that the majority, despite its claims to the contrary, did in fact use some type of heightened scrutiny in this case (Gerstmann 1999, 129–133).

25. Justice Sandra Day O'Connor used the equal protection clause as the justification

for her concurring opinion in *Lawrence v. Texas* (2003), but the majority did not endorse her position, striking down the law as a violation of due process instead. In *United States v. Windsor* (2013) and in *Obergefell v. Hodges* (2015), the Court embraced the language of equal protection but ended up ruling based on due process grounds as well.

26. In his dissent, Scalia questioned how the Court could allow states to use morality as a justification for completely prohibiting "homosexual conduct" in *Bowers* and then could find in *Romer* that morality could not be used as a justification for denying gays and lesbians protection from discrimination (*Romer v. Evans* 1996, 640–642).

27. This is not unique to gay rights, of course; in the Western legal tradition, willingness to grant individual access to equal rights has typically been contingent on the perceived character of the person making the rights claim (Karst 1991; Passavant 2002).

CHAPTER 3. SITES OF CONFLICT: HOW INSTITUTIONS SHAPE THE SAME-SEX MARRIAGE DEBATE

1. Following the passage of this ballot measure the Hawai'i legislature promptly passed a bill defining marriage as between "one man and one woman." In 2013, the legislature passed a bill that overturned this statute and legalized same-sex marriage in the state.

2. Prior to 1988, the US Supreme Court was statutorily obligated to hear all appeals of state supreme court rulings that involved federal constitutional questions.

3. Many advocates of gay rights have been critical of the movement's focus on marriage equality. They argue that the push to legalize same-sex marriage reinforces the power and prestige of marriage and marginalizes individuals and families who do not fit the traditional nuclear family model. Instead of strengthening the legitimacy of marriage in our society, they believe efforts should be made to unmask these stigmas and challenge marriage's dominance. Doing so may help us to better appreciate the benefits of respecting a diverse range of sexual expressions and "alternative" family structures (Warner 1999; Polikoff 2003; Franke 2006; Murray 2012).

4. Attempts to approve the federal marriage amendment, renamed the Marriage Protection Amendment, were resurrected in 2006. Despite strong support from Republicans in Congress and impassioned pleas from President George W. Bush, the amendment came eleven votes shy of gaining cloture in the Senate and failed to attract the necessary two-thirds majority in the House (Mezey 2007, 116).

5. Mississippi passed its marriage amendment in 2004 by 86 percent to 14 percent despite the fact that supporters spent only $7,000 on the campaign. Supporters of Oklahoma's marriage amendment spent less than $22,000 on their campaign in 2004 and still received 76 percent of the vote. No money was spent for or against Alabama's marriage amendment in 2006. It passed 81 percent to 19 percent (see Appendix A).

6. Proponents of marriage equality raised more than $50 million to fund ballot measure campaigns in 2012, whereas their conservative opponents raised slightly more than $22 million. In some states this margin was even wider. In Washington state, for example, proponents of marriage equality raised more than five times as much as their conservative opponents, outspending them $15 million to $2.7 million (see Appendix A).

7. In *Baker* the Vermont Supreme Court ruled that it was unconstitutional to deny the benefits of marriage to same-sex couples, but left it to the legislature to determine how to rectify this problem. As a result of this decision, the Vermont state legislature granted same-sex couples the ability to enter into civil unions with rights equivalent to marriage, making it the first state to do so.

8. The choice of New England for these efforts was not coincidental. In addition to being waged on the anniversary of *Goodridge,* the campaign also coincided with an increase in Democratic political power in the region and a rise in public support for same-sex marriage. Also, the fact that most New England states lack a robust citizens' initiative process would make it more difficult for conservatives to challenge these laws.

9. The group was named after the Arlington-based condominium in which the first meeting occurred. The name stuck even after the group began meeting in Washington, DC (Weyrich 2004).

10. The ADF was founded in 1994 as the Alliance Defense Fund. It changed its name to Alliance Defending Freedom in 2012. I will occasionally refer to the organization by its original name when referencing documents produced by the ADF prior to 2012.

11. Although these categories are treated as distinct for the purposes of this study, this is a somewhat artificial construct used to identify broad discursive patterns. In reality, these categories are not mutually exclusive. Instead, arguments made by activists contain elements of multiple ideological perspectives that interact to form a complex and interrelated worldview.

12. Documents were obtained from the following campaigns: Alaska Ballot Measure 2, 1998; Oregon Measure 36, 2004; Colorado Amendment 43, 2006; South Dakota Amendment C, 2006; Wisconsin Referendum 1, 2006; Arizona Proposition 102, 2008; California Proposition 8, 2008; Florida Amendment 2, 2008; Maine Question 1, 2009; Maine Question 1, 2012; Maryland Question 6, 2012; Minnesota Amendment 1, 2012; North Carolina Amendment 1, 2012; and Washington Referendum 74, 2012.

13. This database used to be hosted at domawatch.org. The website no longer exists, but an archived version of it can be accessed at https://web.archive.org/web/2010 1230022310/http://www.domawatch.org/case_names_index.html.

14. Documents were obtained from the following court cases: *Baker v. State of Vermont* (1999); *Standhardt v. Superior Court County of Maricopa* (2003); *Morrison v. Sadler* (2005); *Goodridge v. Department of Public Health* (2003); *Li and Kennedy v. State of Oregon* (2005); *Forum for Equality v. McKeithen* (2005); *Anderson v. King County*

(2006); *Citizens for Equal Protection v. Bruning* (2006); *Lewis v. Harris* (2006); *Hernández v. Robles* (2006); *Chambers v. Ormiston* (2007); *Conaway v. Deane* (2007); *In re Marriage Cases* (2008); *Kerrigan v. Commissioner of Public Health* (2008); *In re Marriage of J.B. and H.B.* (2010); *Perry v. Schwarzenegger* (2010); *Gill et al. v. Office of Personnel Management* (2010).

15. Documents were obtained from the following interest groups: Alliance Defense Fund, American Family Association, Concerned Women for America, Family Research Council, Focus on the Family, Heritage Foundation, National Organization for Marriage, Traditional Values Coalition, *Weekly Standard*, and Witherspoon Institute.

16. This procedure involves adding the number of cases coded the same way by two coders and dividing by the total number of cases coded (Cohen 1960). This formula results in an integer between zero and one, with zero being a level of agreement expected only through chance and one being perfect agreement.

17. This advertisement is no longer available online. I will make an offline version of it available to interested parties upon request.

18. This argument is not without its problems, however. Proponents of marriage equality often counter this position by pointing out that not all married opposite-sex couples decide to procreate and that many children are born outside the bounds of marriage. If the state is truly interested in using marriage as a means of controlling procreation, they argue, then it would need to take steps to prevent these actions from occurring as well.

19. Conservatives often cite a study by sociologist Mark Regnerus (2012) as support for this position. The study claimed that children raised in same-sex households were more likely to face serious problems as adults, such as attempting suicide, using drugs, and experiencing sexual abuse, than those raised by opposite-sex parents. This is the only study published in a peer-reviewed academic journal that has come to these conclusions. It has, however, been found to have serious methodological issues that completely discredit its findings—most notably that Regnerus did not use a "random sample" and that he classified children as being "raised by same-sex households" if they reported feeling like their parent had a "romantic relationship with someone of the same sex" during the time that they were under the age of eighteen. Regnerus later admitted that only two of the children in his sample were actually raised by two parents of the same gender (Schlatter 2013).

CHAPTER 4. NO RIGHT TO OBJECT? OPPOSITION TO SAME-SEX MARRIAGE IN THE GOLDEN STATE

1. A traveler could go from Chicago to San Francisco in just six days on the railroad. Prior to this, getting to California from the eastern United States required a treacherous

three- to six-month journey by ship beginning in the port of Boston, traveling around Cape Horn, and eventually arriving in San Francisco. Many did not survive the voyage. For a vivid account of this experience, see Richard Henry Dana Jr.'s *Two Years before the Mast* (Dana 1936). Those who did not want to travel by ship could take a much longer (and no less dangerous) overland route through "hostile" Indian territory.

2. These powers were granted via a constitutional amendment placed on the ballot by the state legislature and ratified by popular referendum.

3. Although Nixon was born in Orange County, California, and raised in nearby Whittier, he was a much more pragmatic politician than the more ideologically motivated Goldwater and Reagan. Nixon's stint as vice-president during the moderate Eisenhower administration and his support for internationalist foreign policy linked him, in the eyes of many conservatives, to the eastern establishment of the "Old Right." Though Nixon was able to use populist appeals to the "silent majority" and calls for "law and order" to ride to the presidency in 1968 a wave of frustration and resentment felt by many, he was never fully embraced by the movement faithful (Critchlow 2007, 42–52).

4. The Department of Defense awarded California $50 billion worth of defense contracts from 1952 to 1962. This represented 25 percent of all defense contracts granted—twice the amount received by any other state. Almost all of this defense spending was located in Southern California. By 1958, this area was doing 90 percent of all the defense-related business in the state (Lotchin 1992).

5. Evangelical churches and religious organizations have deep roots in Southern California. The Stewart brothers began publishing an influential series of religious pamphlets called *Fundamentals* in Southern California in 1910. These pamphlets are widely recognized as the beginning of the fundamentalist Christian movement in the United States. During the 1920s, Pentecostalism was founded on Azusa Street in Los Angeles. In the 1940s, Reverend Charles Fuller of Placentia, California, hosted the "Old-Fashioned Revival Hour," the most popular radio evangelist program in the country at that time. In the 1960s, fundamentalist religious leader Reverend Chuck Smith, known by his followers as "Pastor Chuck," helped found the Jesus movement in Southern California, dedicated to spreading the gospel among Southern California youth. In the 1970s, Southern California religious leader Bob Schuller became one of the most influential early television evangelists in the country (for a more detailed look at this history, see McGirr 2001, 241–254).

6. Newsom was a young, first-term mayor of San Francisco at the time. He had just won a close runoff election in which he ran as a moderate-centrist Democrat against liberal Green Party candidate Matt Gonzalez. Some speculated that his decision to issue marriage licenses to same-sex couples was designed to help him shore up liberal support in the city. Newsom's actions made him a symbol of gay activism in the state and helped him curry favor with San Francisco's large gay and lesbian community.

He went on to serve two terms as mayor of San Francisco and was elected lieutenant governor of California in 2010.

7. Leno had introduced a different version of the same bill (AB 19) three months earlier, but it came up four votes shy of a needed forty-one-vote majority after seven Democrats in the state assembly abstained from voting on it. One month after being declared "dead for the year," the bill was resurrected through a parliamentary maneuver known as a "gut and amend." Using this procedure, Leno was able to take a bill regarding marine fisheries research pending in the Senate (AB 849), strip it of its contents, and insert the language of his failed assembly bill.

8. The group originally drafted two versions of the ballot measure—one that would limit marriage to a relationship between "one man and one woman" and another that would have also repealed all legal rights of same-sex domestic partners who formed civil unions. The campaign ultimately decided against the latter approach because, according to Ron Prentice, director of ProtectMarriage.com, its leaders thought Californians would be reluctant to back a proposal to eliminate existing rights (Mesko 2007).

9. Frank Schubert founded Schubert and Flint Public Affairs in 2003. By 2008, the California-based public relations firm had gained a reputation for organizing successful ballot measure campaigns defending corporations, including defeating a tobacco tax increase and a requirement that restaurants provide health care to employees. Schubert left Schubert and Flint Public Affairs in 2012 to found a new firm, Mission: Public Affairs, dedicated to promoting conservative social causes (Eckholm 2012).

10. This change angered opponents of same-sex marriage, who saw the new title as prejudicial. Supporters of Proposition 8 attempted to challenge the title change in court but were ultimately unsuccessful (Kerns 2008).

11. This strategy was not new; church networks have often been fertile ground for the construction of grassroots social movements on both the left and the right. The civil rights movement, for example, relied heavily on southern church networks to help recruit and mobilize volunteers and organize boycotts and protests (Chappell 2004).

12. A sense of religious purpose is often a driving force for rights-based social movements. Historian David Chappell argues, for example, that the civil rights movement was not a political protest with religious dimensions but a religious revival with social and political implications (Chappell 2004).

13. Volunteers collected almost 500,000 of the more than 1 million total signatures gathered in support of the petition. The rest of the signatures were collected by paid signature gatherers. The use of paid signature gatherers to qualify initiatives for the ballot is extremely common in California because of the state's large size and the requirement that signatures be gathered in a 150-day period (Broder 2000).

14. The Yes on 8 campaign had originally written that teachers "will" be required to teach same-sex marriage if Proposition 8 passed. The California Superior Court

found the wording misleading, however, and insisted that the word "will" be changed to "could" (Egelko 2008).

15. Obama did state that he believed marriage should be between one man and one woman during his first presidential run in 2008, but he also stated that he opposed Proposition 8 and other constitutional amendments like it because he believed they were divisive and discriminatory. The Obama campaign released a response to the mailer reiterating his opposition to Proposition 8.

16. Some quotes were clearly tailored to an African American audience. One from Bishop Donald E. Green, for example, took exception to the comparison between the drive for marriage equality and the civil rights movement. Green states, "We strongly reject and find it insulting that radical gay activists try to equate the civil rights movement to people of the same sex demanding that the definition of marriage be forever changed. A person's skin color is completely different than someone's sexual practices; same-sex marriages are in no way comparable to the black experience for [*sic*] civil rights" (ProtectMarriage.com 2008h).

17. This trope of conservatives as part of an oppressed majority whose rights are being violated by subversive minorities is a common component of New Right political discourse. George Wallace was one of the first to successfully hone a populist image of himself and his supporters as part of a virtuous middle under siege from a number of deviant "outsiders," including liberal judges, Washington bureaucrats, lazy welfare recipients, criminals, protesters, and rioters (Kazin 1995, 221–242). Nixon used a similar approach, frequently making reference to the "forgotten" or "silent" majority of "Middle Americans" besieged by powerful liberal elites (Kazin 1995, 246–255; Mason 2004, 5–76).

18. Such tactics have also been used, for example, by opponents of affirmative action. New Right political activists have effectively branded this policy as "reverse racism" in conflict with the promise of a "color-blind society" envisioned by members of the civil rights movement (Crenshaw 1988; Hall 2005; López 2006, 143–162).

19. These fears suggest that members of "in groups" are motivated to demonize members of "out groups" not because they find their lifestyle revolting but because they find it secretly attractive. Psychological studies have found that those who oppose gay rights most vociferously often have a subconscious longing or forbidden desire for what is perceived to be a more sexually permissive gay lifestyle (Weinstein and Ryan et al., 2012). A similar longing for what was perceived to be a more liberating and passionate lifestyle may have also motivated earlier depictions of groups such as American Indians as lazy and undeserving others (Slotkin 1973).

20. It is unclear whether Section 51933 would require schools that choose to teach sex education to teach about same-sex marriage as well because the provision does not mention same-sex marriage specifically. It would be up to a court to interpret the law

and determine if instruction about marriage that did not mention same-sex relationships would fulfill this requirement.

21. The court had previously overturned another same-sex marriage ballot measure, Proposition 22 (*In re Marriage Cases* 2008), but Proposition 8 posed a different challenge because it was a constitutional amendment, whereas Proposition 22 was a statutory prohibition.

22. This decision left supporters of same-sex marriage divided over how to proceed. A joint statement released by many of the organizations behind the push to legalize same-sex marriage, including the American Civil Liberties Union, Gay and Lesbian Advocates and Defenders, National Center for Lesbian Rights, and Human Rights Campaign cautioned against further legal action at the federal level and argued instead for an attempt to repeal Proposition 8 through the ballot measure process (American Civil Liberties Union et al. 2009). Others argued that ballot measure campaigns inherently favor opponents of same-sex marriage and that the time was right to take the issue to federal court (Talbot 2010).

23. A brief crafted by Governor Schwarzenegger's attorney stated that the case posed "interesting constitutional questions" and that the state would "like to remain neutral on the issue" (Mennemeier 2009). A separate brief filed by then attorney general Brown actually argued that Proposition 8 should be found unconstitutional (Brown 2009).

24. Walker was randomly assigned to the case by the court's computer system, but his background made him an interesting choice to oversee this trial. Originally nominated to the court by Reagan, Walker had a reputation as a conservative jurist with libertarian leanings. He was also the first known gay person to serve as a US federal judge. This fact caused some conservatives to argue that he was biased and should have recused himself from the case (Boyles 2010; Liberty Counsel 2010).

25. The Coalition for California Families, represented by the conservative legal organization Liberty Counsel and officials representing California's Imperial County, also filed motions requesting to join the case on the side of the defense. Their requests were opposed by the ADF, citing a desire to present a coherent legal strategy. Walker found that the Protect Marriage Coalition could adequately represent the interests of the defense by itself and denied these motions (Walker 2009b).

26. Although this summary dismissal technically makes the Minnesota Supreme Court's decision binding precedent, some have argued that summary dismissals should not be given the same precedential weight as a typical decision and should instead be evaluated more as a denial of cert than as a decision on the merits (Harvard Law Review Board 1980, 1274).

27. Conservatives often argue that "moral" and "political" questions are not appropriate for judicial inquiry because judges will inevitably be influenced by their own ideological preferences when answering such questions rather than conducting

an unbiased interpretation of the law. However, despite tough talk to the contrary, conservative jurists are by no means immune from using legal reasoning as a cover for advancing their own personal moral or political ideals (Keck 2004).

28. The defense never advanced more than token arguments suggesting that Proposition 8 could survive strict scrutiny review. Although the attorneys did argue that the government's interest in promoting responsible procreation was compelling, they never provided an answer for the plaintiffs' argument that Proposition 8 was not narrowly tailored to meet this interest because it allowed opposite-sex couples unable or uninterested in procreation to marry and did not prohibit same-sex couples who could not marry from raising children (*Perry v. Schwarzenegger* 2010, 994–995).

29. Blankenhorn has since renounced his opposition to same-sex marriage and is now working to create a coalition of gay and straight people with a mutual interest in strengthening the institution of marriage.

30. Blankenhorn has a master of arts in comparative social history from the University of Warwick. Both of his books were published through his organization; neither was subjected to the peer-review process. Blankenhorn based his conclusions on his own reading of the existing scholarly literature and discussions with experts in the field.

31. Walker seemed to agree with Olson's conclusion. In his opinion he speculated, "Perhaps recognizing that Proposition 8 must advance a secular purpose to be constitutional, proponents abandoned previous arguments from the campaign that had asserted the moral superiority of opposite-sex couples" (*Perry v. Schwarzenegger* 2010, 931).

32. The logic used here echoes the rationale employed by Justice Anthony Kennedy to invalidate Colorado's Amendment 2 in the case of *Romer v. Evans* (1996).

CHAPTER 5. "A PLACE APART": OPPOSITION TO
SAME-SEX MARRIAGE IN MAINE

1. Although Massachusetts allows citizens' initiatives, the process of getting an issue on the ballot is governed by some of the most restrictive laws in the nation, and it is therefore rarely used (Gray and Kiley 1991). In order to qualify their issue for the ballot, petitioners must gather signatures equaling 3 percent of the votes cast in the previous gubernatorial election. Successful petitions must then go before the state legislature for consideration. If the legislature refuses to pass the law, supporters must then collect a second round of signatures equal to .5 percent of the votes cast for governor in the previous election. The state legislature must then consider the petition in two consecutive legislative sessions, and it must receive support from at least 25 percent of state legislators each time before it can be placed on the ballot.

2. Comparing two campaigns occurring three years apart presents some methodological difficulties that the other case studies detailed in this book, which examined relatively contemporaneous events, did not have. This extended time frame makes it impossible to isolate the instrumental impact rights discourse had on the outcome of these two campaigns because I cannot hold constant other factors that might have also affected the outcome. I acknowledge these limitations by discussing how a host of other variables might have also helped to account for these changing results. I also provide exit polling data that suggest rights discourse did have some instrumental impact on the campaign. I conclude the section by exploring the constitutive implications of this discourse, analysis unaffected by this extended time frame.

3. Democrats in the state wanted to give citizens the right to propose constitutional amendments, but Republicans would only support a law that allowed citizens to make statutory changes because they feared that a more expansive initiative process could lead to overturning the Maine Law (Black 1912, 165–167). Passed in 1851, this law prohibited the consumption of alcohol in the state except for medicinal purposes. Though the Republican position eventually prevailed, the Maine Law was successfully put to a vote by legislative initiative in 1911. Voters narrowly agreed to keep the law, however. Maine did not repeal its prohibition on alcohol until the passage of the Twenty-First Amendment in 1933.

4. In 1911 voters approved a referendum mandating that representatives of political parties be chosen by primary election. In 1935 voters approved a referendum regulating the use of state highway funds (Maine State Law and Legislative Reference Library 2011).

5. Defeating the repeal effort was a considerable victory for supporters of gay and lesbian rights—a similar law had been successfully repealed by Maine voters in 1997.

6. One highly publicized effort to build support for same-sex marriage took place on Election Day in 2005, when Equality Maine volunteers working outside polling places asked citizens to send postcards pledging their support for same-sex marriage to their state representatives. More than 33,000 such postcards were sent, far more than supporters had anticipated (Wickenheiser 2008).

7. These gains were particularly important in the Senate, where the Democratic majority increased from a narrow one-vote lead to a more secure five-vote margin.

8. Stand for Marriage Maine was cofounded by Reverend Bob Emrich, an evangelical pastor who founded the Maine Marriage Alliance, an organization opposed to same-sex marriage, and also directed the Maine Jeremiah Project, a coalition of Protestant pastors dedicated to promoting a variety of social conservative causes in the state.

9. In 2008 the organization changed its name to Maine Family Policy Council.

10. One member of the Judiciary Committee, Senator David Hastings (R-Oxford), supported an amendment to the bill that would have sent it directly to the people for a referendum without a vote of the legislature.

11. LD 1020 had been set to go into effect ninety days after its passage, but the legislation was put on hold pending the results of the referendum campaign. It never became law.

12. The largest of these donors were the National Organization for Marriage, which gave $1.6 million, and the Roman Catholic Dioceses of Portland, which donated a little more than $500,000 (Evilsizer 2009).

13. It is a bit ironic that conservatives, who often decry efforts to legalize same-sex marriage as the work of subversive elites and outsiders, would use a Harvard-educated law professor from Massachusetts as a spokesperson for their campaign in Maine.

14. Campaign materials frequently argued that "the people," not elites, should be the ones to define marriage (Stand for Marriage Maine 2009g, 2009h, 2009j, 2009k). In contrast, proponents of same-sex marriage were typically depicted by the campaign as members of "special interest groups" and the "homosexual lobby" (Stand for Marriage Maine 2009e, 2009f, 2009h, 2009i, 2009j). These images equate same-sex marriage with the values of a small cadre of highly organized elites, not the majority of citizens.

15. In many cases, signs that disappeared were not actually stolen at all but removed by the Department of Transportation because they had been placed in "restricted areas" (Adams 2009).

16. Janet Mills (2009) pointed out that the "Maine Learning Results statute, 20-A M.R.S.A. sec. 6209, requires 'accommodation provisions for instances where course content conflicts with sincerely held religious beliefs and practices of a student's parent or guardian.'"

17. Although this characterization of the Yes on 1 campaign is fair, it should be noted that Equality Maine also received considerable financial donations from out-of-state donors and coordinated its campaign strategy with national organizations such as the Human Rights Campaign and Gay and Lesbian Advocates and Defenders.

18. Republicans gained five seats in the Maine Senate to earn a twenty-to-fourteen-to-one majority, with one Independent. In the House, Republicans gained twenty-three seats to win a narrow, seventy-eight-to-seventy-two majority. The Republican governor, Paul LePage, also won with 38 percent of the vote in a close, three-candidate race.

19. Although 55 percent of Mainers had voted in 2009 (a record number for a non-presidential election year), 71 percent voted in the 2008 presidential election. Perhaps recognizing that a larger turnout put them at a disadvantage, Republicans in the state legislature passed a law repealing Maine's thirty-eight-year-old same-day voter registration law in 2011. This legislation was itself repealed, however, by a popular referendum later that year—a victory many proponents of same-sex marriage believed was crucial to their efforts to pass Question 1 in 2012. Voters who register on Election Day are typically younger, more liberal, and thus generally more supportive of same-sex marriage.

20. The campaign's biggest fundraising drive was a highly publicized Father's Day event at which parishioners across the state of Maine were asked to donate money to the campaign via church collection plates (Canfield 2012b).

21. Many of the advertisements used by the campaign featured people, often seniors, frankly admitting that they were not always supportive of same-sex marriage themselves, but that after careful reflection, they had changed their minds on the issue (Mainers United for Marriage 2012c, 2012f, 2012g). Such appeals invite voters to reconsider their own positions on same-sex marriage as well. This strategy might have been particularly effective at helping the campaign appeal to older voters, who tend to be less supportive of same-sex marriage.

22. One advertisement used by the campaign implied that a lesbian and her partner were among a group of family members seated at the kitchen table, but the gay family member was never identified in the advertisement and never spoke (Mainers United for Marriage 2012b). Three of the campaign's advertisements showed pictures of the gay family members being discussed (Mainers United for Marriage 2012c, 2012g, 2012k), but most did not show gays or lesbians at all (Mainers United for Marriage 2012a, 2012d, 2012e, 2012f, 2012h, 2012i, 2012j, 2012l).

23. In "Brotherhood," a group of firefighters discussed what it was like to work with a gay fireman. At one point the gay fireman in question, Ryan Michel, said, "These guys are all straight, so when I joined the department I wondered how a brotherhood so tight like that would be accepting of someone who is gay" (Mainers United for Marriage 2012m). The other firefighters quickly appeased Michel's concerns, however. One argued, "If a guy works hard and does his job, I'm not gonna judge him" (Mainers United for Marriage 2012m).

24. This number included Maine, which later had its marriage equality legislation overturned via popular referendum.

CHAPTER 6. TAKING (OR LEAVING) THE INITIATIVE PROCESS

1. The military's "Don't Ask, Don't Tell" policy, which allowed gays and lesbians to serve as long as they kept their sexual orientation secret, was repealed in 2011.

2. Perhaps the best example of this is *Planned Parenthood v. Casey* (1992), in which the Supreme Court declined to overturn *Roe v. Wade* (1973) but did allow states to place a number of restrictions on abortion if they so choose. Similarly, in both *Gratz v. Bollinger* (2003) and *Grutter v. Bollinger* (2003), the Court declined to rule the policy of affirmative action unconstitutional but did allow for considerable restrictions to be placed on how universities construct these policies.

3. Scholars have offered a number of different potential reasons for the decline in the use of the ballot measure process during this period. Some have theorized that the

decline might be indicative of the disillusionment felt by many Americans about the political system at that time; others argue that it might be a product of the fact that petition thresholds needed to get measures on the ballot rose sharply during that period because western states experienced extensive population growth (Schmidt 1989, 21–23).

4. Although this book is focused primarily on how New Right conservatives have used the ballot measure process, I do not mean to suggest that they are the only ones to do so. Many left-leaning and libertarian activists have used the ballot measure process to push for the legalization of marijuana or physician-assisted suicide, for example. Twelve states have legalized medical marijuana through the ballot measure process, and voters in four states and the District of Columbia have legalized recreational marijuana use via citizens' initiatives (Marijuana Policy Project 2016). Both Oregon and Washington have passed ballot measures legalizing physician-assisted suicide, and three states have rejected such initiatives (Nightingale Alliance 2012).

5. Four states have instituted parental notification laws as a result of ballot measures: Colorado voters ratified Amendment 12 in 1998, Florida passed Amendment 1 in 2000, Alaska passed Ballot Measure 2 in 2010, and Montana passed L-R 120 in 2012. Oregon voters rejected a proposed parental notification law in 2006 (Ballot Measure 43). California voters have rejected proposed parental notification laws three times (Proposition 73 in 2005, Proposition 85 in 2006, and Proposition 4 in 2008).

6. Washington state passed Initiative 200 in 1998, Michigan passed Proposition 2 in 2006, Nebraska passed Initiative 424 in 2008, Arizona passed Proposition 107 in 2010, and Oklahoma passed State Question 759 in 2012. Colorado voters rejected a ballot measure that would have prohibited affirmative action in the state in 2008.

Works Cited

Abrajano, Marisa. 2010. "Are Blacks and Latinos Responsible for Passing Proposition 8? Analyzing Voter Attitudes on California's Proposal to Ban Same-Sex Marriage in 2008." *Political Research Quarterly* 63, no. 4: 922–932.

Ackley, Ralph, et al. 2009. "Letter to the Elected Members of the Maine Legislature." http://www.asmainegoes.com/content/maine-church-leaders-support-traditional -marriage. Accessed July 25, 2011.

Adam, Barry D. 1987. *The Rise of a Gay and Lesbian Movement.* Boston, MA: Twayne.

Adams, Betty. 2009. "Sign-Theft Complaints Rise as Vote Nears: The DOT Removes Political Signs from I-95, and Reports of Tampering with 'Yes on 1' Signs Escalate." *Portland Press Herald*, October 25, B7.

Alan, Sears, and Craig Osten. 2005. *The ACLU vs. America: Exposing the Agenda to Redefine Moral Values.* Nashville, TN: B&H Books.

Alexander, Michelle. 2010. *The New Jim Crow: Mass Incarceration in the Age of Colorblindness.* New York: New Press.

Alliance Defense Fund. 2008. "Issues by State." https://web.archive.org/web/201202 06020702/http://www.domawatch.org/stateissues/index.html. Accessed February 9, 2016.

———. 2009a. "Defendant-Intervenors' Notice of Motion and Motion for Summary Judgment, and Memorandum of Points and Authorities in Support of Motion for Summary Judgment." http://www.domawatch.org/cases/9thcircuit/Perry_v _Schwarzenegger/District%20Court/MSJ/PvS_DN_172_1_Def_Intrvnr_MSJ_and _Memo_090909.pdf. Accessed September 1, 2010.

———. 2009b. "Trial Memorandum." http://oldsite.alliancedefensefund.org/userdocs /SchwarzeneggerTrialBrief.pdf. Accessed September 1, 2010.

———. 2010. "Answers to Questions for Closing Argument." June 15. http://oldsite .alliancedefensefund.org/userdocs/SchwarzeneggerAnswers.pdf. Accessed September 1, 2010.

Allport, G. W. 1954. *The Nature of Prejudice.* New York: Doubleday.

American Civil Liberties Union et al. 2009. "Why the Ballot Box and Not the Courts Should Be the Next Step on Marriage Equality." http://www.aclu.org/pdfs/lgbt /ballot_box_20090527.pdf. Accessed April 1, 2011.

American Psychiatric Association. 1952. *Diagnostics and Statistical Manual of Mental Disorders.* Washington, DC: American Psychiatric Association Mental Hospital Service.

Andersen, Ellen Ann. 2005. *Out of the Closets and into the Courts: Legal Opportunity Structure and Gay Rights Litigation.* Ann Arbor: University of Michigan Press.

Anderson, Jane, Robert Bolingbroke, and Jeralee Smith. 2008. "Rebuttal to Arguments against Proposition 8." *California General Election 2008 Official Voter Information Guide.* http://www.voterguide.sos.ca.gov/past/2008/general/argu-rebut/argu -rebutt8.htm.

Armstrong, Elizabeth A. 2002. *Forging Gay Identities: Organizing Sexuality in San Francisco, 1950–1994.* Chicago, IL: University of Chicago Press.

Armstrong, Elizabeth, and Suzanne Crage. 2006. "Movements and Memory: The Making of the Stonewall Myth." *American Sociology Review* 71: 724–751.

Austin, John. 1879. *Lectures on Jurisprudence; or, the Philosophy of Positive Law.* Edited by Robert Campbell. Charleston, SC: Nabu Press.

Bachrach, Paul, and Morton S. Baratz. 1962. "The Two Faces of Power." *American Political Science Review* 56, no. 4: 947–952.

Badgett, Lee. 2010a. "Expert Testimony." Transcript of Trial Day Six, January 19. *Perry v. Schwarzenegger.* http://www.afer.org/wpcontent/uploads/2010/01/Perry-Vol-6-1 -19-10.pdf. Accessed September 1, 2010.

———. 2010b. *When Gay People Get Married: What Happens When Societies Legalize Same-Sex Marriage.* New York: New York University Press.

Badgett, M. V. Lee, Laura E. Durso, and Alyssa Schneebaum. 2013. "New Patterns of Poverty in the Lesbian, Gay, and Bisexual Community." Williams Institute. http ://williamsinstitute.law.ucla.edu/research/census-lgbt-demographics-studies/lgbt -poverty-update-june-2013/. Accessed December 16, 2015.

Baum, Lawrence. 2006. *Judges and Their Audiences: A Perspective on Judicial Behavior.* Princeton, NJ: Princeton University Press.

Beckett, Katherine. 1997. *Making Crime Pay: Law and Order in Contemporary American Politics.* New York: Oxford University Press.

Bell, Derrick A., Jr. 1978. "The Referendum: Democracy's Barrier to Racial Equality." *Washington Law Review* 54: 1–30.

Bell, Ellyne, Rachael Salcido, and Delaine Eastin. 2008. "Rebuttal to Argument in Favor of Proposition 8." *California General Election 2008 Official Voter Information Guide.* http://voterguide.sos.ca.gov/past/2008/general/argu-rebut/argu-rebutt8.htm.

Benford, Robert D., and David Snow. 2000. "Framing Processes and Social Movements: An Overview and Assessment." *Annual Review of Sociology* 26: 611–639.

Berg, Thomas C., Carl Esbeck, Robin Wilson, and Richard Garnett. 2009. "Religious Liberty Implications of S.P. 384." http://www.standformarriagemaine.com/docs /SP384lettertoGovernor.pdf. Accessed July 17, 2011.

Berube, Allan. 2010. *Coming Out under Fire: The History of Gay Men and Women during World War II.* Chapel Hill: University of North Carolina Press.

Bickford, Bruce. 2009. "Legislative Record." *One Hundred and Twenty-Fourth Legislature*

First Regular Session 34th Legislative Day. http://www.maine.gov/legis/house/rec ords/124hrecindx.htm#may09. Accessed July 17, 2011.

Bickle, Alexander M. 1962. *The Least Dangerous Branch: The Supreme Court at the Bar of Politics.* New Haven, CT: Yale University Press.

Black, William J. 1912. "Maine's Experience with the Initiative and Referendum." *Annals of the American Academy of Political Science* 43: 159–178.

Blankenhorn, David. 1996. *Fatherless America: Confronting Our Most Urgent Social Problems.* New York: HarperPerennial.

———. 2007. *The Future of Marriage.* Jackson, TN: Encounter Books.

———. 2010. "Expert Testimony." Transcript of Trial Day Eleven, January 26. *Perry v. Schwarzenegger.* http://www.afer.org/wp-content/uploads/2010/01/Perry-Vol-11-1 -26-10.pdf. Accessed September 1, 2010.

Boies, David. 2010a. "Cross Examination of Kenneth Miller." Transcript of Trial Day Ten, January 25. *Perry v. Schwarzenegger.* http://www.afer.org/wpcontent/uploads /2010/01/Perry-Vol-10-1-25-10.pdf. Accessed September 1, 2010.

———. 2010b. "Voir Dire of David Blankenhorn." Transcript of Trial Day Eleven, January 26. *Perry v. Schwarzenegger.* http://www.afer.org/wpcontent/uploads/2010/01 /Perry-Vol-11-1-26-10.pdf. Accessed September 1, 2010.

———. 2010c. "Direct Examination of William Tam." Transcript of Trial Day Eight, January 21. *Perry v. Schwarzenegger.* http://www.afer.org/wp-content/uploads/ 2010 /01/Perry-Vol-8-1-21-10.pdf. Accessed September 1, 2010.

Bork, Robert H. 1991. *The Tempting of America: The Political Seduction of the Law.* New York: Touchstone Books.

Bossin, Phyllis. 2005. "Same-Sex Unions: The New Civil Rights Struggle or an Assault on Traditional Marriage?" *Tulsa Law Review* 40: 381–420.

Boyles, Dean R. 2010. "A Result Looking for a Rationale." *Daily Journal,* August 30. http://www.protectmarriage.com/article/-a-result-looking-for-a-rationale-daily -journal. Accessed December 1, 2010.

Brandwein, Pamela. 2011. *Rethinking the Judicial Settlement of Reconstruction.* Cambridge, UK: Cambridge University Press.

Briggs, Sheryl. 2009. "Legislative Record." *One Hundred and Twenty-Fourth Legislature First Regular Session 34th Legislative Day.* http://www.maine.gov/legis/house /records/124hrecindx.htm#may09. Accessed July 17, 2011.

Brigham, John. 1987. *The Cult of the Court.* Philadelphia, PA: Temple University Press.

———. 1996. *The Constitution of Interests: Beyond the Politics of Rights.* New York: New York University Press.

Broder, David S. 2000. *Democracy Derailed: Initiative Campaigns and the Power of Money.* New York: Harcourt.

Brown, Edmund G. 2009. "Answer of Attorney General Edmund G. Brown Jr." June 12. http://www.domawatch.org/cases/9thcircuit/Perry_v_Schwarzenegger/District

%20Court/Answers/PvS_DN_39_Answer_of_AG_Brown_to_Complaint_061209
.pdf. Accessed September 1, 2010.

Brown, Sonja Eddings. 2008. "News Media at a Loss for Words." http://www.protect
marriage.com/blog/2008/?w=42. Retrieved from Internet Archiver September 10,
2010.

Brown, Steven P. 2002. *Trumping Religion: The New Christian Right, the Free Speech
Clause, and the Courts.* Tuscaloosa: University of Alabama Press.

Bryan, Frank M. 2004. *Real Democracy: The New England Town Meeting and How It
Works.* Chicago, IL: University of Chicago Press.

Burns, David. 2009. "Legislative Record." *One Hundred and Twenty-Fourth Legislature
First Regular Session 34th Legislative Day.* http://www.maine.gov/legis/house/rec
ords/124hrecindx.htm#may09. Accessed July 17, 2011.

Burstein, Paul. 1991. "Legal Mobilization as a Social Movement Tactic: The Struggle for
Equal Employment Opportunity." *American Journal of Sociology* 96, no. 5: 1201–
1225.

Cahill, Sean. 2007. "The Anti–Gay Marriage Movement." In *The Politics of Same-Sex
Marriage.* Edited by Craig A. Rimmerman and Clyde Wilcox. Chicago, IL: University of Chicago Press, 155–191.

California Ballot Pamphlet. 1996. "Proposition 209: Text of Proposed Law." *California
Ballot Pamphlet: General Election, November 5, 1996.* http://vote96.sos.ca.gov/bp
/209text.htm. Accessed March 30, 2012.

California Department of Education. 2011. "Frequently Asked Questions." http://www
.cde.ca.gov/ls/he/se/faq.asp. Accessed June 15, 2012.

Canfield, Clarke. 2012a. "Changed Minds on Gay Marriage Viewed as Key: Advocates
of Equal Rights for Same-Sex Couples Believe They Have Gained Votes since
2009." *Portland Press Herald,* November 3. http://www.pressherald.com/news
/changed-minds-on-gay-marriage-viewed-as-key_2012-11-04. Accessed October
2, 2013.

———. 2012b. "Maine Churches Expected to Collect Money against Gay Marriage,
but Other Churches of Various Denominations Are Working to Support the Ballot Measure." *Portland Press Herald,* May 26. http://www.pressherald.com/news
/churches-expected-to-collect-money-against-gay-marriage_2012-05-26. Accessed
October 2, 2013.

Carpenter, Dale. 2012. *Flagrant Conduct: The Story of* Lawrence v. Texas. New York:
Norton.

Carter, David. 2004. *Stonewall: The Riots That Sparked the Gay Revolution.* New York:
St. Martin's.

Celli, Michael. 2009. "Legislative Record." *One Hundred and Twenty-Fourth Legislature First Regular Session 34th Legislative Day.* http://www.maine.gov/legis/house
/records/124hrecindx.htm#may09. Accessed July 17, 2011.

Chambers, Alan. 2008. "Love, Power, and Sound Mind." *Church Communication Network Simulcast.* Transcribed by Yvonne T. Boggs, December 13, 2009.

Chappell, David L. 2004. *A Stone of Hope: Prophetic Religion and the Death of Jim Crow.* Chapel Hill: University of North Carolina Press.

Charles, Douglas M. 2015. *Hoover's War on Gays: Exposing the FBI's "Sex Deviates" Program.* Lawrence: University Press of Kansas.

Chase, Kathleen. 2009. "Legislative Record." *One Hundred and Twenty-Fourth Legislature First Regular Session 34th Legislative Day.* http://www.maine.gov/legis/house /records/124hrecindx.htm#may09. Accessed July 17, 2011.

Chauncey, George. 1995. *Gay New York: Gender, Urban Culture, and the Making of the Gay Male World, 1890–1940.* New York: Basic Books.

———. 2004. *Why Marriage? The History Shaping Today's Debate over Gay Equality.* New York: Basic Books.

———. 2010. "Expert Testimony." Transcript of Trial Day Two, January 12. *Perry v. Schwarzenegger.* http://www.afer.org/wp-content/uploads/2010/01/Perry-Vol-2-1 -12-10.pdf. Accessed September 1, 2010.

Clendinen, Dudley, and Adam Nagourney. 1999. *Out for Good: The Struggle to Build a Gay Rights Movement in America.* New York: Simon and Schuster.

CNN. 2008. "California Proposition 8: Ban on Gay Marriage Exit Polls." http://www .cnn.com/ELECTION/2008/results/polls/#CAI01p1. Accessed February 14, 2011.

Cohen, Jacob. 1960. "A Coefficient of Agreement for Nominal Scales." *Educational and Psychological Measurement* 20: 37–46.

Colorado State Legislative Council. 1992. "Ballot History." http://www.leg.state.co.us /lcs/ballothistory.nsf/835d2ada8de735e787256ffe0074333d/f92307749e2caea387256 ffd006a4986?OpenDocument. Accessed July 23, 2014.

Comaroff, John L., and Jean Comaroff. 1991. *Of Revelation and Revolution.* Vol. 2: *Dialectics of Modernity on a South African Frontier.* Chicago, IL: University of Chicago Press.

Cooper, Charles J. 2010a. "Opening Statement." Transcript of Trial Day One, January 11. *Perry v. Schwarzenegger.* http://www.afer.org/wp-content/uploads/2010/01/Perry -Vol-1-1-11-10.pdf. Accessed September 1, 2010.

———. 2010b. "Cross Examination of Lee Badgett." Transcript of Trial Day Six, January 19. *Perry v. Schwarzenegger.* http://www.afer.org/wp-content/uploads/2010/01 /Perry-Vol-6-1-19-10.pdf. Accessed September 1, 2010.

———. 2010c. "Closing Arguments." Closing Arguments Transcript, June 16. *Perry v. Schwarzenegger* http://www.afer.org/legal-filings/hearing-transcripts/perry -trial-closing-arguments-transcript/attachment/perry-vol-13–6-16–10-amended/. Accessed September 1, 2010.

Cott, Nancy. 2000. *Public Vows: A History of Marriage and the Nation.* Cambridge, MA: Harvard University Press.

Courtney, Jonathan. 2009. "Legislative Record." *State of Maine One Hundred and Twenty-Fourth Legislature First Regular Session Journal of the Senate*. http://maine.gov/legis/senate/124th-records.html. Accessed July 17, 2011.

Cover, Robert M. 1983. "Foreword: *Nomos* and Narrative." *Harvard Law Review* 97, no. 1: 4–67.

Cover, Susan M. 2009a. "Emotional Battle Ahead on Gay Marriage: Those Leading the Effort to Repeal the Law Say They Are Already Being Harassed, in Public and at Home." *Portland Press Herald*, June 13, A2.

———. 2009b. "AG Says Marriage Law Not a School Issue: Janet Mills Says She Could Find No Reference in Maine Law Regarding Marriage in the Public School Curriculum." *Portland Press Herald*, October 16, A1.

———. 2009c. "Same-Sex Marriage Foes Slam AG Mills: Her Finding That the Law Would Have No Bearing on Schools Is a 'Shameless Political Ploy,' Says Marc Mutty of Yes on 1. Marc Mutty Insists There's a Correlation between the Same-Sex Marriage Law and What's Taught in Schools." *Portland Press Herald*, October 17, A1.

Cox, Gary, and Mathew McCubbins. 1993. *Legislative Leviathan: Party Government in the House*. Berkeley: University of California Press.

Crawford, Alan. 1980. *Thunder on the Rights: The "New Right" and the Politics of Resentment*. New York: Pantheon Books.

Crenshaw, Kimberlé Williams. 1988. "Race, Reform, and Retrenchment: Transformation and Legitimation in Antidiscrimination Law." *Harvard Law Review* 101, no. 7: 1331–1387.

Critchlow, Donald T. 2007. *The Conservative Ascendancy: How the GOP Right Made Political History*. Cambridge, MA: Harvard University Press.

Cronin, Thomas E. 1989. *Direct Democracy: The Politics of Initiative, Referendum, and Recall*. Cambridge, MA: Harvard University Press.

Cummings, Scott L., and Douglas NeJaime. 2010. "Lawyering for Marriage Equality." *UCLA Law Review* 57: 1235–1331.

Cunningham, Laura Saucedo. 2008. "Protect Marriage—Yes on Prop. 8 Launches Campaign Theme for Latinos: Family Is Sacred—Protect Children's Education." http://www.protectmarriage.com/article/protectmarriageyes-on-prop-8-launches-campaign-theme-for-latinos. Retrieved from Internet Archiver September 10, 2010.

Curtis, Phil. 2009. "Legislative Record." *One Hundred and Twenty-Fourth Legislature First Regular Session 34th Legislative Day*. http://www.maine.gov/legis/house/records/124hrecindx.htm#may09. Accessed July 17, 2011.

Dana, Richard Henry, Jr. 1936. *Two Years before the Mast*. New York: Random House.

Daniels, Cynthia R. 2000. *Lost Fathers: The Politics of Fatherlessness in America*. New York: Palgrave Macmillan.

Darian-Smith, Eve. 2010. *Religion, Race, and Rights: Landmarks in the History of Modern Anglo-American Law*. Oxford, UK: Hart.

Dawson, Michael. 1994. *Behind the Mule: Race and Class in African American Politics*. Princeton, NJ: Princeton University Press.

Defense of Marriage Coalition. 2004. "Oregon Marriage Amendment Commercial."

D'Emilio, John. 1983. *Sexual Politics, Sexual Communities: The Making of a Homosexual Minority in the United States, 1940–1970*. Chicago, IL: University of Chicago Press.

den Dulk, Kevin R. 2006. "In Legal Culture but Not of It: The Role of Cause Lawyers in Evangelical Legal Mobilization." In *Cause Lawyers and Social Movements*. Edited by Austin Sarat and Stuart Scheingold. Cambridge, UK: Cambridge University Press, 197–220.

———. 2008. "Purpose-Driven Lawyers: Evangelical Cause Lawyering and the Culture War." In *The Cultural Lives of Cause Lawyers*. Edited by Austin Sarat and Stuart Scheingold. Cambridge, UK: Cambridge University Press, 56–79.

Diamond, Sara. 1995. *Roads to Dominion: Right-Wing Movements and Political Power in the United States*. New York: Guilford.

DiCamillo, Mark, and Mervin Field. 2008. "Prop. 8 (Same-Sex Marriage Ban) Dividing 49% No–44% Yes, with Many Voters in Conflict." Field Research Corporation. http://www.field.com/fieldpollonline/subscribers/Rls2292.pdf. Accessed June 7, 2013.

Donovan, Charles A. 2011. "A Marshall Plan for Marriage: Rebuilding Our Shattered Homes." *Backgrounder*. Heritage Foundation No. 2567, 1–13.

Douglass, David. 1997. "Taking the Initiative: Anti-Homosexual Propaganda of the Oregon Citizen's Alliance." In *Anti-Gay Rights: Assessing Voter Initiatives*. Edited by Stephanie L. Witt and Suzanne McCorkle. Westport, CT: Praeger, 17–33.

Downs, Anthony. 1957. *An Economic Theory of Democracy*. New York: HarperCollins.

Doyle, William, and Josephine F. Milburn. 1981. "Citizen Participation in New England Politics: Town Meetings, Political Parties, and Interest Groups." In *New England Politics*. Edited by Josephine F. Milburn and Victoria Schuck. Cambridge, MA: Schenkman.

Dudas, Jeffrey R. 2008. *The Cultivation of Resentment: Treaty Rights and the New Right*. Palo Alto, CA: Stanford University Press.

Dugan, Kimberly. 2005. *The Struggle over Gay, Lesbian, and Bisexual Rights: Facing Off in Cincinnati*. New York: Routledge.

Dumais, Paul. 2009. "Testimony before Maine Judiciary Committee Public Hearing on Legislative Documents 1020 and 1118." http://www.youtube.com/watch?v=pp O-RP4usFE&feature=related. Accessed July 17, 2011.

Durso, Laura E., and Gary J. Gates. 2012. "Serving Our Youth: Findings from a National Survey of Service Providers Working with Lesbian, Gay, Bisexual, and Transgender Youth Who Are Homeless or at Risk of Becoming Homeless." Williams Institute. http://williamsinstitute.law.ucla.edu/wp-content/uploads/Durso-Gates-LGBT -Homeless-Youth-Survey-July-2012.pdf. Accessed December 15, 2015.

Eckholm, Erik. 2012. "One Man Guides the Fight against Gay Marriage." *New York*

Times, October 9. http://www.nytimes.com/2012/10/10/us/politics/frank-schubert -mastermind-in-the-fight-against-gay-marriage.html?_r=1&hp. Accessed October 10, 2012.

Egan, Patrick J., and Kenneth Sherrill. 2009. "California's Proposition 8: What Happened and What Does the Future Hold?" National Gay and Lesbian Task Force. http:// www.wwww.thetaskforce.org/downloads/reports/reports/pi_prop8_1_6_09.pdf. Accessed May 21, 2014.

Egelko, Bob. 2008. "Judge Refuses to Order Change in Prop. 8 Title." *San Francisco Chronicle*, August 9, B1.

Ellis, Richard. 2014. *Judging the Boy Scouts of America: Gay Rights, Freedom of Association, and the Dale Case.* Lawrence: University Press of Kansas.

Engel, David M., and Frank W. Munger. 2003. *Rights of Inclusion: Law and Identity in the Life Stories of Americans with Disabilities.* Chicago, IL: University of Chicago Press.

Epp, Charles. 1998. *The Rights Revolution: Lawyers, Activists, and Supreme Courts in Comparative Perspective.* Chicago, IL: University of Chicago Press.

———. 2009. *Making Rights Real: Activists, Bureaucrats, and the Creation of the Legalistic State.* Chicago, IL: University of Chicago Press.

Equality Maine. 2009a. "Proud." http://www.youtube.com/watch?v=3s3FURNG2wA. Accessed September 21, 2011.

———. 2009b. "Book." http://www.youtube.com/watch?v=u0qcpfJ-09M. Accessed September 21, 2011.

———. 2009c. "Clearing Up Distortions." http://www.youtube.com/watch?v=2Gm7 HvaCW2k. Accessed September 21, 2011.

———. 2009d. "Together." http://www.youtube.com/watch?v=74kiByvu8R4. Accessed September 21, 2011.

———. 2009e. "Stand." http://www.youtube.com/watch?v=ID8q02opSiU. Accessed September 21, 2011.

———. 2009f. "All Families." http://www.youtube.com/watch?v=3QLirv1-vBY. Accessed September 29, 2013.

———. 2009g. "Clear." http://www.youtube.com/watch?v=vPS-fMX0gsg. Accessed September 29, 2013.

Eves, Mark. 2009. "Legislative Record." *One Hundred and Twenty-Fourth Legislature First Regular Session 34th Legislative Day.* http://www.maine.gov/legis/house/rec ords/124hrecindx.htm#may09. Accessed July 17, 2011.

Evilsizer, Tyler. 2009. "The Money behind the Maine Marriage Measure." National Institute on Money in State Politics. FollowtheMoney.org. Accessed August 31, 2011.

Ewers, Justin. 2008. "California Same-Sex Marriage Initiative Campaigns Shatter Spending Records." *U.S. News and World Report.* http://www.usnews.com/news /national/articles/2008/10/29/california-same-sex-marriage-initiative-campaigns -shatter-spending-records. Accessed July 7, 2011.

Ewick, Patricia, and Susan S. Silbey. 1998. *The Common Place of Law: Stories from Everyday Life.* Chicago, IL: University of Chicago Press.

Fagan, Dan. 2009. "Parents Need a Say in Abortion Decision." *Anchorage Daily News.* http://www.adn.com/2009/01/24/666711/parents-need-a-say-in-abortion.html. Accessed March 29, 2012.

Family Research Council. 2005. "Brief of Family Research Council as Amicus Curiae." https://web.archive.org/web/20101230090549/http://www.domawatch.org/cases /connecticut/kerriganvstate/Gallagher_Law_Firm_Amicus.pdf. Accessed July 24, 2015.

———. 2014. "Hostility to Religion: The Growing Threat to Religious Liberty in the United States." http://downloads.frc.org/EF/EF14G83.pdf. Accessed September 2, 2014.

Feeley, Malcolm M. 1992. "Hollow Hopes, Flypaper, and Metaphors." *Law and Social Inquiry* 17: 745–760.

Fejes, Fred. 2008. *Gay Rights and Moral Panic: The Origins of America's Debate on Homosexuality.* New York: Palgrave Macmillan.

Fishkin, James S. 1991. *Democracy and Deliberation: New Directions for Democratic Reform.* New Haven, CT: Yale University Press.

Fitzhugh, George. 1960. *Cannibals All! Or, Slaves without Masters.* Edited by C. Vann Woodward. Cambridge, MA: Harvard University Press.

Fitzpatrick, Peter. 1992. *The Mythology of Modern Law.* New York: Routledge.

Florida4Marriage.org. 2008. "One Thing." https://www.youtube.com/watch?v=zgOt _s87nXg. Accessed July 24, 2015.

Foucault, Michel. 1990. *The History of Sexuality.* Vol. 1: *An Introduction.* New York: Vintage Books.

Franke, Katherine M. 2006. "The Politics of Same-Sex Marriage Politics." *Columbia Journal of Law and Gender* 15, no. 1: 236–248.

Frankowski, Barbara L. 2004. "Sexual Orientation and Adolescents." *Pediatrics* 113, no. 6: 1827–1832.

Fry, Richard. 2014. "New Census Data Show More Americans Are Tying the Knot, but Mostly It's the College Educated." Pew Research Center. http://www.pewresearch .org/fact-tank/2014/02/06/new-census-data-show-more-americans-are-tying-the -knot-but-mostly-its-the-college-educated/. Accessed April 8, 2014.

Fryrear, Melissa. 2008. "ABC Protecting Marriage." Simulcast, October 20. Transcribed by Laura L. Springate, December 16, 2009.

Galanter, Marc. 1983. "The Radiating Effects of Courts." In *Empirical Theories of Courts.* Edited by Keith D. Boyum and Lynn Mather. New York: Longman, 117–142.

Gallagher, Maggie. 2008. "Love, Power, and Sound Mind." Church Communication Network Simulcast. Transcribed by Yvonne T. Boggs, December 13, 2009.

Gallup. 2014. "Same-Sex Marriage Support Reaches New High at 55%." http://www

.gallup.com/poll/169640/sex-marriage-support-reaches-new-high.aspx. Accessed August 15, 2014.

Gamble, Barbara S. 1997. "Putting Civil Rights to a Popular Vote." *American Journal of Political Science* 91: 245–269.

Gamson, William A., and Andre Modigliani. 1989. "Media Discourse and Public Opinion on Nuclear Power: A Constructionist Approach." *American Journal of Sociology* 95, no. 1: 1–37.

Garlow, Jim. 2008a. "ABC Protecting Marriage." Simulcast, October 20, 2008. Transcribed by Laura L. Springate, December 16, 2009.

———. 2008b. "Love, Power, and Sound Mind." Church Communication Network Simulcast. Transcribed by Yvonne T. Boggs, December 13, 2009.

Garrison, Jessica, Cara Mia DiMassa, and Richard C. Paddock. 2008. "Voters Approve Proposition 8 Banning Same-Sex Marriages: Passage of Prop. 8 Throws Thousands of Same-Sex Unions into Doubt." *Los Angeles Times*, November 5. http://www.latimes.com/news/local/la-me-gaymarriage5-2008nov05,0,1545381.story. Accessed September 10, 2010.

Gates, Gary J. 2013. "LGBT Parenting in the United States." Williams Institute. http://williamsinstitute.law.ucla.edu/research/census-lgbt-demographics-studies/lgbt-parenting-in-the-united-states/. Accessed December 16, 2015.

Gaventa, John. 1980. *Power and Powerlessness: Quiescence and Rebellion in an Appalachian Valley.* Urbana-Champaign: University of Illinois Press.

Gay and Lesbian Advocates and Defenders (GLAD). 2008. "5 Years after *Goodridge*, GLAD Announces '6x12': Marriage Is Possible in All Six New England States by 2012, Says GLAD." Press Release. http://www.glad.org/current/pr-detail/5-years-after-goodridge-glad-announces-6x12/. Accessed August 9, 2011.

Gerstmann, Evan. 1999. *The Constitutional Underclass: Gays, Lesbians, and the Failure of Class-Based Equal Protection.* Chicago, IL: University of Chicago Press.

———. 2008. *Same-Sex Marriage and the Constitution.* Cambridge, UK: Cambridge University Press.

Ghaziani, Amin. 2011. "Post-Gay Collective Identity Construction." *Social Problems* 58, no. 1: 99–125.

Gilliom, John. 2001. *Overseers of the Poor: Surveillance, Resistance, and the Limits of Privacy.* Chicago, IL: University of Chicago Press.

Gillman, Howard, and Cornell Clayton. 1999. "Introduction." In *The Supreme Court in American Politics: New Institutionalist Interpretations.* Edited by Howard Gillman and Cornell Clayton. Lawrence: University Press of Kansas.

Glendon, Mary Ann. 1993. *Rights Talk: The Impoverishment of Political Discourse.* New York: Free Press.

Goldberg, Chad Alan. 2007. *Citizens and Paupers: Relief, Rights, and Race, from the Freedmen's Bureau to Workfare.* Chicago, IL: University of Chicago Press.

Goldberg-Hiller, Jonathan. 2002. *The Limits to Union: Same-Sex Marriage and the Politics of Civil Rights.* Ann Arbor: University of Michigan Press.

Goldberg-Hiller, Jonathan, and Neal Milner. 2003. "Rights as Excess: Understanding the Politics of Special Rights." *Law and Social Inquiry* 28, no. 4: 1075–1118.

Government Accountability Office. 1996. *Content Analysis: A Methodology for Structuring and Analyzing Written Material.* GAO/PEMD-10.3.1. Washington, DC: Government Printing Office.

———. 1997. Defense of Marriage Act. GAO/OGC-97–16. Washington, DC: Government Printing Office.

Gray, Alexander, Jr., and Thomas R. Kiley. 1991. "The Initiative and Referendum in Massachusetts." *New England Law Review* 26: 27–110.

Gutmann, Amy, and Dennis Thompson. 2002. "Deliberative Democracy beyond Process." *Journal of Political Philosophy* 10, no. 2: 153–174.

Hacker, Hans J. 2005. *The Culture of Conservative Christian Litigation.* Lanham, MD: Rowman and Littlefield.

Haldeman, Douglas C. 1994. "The Practice and Ethics of Sexual Orientation Conversion Therapy." *Journal of Consulting and Clinical Psychology* 62, no. 2: 221–227.

Hall, Jacquelyn Dowd. 2005. "The Long Civil Rights Movement and the Political Uses of the Past." *Journal of American History* 91, no. 4: 1233–1259.

Halley, Janet E. 1994. "Sexual Orientation and the Politics of Biology: A Critique of the Argument from Immutability." *Stanford Law Review* 46, no. 3: 503–568.

Haltom, William, and Michael McCann. 2004. *Distorting the Law: Politics, Media, and the Litigation Crisis.* Chicago, IL: University of Chicago Press.

Hancock, Ange-Marie. 2004. *The Politics of Disgust: The Public Identity of the Welfare Queen.* New York: New York University Press.

Hardisty, Jean. 1999. *Mobilizing Resentment: Conservative Resurgence from the John Birch Society to the Promise Keepers.* Boston, MA: Beacon.

Harvard Law Review Board. 1980. "Developments in the Law: The Constitution and the Family." *Harvard Law Review* 93: 1156–1383.

Hastings, David. 2009. "Legislative Record." *State of Maine One Hundred and Twenty-Fourth Legislature First Regular Session Journal of the Senate.* http://maine.gov/legis/senate/124th-records.html. Accessed July 17, 2011.

Hatalsky, Lanae, and Sarah Trumble. 2012. "How Marriage Won in Washington State." Third Way Social Policy and Politics Program.

Hatcher, Laura. 2005. "Economic Libertarians, Property, and Institutions: Linking Activism, Ideas, and Identities among Property Rights Activists." In *The Worlds Cause Lawyers Make: Structure and Agency in Legal Practice.* Edited by Austin Sarat and Stuart Scheingold. Palo Alto, CA: Stanford University Press.

Hawkesworth, Mary. 2006. "Contending Conceptions of Science and Politics: Methodology and the Constitution of the Political." In *Interpretation and Method:*

Empirical Research Methods and the Interpretive Turn. Edited by Dvora Yanow and Peregrine Schwartz-Shea. New York: M. E. Sharpe, 27–49.

Heinz, John P., et al. 2003. "Lawyers for Conservative Causes: Clients, Ideology, and Social Distance." *Law and Society Review* 37, no. 1: 5–50.

Herek, Gregory. 2010a. "Sexual Orientation Differences as Deficits: Science and Stigma in the History of American Psychology." *Perspectives on Psychological Science* 5: 693–699.

———. 2010b. "Expert Testimony." Transcript of Trial Day Nine, January 22. *Perry v. Schwarzenegger.* http://www.afer.org/wp-content/uploads/2010/01/Perry-Vol-9-1-22-10.pdf. Accessed September 1, 2010.

Herman, Didi. 1994. *Rights of Passage: Struggles for Lesbian and Gay Legal Equality.* Toronto, ON: University of Toronto Press.

———. 1997. *The Antigay Agenda: Orthodox Vision and the Christian Right.* Chicago, IL: University of Chicago Press.

———. 2000. "The Gay Agenda Is the Devil's Agenda: The Christian Right's Vision and the Role of the State." In *The Politics of Gay Rights.* Edited by Craig A. Rimmerman, Kenneth D. Wald, and Clyde Wilcox. Chicago, IL: University of Chicago Press, 139–160.

Hirshman, Linda. 2012. *Victory: The Triumphant Gay Revolution.* New York: HarperCollins.

Hofstadter, Richard. 1974. *The Age of Reform: From Bryan to F.D.R.* New York: Knopf.

Holmes, Oliver Wendell, Jr. 1897. "The Path of the Law." *Harvard Law Review* 10: 457. http://www.constitution.org/lrev/owh/path_law.htm.

Holsti, O. R. 1969. *Content Analysis for the Social Sciences and Humanities.* Reading, MA: Addison-Wesley.

Hull, Katherine. 2006. *Same-Sex Marriage: The Cultural Politics of Love and Law.* Cambridge, UK: Cambridge University Press.

Ingle, Lou. 2008. "Love, Power, and Sound Mind." Church Communication Network Simulcast. Transcribed by Yvonne T. Boggs, December 13, 2009.

Initiative and Referendum Institute. 2010. "Signature, Geographic Distribution, and Single Subject (SS) Requirements for Initiative Petitions." University of Southern California School of Law. http://www.iandrinstitute.org/statewide_i%26r.htm. Accessed December 1, 2010.

Jackson, Troy. 2009. "Legislative Record." *State of Maine One Hundred and Twenty-Fourth Legislature First Regular Session Journal of the Senate.* http://maine.gov/legis/senate/124th-records.html. Accessed July 17, 2011.

Jenkins, Phillip. 2004. *Moral Panic: Changing Conceptions of the Child Molester in Modern America.* New Haven, CT: Yale University Press.

Johnson, David K. 2004. *The Lavender Scare: Cold War Persecution of Gays and Lesbians in the Federal Government.* Chicago, IL: University of Chicago Press.

Kahn, Ronald. 1999. "Institutional Norms and Supreme Court Decision-Making: The

Rehnquist Court on Privacy and Religion." In *Supreme Court Decision-Making: New Institutionalist Approaches.* Chicago, IL: University of Chicago Press, 175–198.

Karst, Kenneth L. 1991. *Belonging to America: Equal Citizenship and the Constitution.* New Haven, CT: Yale University Press.

Katami, Paul. 2010. "Testimony." Transcript of Trial Day One, January 11. *Perry v. Schwarzenegger.* http://www.afer.org/wp-content/uploads/2010/01/Perry-Vol-1-1-11 -10.pdf. Accessed September 1, 2010.

Kazin, Michael. 1995. *The Populist Persuasion: An American History.* New York: Basic Books.

Keck, Thomas M. 2004. *The Most Activist Supreme Court in History: The Road to the Modern Judicial Conservatism.* Chicago, IL: University of Chicago Press.

———. 2009. "Beyond Backlash: Assessing the Impact of Judicial Decisions on LGBT Rights." *Law and Society Review* 43, no. 1: 151–186.

Kerns, Jennifer. 2008. "Proposition 8 to Protect Marriage Receives $1 Million Donation from Knights of Columbus Catholic Organization." *Christian Newswire.* http:// www.christiannewswire.com/news/863947548.html. Accessed July 7, 2011.

Kinsey, Alfred. 1948. *Sexual Behavior in the Human Male.* Bloomington: Indiana University Press.

———. 1953. *Sexual Behavior in the Human Female.* Bloomington: Indiana University Press.

Kirwan Institute for the Study of Race and Ethnicity. 2008. "Anti-Affirmative Action Ballot Initiatives." http://research.kirwaninstitute.org/publications/antiaffirmative _action_ballot_initiatives_report.pdf. Accessed March 29, 2012.

Kissack, Terence. 1995. "Freaking Fag Revolutionaries: New York's Gay Liberation Front, 1969–1971." *Radical History Review* 62: 104–134.

Klarman, Michael. 2006. *From Jim Crow to Civil Rights: The Supreme Court and the Struggle for Racial Equality.* New York: Oxford University Press.

———. 2012. *From the Closet to the Altar: Courts, Backlash, and the Struggle for Same-Sex Marriage.* New York: Oxford University Press.

Kramer, Larry. 1985. *The Normal Heart.* New York: Samuel French.

Krippendorff, K. 1980. *Content Analysis: An Introduction to Its Methodology.* Newbury Park, CA: Sage.

Lamb, Michael. 2010. "Expert Testimony." Transcript of Trial Day Five, January 15. *Perry v. Schwarzenegger.* http://www.afer.org/wpcontent/uploads/2010/01/Perry-Vol-5-1 -15-10.pdf. Accessed September 1, 2010.

Laycock, Douglas. 2009. "Religious Liberty Implications of SP 0384, LD 1020." http:// www.standformarriagemaine.com/docs/ProfessorLaycockLettertoGovBaldacci .pdf. Accessed July 17, 2011.

Ley, Aaron. 2014. "The Costs and Benefits of American Policy-Making Venues." *Law and Society Review* 48, no. 1: 91–126.

Liberty Counsel. 2010. "California Judge Strikes Down Prop. 8 Marriage Amendment." August 4. http://lc.org/index.cfm?PID=14100&PRID=960. Accessed September 1, 2010.

Lockard, Duane. 1959. *New England State Politics.* Princeton, NJ: Princeton University Press.

López, Ian Haney. 2006. *White by Law: The Legal Construction of Race.* New York: New York University Press.

Lorence, Jordan. 2010. *"Perry v. Schwarzenegger* Trial Blog Posts." Alliance Defense Fund, January 15. http://adfmedia.org/News/PRDetail/?CID=12012#. Accessed September 1, 2010.

Lotchin, Roger W. 1992. *Fortress California 1910–1961: From Warfare to Welfare.* New York: Oxford University Press.

Lovell, George I. 2006. "Justice Excused: The Deployment of Law in Everyday Political Encounters." *Law and Society Review* 40, no. 2: 283–324.

———. 2012. *This Is Not Civil Rights: Discovering Rights Talk in 1939 America.* Chicago, IL: University of Chicago Press.

Lucas, DeWayne. 2007. "Same-Sex Marriage in the 2004 Election." In *The Politics of Same-Sex Marriage.* Edited by Craig Rimmerman and Clyde Wilcox. Chicago, IL: University of Chicago Press, 243–271.

Luskin, Robert C., James S. Fishkin, and Roger Jowell. 2002. "Considered Opinions: Deliberative Polling in Britain." *British Journal of Political Science* 32: 455–487.

Madsen, Deborah L. 1998. *American Exceptionalism.* Jackson: University of Mississippi Press.

Maine Marriage Alliance. 2009. "We Need You to Save Marriage in Maine." Maine marriageamendment.com. Retrieved from Internet Archiver August 18, 2011.

Mainers United for Marriage. 2012a. "Pat and Dan Lawson." http://www.youtube.com /watch?v=FdUCLgjxanQ. Accessed October 16, 2013.

———. 2012b. "The Gardner Family." http://www.youtube.com/watch?v=gvJrmMK 8H1o. Accessed October 16, 2013.

———. 2012c. "Cathy and Phil Curtis." http://www.youtube.com/watch?v=TL48 VDCsG-4. Accessed October 16, 2013.

———. 2012d. "Mary and Chris Stevens." http://www.youtube.com/watch?v=J64KS4 ctrGk. Accessed October 16, 2013.

———. 2012e. "Eric and Jen Humphrey." http://www.youtube.com/watch?v=mXpL lNWGo9I. Accessed October 16, 2013.

———. 2012f. "Paul and Jeanette Rediker." http://www.youtube.com/watch?v=rzGLq Wjuu18. Accessed October 16, 2013.

———. 2012g. "Arlene and Will Brewster." http://www.youtube.com/watch?v=rizfht N6UVc. Accessed October 16, 2013.

———. 2012h. "Rob and Amy." http://www.youtube.com/watch?v=PXSUYKgoOSg. Accessed October 16, 2013.

———. 2012i. "Amy Wilton." http://www.youtube.com/watch?v=EmzVeNo_OjY. Accessed October 16, 2013.

———. 2012j. "Michael and Robyn Gray." http://www.youtube.com/watch?v=OlY _Hj72YWU. Accessed October 16, 2013.

———. 2012k. "Brian Arsenault." http://www.youtube.com/watch?v=poVBgAxLiQ8. Accessed October 16, 2013.

———. 2012l. "Stacey Fitts." http://www.youtube.com/watch?v=LV8RogOJWDQ. Accessed October 16, 2013.

———. 2012m. "Brotherhood." http://www.youtube.com/watch?v=y6E6voXmSSM. Accessed October 16, 2013.

Maine State Law and Legislative Reference Library. 2011. "Votes on Initiated Bills 1910– ." http://www.maine.gov/legis/lawlib/inivot.htm. Accessed August 11, 2011.

Malone, Richard. 2009. "Testimony before Maine Judiciary Committee Public Hearing on Legislative Documents 1020 and 1118." http://www.youtube.com/watch?v=Kd -xj6rZbw. Accessed July 17, 2011.

Mansbridge, Jane J. 1983. *Beyond Adversary Democracy.* Chicago, IL: University of Chicago Press.

March, James G., and Johan P. Olsen. 1984. "The New Institutionalism: Organizational Factors in Political Life." *American Political Science Review* 78: 734–749.

Marijuana Policy Project. 2016. "Campaigns." http://www.mpp.org/about/campaigns/. Accessed February 9, 2016.

Marriage Anti-Defamation Alliance. 2014. "About Us." http://marriageada.org/about/. Accessed September 2, 2014.

Marriage Law Project. 2002. "Brief of Amicus Curiae Marriage Law Project." https:// web.archive.org/web/20101230102923/http://www.domawatch.org/cases/massachu setts/goodridgevdepartmentofhealth/20021220_d_mlp_amicus.pdf. Accessed July 24, 2015.

Maryland Marriage Alliance. 2012. "Broken Promises." https://www.youtube.com /watch?v=815BoSjpUrM. Accessed July 24, 2015.

Mason, Robert. 2004. *Richard Nixon and the Quest for a New Majority.* Chapel Hill: University of North Carolina Press.

Mayhew, David. 1974. *Congress: The Electoral Connection.* New Haven, CT: Yale University Press.

McCann, Michael. 1994. *Rights at Work: Pay Equity Reform and the Politics of Legal Mobilization.* Chicago, IL: University of Chicago Press.

———. 1996. "Causal versus Constitutive Explanations (or, on the Difficulty of Being So Positive . . .)." *Law and Social Inquiry* 21: 457–482.

McCormick, Earle. 2009. "Legislative Record." *State of Maine One Hundred and Twenty-Fourth Legislature First Regular Session Journal of the Senate*. http://maine.gov/legis/senate/124th-records.html. Accessed July 17, 2011.

McGirr, Lisa. 2001. *Suburban Warriors: The Origins of the New American Right*. Princeton, NJ: Princeton University Press.

McKinley, Jesse, and Kirk Johnson. 2008. "Mormons Tipped Scale in Ban on Gay Marriage." *New York Times*, November 15. http://www.nytimes.com/2008/11/15/us/politics/15marriage.html. Accessed July 7, 2011.

Meese, Edwin, III. 1985. "Speech before the Federalist Society Lawyers Division." In *The Great Debate: Interpreting Our Written Constitution*. Washington, DC: Federalist Society.

Mennemeier, Kenneth. 2009. "The Administrations Answer to Complaint for Declarative, Injunctive, or Other Relief," June 16. http://www.domawatch.org/cases/9th circuit/Perry_v_Schwarzenegger/District%20Court/Answers/PvS_DN_46_Dfs_Answer_061609.pdf. Accessed September 1, 2010.

Merry, Sally Engle. 1988. "Legal Pluralism." *Law and Society Review* 22, no. 5: 869–896.

———. 2000. *Colonizing Hawaii: The Cultural Power of Law*. Princeton, NJ: Princeton University Press.

Mesko, Jennifer. 2007. "California Marriage Amendment Drive Takes Shape." http://www.citizenlink.com. Retrieved from Internet Archiver September 10, 2010.

Meyer, Ilan. 2010. "Expert Testimony." Transcript of Trial Day Four, January 14. *Perry v. Schwarzenegger*. http://www.afer.org/wpcontent/uploads/2010/01/Perry-Vol-4-1-14-10.pdf. Accessed September 1, 2010.

Mezey, Susan Gluck. 2007. *Queers in Court: Gay Rights Law and Public Policy*. Lanham, MD: Rowman and Littlefield.

Miller, Jodi. 1999. "'Democracy in Free-Fall': The Use of Ballot Initiatives to Dismantle State-Sponsored Affirmative Action Programs." *New York University Annual Survey of American Law*: 1–42.

Miller, Kenneth P. 2001. "Constraining Populism: The Real Challenge of Initiative Reform." *Santa Clara Law Review* 41: 1037–1084.

———. 2010. "Expert Testimony." Transcript of Trial Day Ten, January 25. *Perry v. Schwarzenegger*. http://www.afer.org/wp-content/uploads/2010/01/Perry-Vol-10-1-25-10.pdf. Accessed September 1, 2010.

Miller, Kevin. 2009. "Maine Vote 2009 Analysis; Question 1 Reflects Split in Culture; Urban, Rural Divide Defines Differing Views on Marriage." *Bangor Daily News*, November 5, A1.

Mills, Janet. 2009. "Letter to Commissioner Gendron." http://www.asmainegoes.com/content/ag-mills-says-same-sex-marriage-has-no-affect-maines-schools. Accessed May 16, 2016.

Mills, Peter. 2009. "Legislative Record." *State of Maine One Hundred and Twenty-Fourth Legislature First Regular Session Journal of the Senate.* http://maine.gov/legis/senate /124th-records.html. Accessed July 17, 2011.

Minnesota for Marriage. 2012. "Threat to Marriage." https://www.youtube.com/watch ?v=41KcIgoP4xQ. Accessed July 24, 2015.

Miranda, Robert. 2008. "Love, Power, and Sound Mind." Church Communication Network Simulcast. Transcribed by Yvonne T. Boggs, December 13, 2009.

Mitchell, Elizabeth, et al. 2009. "Memorandum to Members of Maine Media." http ://www.scribd.com/doc/19911316/Maine-Legal-Rebuttal-to-Yes-on-1-Ads. Accessed July 26, 2011.

Mnookin, Robert H., and Lewis Kornhauser. 1979. "Bargaining in the Shadow of the Law: The Case of Divorce." *Yale Law Journal* 88: 950–997.

Moore, Megan. 2007. "The Money behind the 2006 Marriage Amendments." Institute on Money in State Politics. Followthemoney.org. Accessed June 14, 2011.

Morone, James A. 2003. *Hellfire Nation: The Politics of Sin in American History.* New Haven, CT: Yale University Press.

Morse, Roback. 2008. "Love, Power, and Sound Mind." Church Communication Network Simulcast. Transcribed by Yvonne T. Boggs, December 13, 2009.

Moss, Nicole. 2010. "Cross Examination of William Tam." Transcript of Trial Day Eight, January 21. *Perry v. Schwarzenegger.* http://www.afer.org/wp-content/uploads/2010 /01/Perry-Vol-8-1-21-10.pdf. Accessed September 1, 2010.

Murray, Melissa. 2012. "What's So New about the New Illegitimacy?" *American University Journal of Gender, Social Policy, and the Law* 20, no. 3: 387–436.

Mutty, Marc. 2009a. "'Yes on One' Signs Vandalized across State." Stand for Marriage Maine Press Release, October 28. http://www.standformarriagemaine.com/?p=670. Accessed July 23, 2011.

———. 2009b. "Statement Regarding Threat to Yes on One T.V. Ad Spokesman." Stand for Marriage Maine Press Release, October 29. http://www.standformarriagemaine .com/?p=689. Accessed July 23, 2011.

———. 2009c. "Stand for Marriage Maine Responds to Attorney General's 'Independent' Opinion." Press Release. October 16. http://www.prnewswire.com/news -releases/stand-for-marriage-maine-responds-to-attorney-generals-independent -opinion-64522182.html. Accessed July 23, 2011.

Myrdal, Gunnar. 1944. *An American Dilemma.* Vol. 1: *The Negro Problem and Modern Democracy.* New Brunswick, NJ: Transaction.

National Institute on Money in State Politics. 2013. "2011–2012 Ballot Measure Overview." http://beta.followthemoney.org/research/institute-reports/2011-2012-ballot -measure-overview/. Accessed August 15, 2014.

National Organization for Marriage. 2013. "About Us." https://www.nationformarriage .org/about. Accessed September 1, 2013.

NeJaime, Douglas. 2009. "Inclusion, Accommodation, and Recognition: Accounting for Differences Based on Religion and Sexual Orientation." *Harvard Journal of Law and Gender* 32: 303–382.

Nemitz, Bill. 2009a. "His Relevance Fading Away, Heath Exits." *Portland Press Herald*, September 23, B1.

———. 2009b. "This Time, Gays Are Not the Target." *Portland Press Herald*, July 15, B1.

———. 2011. "Documentary Clips Show Sad Face of Yes on 1 Campaign." *Portland Press Herald*, April 17, B1.

———. 2012. "For Enemy of Gay Marriage, Untruths Best Told Quickly." *Portland Press Herald*, October 24. http://www.pressherald.com/news/for-enemy-of-gay -marriage-untruths-best-told-quickly_2012-10-24.html. Accessed October 2, 2013.

Nightingale Alliance. 2012. "Legal Status of Assisted Suicide/Euthanasia in the United States." http://www.nightingalealliance.org/pdf/state_grid.pdf. Accessed April 5, 2012.

Nimocks, Austin R. 2010. "*Perry v. Schwarzenegger* Trial Blog Posts." Alliance Defense Fund, January 21. http://adfmedia.org/News/PRDetail/?CID=12012#. Accessed September 1, 2010.

NoOnProp8.com. 2008a. "Unfair, Unnecessary, and Wrong." http://www.youtube.com /watch?v=JHeTVAE4ZkY&list=UUmbVgavgktLpeTnDjcYXIew&index=46. First aired October 15.

———. 2008b. "Prop. 8 Has Nothing to Do with Schools." http://www.youtube.com /watch?v=CIL7PU124hE. First aired October 22.

———. 2008c. "Ferrera, Plana, and Ortiz Speak Out against Prop. 8." http://www.you tube.com/watch?v=I9HfNwMKZoE&list=UUmbVgavgktLpeTnDjcYXIew&index =34. First aired October 25.

———. 2008d. "Discrimination." http://www.youtube.com/watch?v=OjoxMrsyxE &list=UUmbVgavgktLpeTnDjcYXIew&index=13. First aired October 30.

———. 2008e. "Divisive." http://www.youtube.com/watch?v=_eMXdliDGXs&list =UUmbVgavgktLpeTnDjcYXIew&index=7. First aired November 1.

———. 2008f. "Parents." http://www.youtube.com/watch?v=JlOh6Qni_g&list=UU mbVgavgktLpeTnDjcYXIew&index=4. First aired November 3.

Novkov, Julie. 2008. *Racial Union: Law, Intimacy, and the White State in Alabama, 1865– 1954*. Ann Arbor: University of Michigan Press.

O'Connell, Sue. 2006. "The Money behind the 2004 Marriage Amendments." Institute on Money in State Politics. Followthemoney.org. Accessed June 14, 2011.

Olson, Theodore. 2010. "Closing Arguments." Closing Arguments Transcript, June 16. *Perry v. Schwarzenegger.* http://www.afer.org/legal-filings/hearing-transcripts/perry -trial-closing-arguments-transcript/attachment/perry-vol-13-6-16-10-amended/. Accessed September 1, 2010.

Oregon State Library. 1992. *State of Oregon Official Voters' Pamphlet.* http://library.state.or.us/repository/2010/201003011350161/ORVPGenMari1992.pdf. Accessed July 23, 2014.

Palmer, Kenneth T., G. Thomas Taylor, and Marcus A. Librizzi. 1992. *Maine Politics and Government.* Lincoln: University of Nebraska Press.

Parker, David. 2009. "Testimony before Maine Judiciary Committee Public Hearing on Legislative Documents 1020 and 1118." http://www.youtube.com/watch?v=oJ62 rcZ7yBE&feature=related. Accessed July 17, 2011.

Passavant, Paul. 2002. *No Escape: Freedom of Speech and the Paradox of Rights.* New York: New York University Press.

Pavone, Frank. 2008. "Love, Power, and Sound Mind." Church Communication Network Simulcast. Transcribed by Yvonne T. Boggs, December 13, 2009.

Pelletier, Lawrence Lee. 1951. *The Initiative and Referendum in Maine.* Brunswick, ME: Bowdoin College Bulletin.

Peplau, Ann. 2010. "Expert Testimony." Transcript of Trial Day Three, January 13. *Perry v. Schwarzenegger.* http://www.afer.org/wpcontent/uploads/2010/01/Perry-Vol-3-1 -13-10.pdf. Accessed September 1, 2010.

Perlstein, Rick. 2001. *Before the Storm: Barry Goldwater and the Unmaking of the American Consensus.* New York: Hill and Wang.

Personhood USA. 2014. "What Is Personhood?" http://www.personhoodusa.com /aboutus/what-is-personhood/. Accessed September 2, 2014.

Pew Research Center for the People and the Press. 2011. "Forum on Religion and Public Life: Religious Landscape Study." http://religions.pewforum.org/pdf/report -religious-landscape-study-full.pdf. Accessed August 1, 2011.

Pinello, Daniel R. 2006. *America's Struggle for Same-Sex Marriage.* Cambridge, UK: Cambridge University Press.

Polikoff, Nancy D. 2003. "Ending Marriage as We Know it." *Hofstra Law Review* 32: 201–232.

Pollo, Sarah. 2008. "Protect Marriage Grassroots Meeting Minutes, 8-21-08." Email correspondence with Protect Marriage Coalition members, August 22, 2008.

Prentice, Ron. 2008. "Ron Prentice Addressing Supporters of Proposition 8." http ://www.youtube.com/watch?v=stDJrXv16ko&feature=player_embedded. Accessed February 9, 2011.

———. 2010. "Demonstrating the Intolerance of 'the Tolerant' and the Power of 'the Powerless.'" February 24. http://www.protectmarriage.com/blog/. Accessed February 26, 2010.

Prentice, Ron, Rosemarie Avila, and Bishop George McKinney. 2008. "Argument in Favor of Proposition 8." *California General Election 2008 Official Voter Information Guide.* http://www.voterguide.sos.ca.gov/past/2008/general/argu-rebut/argu -rebutt8.htm.

Preserve Marriage Washington. 2012. "No Right for Parents." https://www.youtube.com /watch?v=_87va3AiHSE. Accessed July 24, 2015.

ProtectMarriage.com. 2008a. "California Protect Marriage Amendment: Three Ways to Conduct an Effective Petition Drive in Your Church." http://www.protectmarriage .com. Retrieved from Internet Archiver September 10, 2010.

———. 2008b. "Whether You Like It or Not." http://protectmarriage.com/video/view /2. First aired September 28.

———. 2008c. "It's Already Happened." http://protectmarriage.com/video/view/5. First aired October 8.

———. 2008d. "Everything to Do with Schools." http://protectmarriage.com/video /view/7. First aired October 24.

———. 2008e. "Robb and Robin Wirthlin's Story." http://protectmarriage.com/video /view/6. Accessed February 7, 2011.

———. 2008f. "Finally the Truth." http://protectmarriage.com/video/view/8. First aired October 28.

———. 2008g. "Barack Obama Does Not Support Gay Marriage." Campaign mailer.

———. 2008h. "Esto Ya Ocurrio." http://protectmarriage.com/video/view/4. First aired October 8.

———. 2008i. "4 Men in Black." http://protectmarriage.com/video/view/1. Accessed February 21, 2011.

———. 2008j. "Have You Thought about It?" https://www.youtube.com/watch?v=3 YRQZwNfQoo. First aired October 29. Accessed February 9, 2016.

———. 2008k. "Myths and Facts about Proposition 8." http://www.protectmarriage .com/files/myths.pdf. Accessed February 21, 2011.

———. 2008l. "Fact Sheet." http://www.protectmarriage.com/files/fact_sheet.pdf. Accessed February 21, 2011.

———. 2008m. "Questions and Answers about Proposition 8." http://www.protect marriage.com/files/faq.pdf. Accessed February 21, 2011.

Protect Marriage Maine. 2012a. "Parkers." http://www.youtube.com/watch?v=MER 3qEaQlkY. Accessed October 7, 2013.

———. 2012b. "Don Mendel." http://www.youtube.com/watch?v=Us6Uzs_Yhqo. Accessed October 7, 2013.

———. 2012c. "I Was Fired." http://www.youtube.com/watch?v=rd_vn41m2gg. Accessed October 7, 2013.

———. 2012d. "They Sued Us." http://www.youtube.com/watch?v=esQgxaT6kAo. Accessed October 7, 2013.

———. 2012e. "Marriage Serves Maine." http://www.youtube.com/watch?v=VCW -cMx142Y. Accessed October 7, 2013.

Pugno, Andrew. 2008. "Statement of Unity." Email correspondence with Bill Tam, July 21, 2008.

Quist, Peter. 2009. "The Money behind the 2008 Same-Sex Partnership Ballot Measures." Institute on Money in State Politics. Followthemoney.org. Accessed June 14, 2011.

Rabinow, Paul, and William Sullivan. 1988. *Interpretive Social Science: A Second Look.* Berkeley: University of California Press.

Rasmussen, Claire E. 2006. "We're No *Metrosexuals*: Identity, Place, and Sexuality in the Struggle over Gay Marriage." *Social and Cultural Geography* 7, no. 5: 807–825.

Rauch, Jonathan. 2004. *Gay Marriage: Why It Is Good for Gays, Good for Straights, and Good for America.* New York: Times Books.

Raum, Brian W. 2010. "Cross Examination of Jerry Sanders." Transcript of Trial Day Six, January 19. *Perry v. Schwarzenegger.* http://www.afer.org/wpcontent/uploads/2010/01/Perry-Vol-6-1-19-10.pdf. Accessed September 1, 2010.

Rawls, John. 1997. "The Idea of Public Reason." In *Deliberative Democracy: Essays on Reason and Politics.* Edited by James Bohman and William Rehg. Cambridge: Massachusetts Institute of Technology Press, 93–144.

Raye, Kevin. 2009. "Legislative Record." *State of Maine One Hundred and Twenty-Fourth Legislature First Regular Session Journal of the Senate.* http://maine.gov/legis/senate/124th-records.html. Accessed July 17, 2011.

Rector, Chris. 2009. "Legislative Record." *State of Maine One Hundred and Twenty-Fourth Legislature First Regular Session Journal of the Senate.* http://maine.gov/legis/senate/124th-records.html. Accessed July 17, 2011.

Regnerus, Mark. 2012. "How Different Are the Adult Children of Parents Who Have Same-Sex Relationships? Findings from the New Family Structures Study." *Social Science Research* 41: 752–770.

Richman, Kimberly. 2014. *License to Wed: What Legal Marriage Means to Same-Sex Couples.* New York: New York University Press.

Ricoeur, Paul. 1973. "The Model of Text: Meaningful Action Considered as a Text." *New Literary History* 5, no. 1: 91–117.

Riker, William H. 1980. "Implications from the Disequilibrium of Majority Rule for the Study of Institutions." *American Political Science Review* 74: 432–446.

Rogin, Michael Paul. 1975. *Fathers and Children: Andrew Jackson and the Subjugation of the American Indian.* New Brunswick, NJ: Transaction.

———. 1986. "The Counter-Subversive Tradition in American Politics." *Berkeley Journal of Sociology* 31: 1–33.

———. 1996. *Blackface, White Noise: Jewish Immigrants in the Hollywood Melting Pot.* Berkeley: University of California Press.

Rosenberg, Gerald L. 1991. *The Hollow Hope: Can Courts Bring about Social Change?* Chicago, IL: University of Chicago Press.

Russo, Vito. 1987. *The Celluloid Closet: Homosexuality in the Movies.* New York: Harper and Row.

Scalia, Antonin. 1997. *A Matter of Interpretation: Federal Courts and the Law.* Princeton, NJ: Princeton University Press.

Schacter, Jane S. 1994. "The Gay Civil Rights Debate in the States: Decoding the Discourse of Equivalents." *Harvard Civil-Rights Civil-Liberties Law Review* 29: 283–317.

———. 1997. "Skepticism, Culture, and the Gay Civil Rights Debate in a Post-Civil-Rights Era." *Harvard Law Review* 110: 684–731.

Schattschneider, E. E. 1960. *The Semisovereign People: A Realist's View of Democracy in America.* New York: Holt, Rinehart, and Winston.

Scheingold, Stuart A. 1974. *The Politics of Rights: Lawyers, Public Policy, and Political Change.* Ann Arbor: University of Michigan Press.

Schlatter, Evelyn. 2013. "Suspect 'Science.'" https://www.splcenter.org/fighting-hate/intelligence-report/2013/suspect-science#.UaYTvpWj3F8. Accessed August 4, 2015.

Schmidt, David. 1989. *Citizen Lawmakers: The Ballot Initiative Revolution.* Philadelphia, PA: Temple University Press.

Schneider, Yvette. 2008. "The Fine Line." Simulcast. October 1. http://www.protectmarriage.com. Accessed February 14, 2011.

Schragg, Peter. 1998. *Paradise Lost: California's Experience, America's Future.* New York: Free Press.

———. 2008. *California: America's High-Stakes Experiment.* Berkeley: University of California Press.

Schubert, Frank, and Jeff Flint. 2009. "Passing Prop 8: Smart Timing and Messaging Convinced California Voters to Support Traditional Marriage." *Politics Magazine,* 44–47.

Segal, Jeffrey A., and Harold J. Spaeth. 1993. *The Supreme Court and the Attitudinal Model.* Cambridge, UK: Cambridge University Press.

Segura, Gary. 2010. "Expert Testimony." Transcript of Trial Day Seven, January 20. *Perry v. Schwarzenegger.* http://www.afer.org/wpcontent/uploads/2010/01/Perry-Vol-7-1-20-10.pdf. Accessed September 1, 2010.

Shilts, Randy. 1987. *And the Band Played On: Politics, People, and the AIDS Epidemic.* New York: St. Martin's.

Shoofs, Mark. 2008. "Mormons Boost Anti-Gay Marriage Effort: Group Has Given Millions in Support of California Fund." *Wall Street Journal,* September 20. http://online.wsj.com/article/SB122186063716658279.html. Accessed July 7, 2011.

Simon, Jonathan. 1992. "'The Long Walk Home' to Politics." *Law and Society Review* 26, no. 4: 923–941.

Slotkin, Richard. 1973. *Regeneration through Violence: The Mythology of the American Frontier, 1600–1860.* Norman: University of Oklahoma Press.

———. 1992. *Gunfighter Nation: The Myth of the Frontier in Twentieth-Century America.* Norman: University of Oklahoma Press.

Smith, Mark A. 2007. *The Right Talk: How Conservatives Transformed the Great Society into the Economic Society.* Princeton, NJ: Princeton University Press.

Smith, Miriam. 2008. *Political Institutions and Lesbian and Gay Rights in the United States and Canada.* New York: Routledge.

Smith, Rogers. 1988. "Political Jurisprudence, the 'New Institutionalism,' and the Future of Public Law." *American Political Science Review* 82, no. 1: 89–108.

———. 1993. "Beyond Tocqueville, Myrdal, and Hartz: The Multiple Traditions in America." *American Political Science Review* 87, no. 3: 549–566.

Snow, David, and Robert D. Benford. 1988. "Ideology, Frame Resonance, and Participant Mobilization." *International Social Movement Research* 1: 197–218.

Southworth, Ann. 2008. *Lawyers of the Right: Professionalizing the Conservative Coalition.* Chicago, IL: University of Chicago Press.

Sprigg, Peter. 2006. "The Other Side of Tolerance." Family Research Council. http://www.frc.org/. Accessed December 1, 2009.

———. 2007. "Homosexuality Is Not a Civil Right." Family Research Council. http://www.frc.org/. Accessed December 1, 2009.

———. 2010. "The Top Ten Myths about Homosexuality." http://downloads.frc.org/EF/EF10F01.pdf. Accessed July 24, 2015.

———. 2011. "The Top Ten Harms of Same-Sex Marriage." http://downloads.frc.org/EF/EF11B30.pdf. Accessed July 24, 2015.

Sprigg, Peter, and Timothy Dailey. 2004. *Getting It Straight: What the Research Shows about Homosexuality.* Washington, DC: Family Research Council.

Stand for Marriage Maine. 2009a. "Consequences." http://www.standformarriagemaine.com/?page_id=457. Accessed July 1, 2011.

———. 2009b. "Everything to Do with Schools." http://www.standformarriagemaine.com/?page_id=457. Accessed July 1, 2011.

———. 2009c. "Safe Schools." http://www.standformarriagemaine.com/?page_id=457. Accessed July 1, 2011.

———. 2009d. "Give Me a Break." http://www.standformarriagemaine.com/?p=525. Accessed July 1, 2011.

———. 2009e. "It's Already Happening." http://www.standformarriagemaine.com/?p=675. Accessed July 1, 2011.

———. 2009f. "They Said." http://www.standformarriagemaine.com/?p=597. Accessed July 1, 2011.

———. 2009g. "Fact Sheet." http://www.standformarriagemaine.com/?page_id=471. Accessed February 26, 2010.

———. 2009h. "Myths and Facts about the People's Veto of Homosexual Marriage Legislation (LD 1020)." http://www.standformarriagemaine.com/?page_id=271. Accessed February 26, 2010.

———. 2009i. "The Threat to Marriage." http://www.standformarriagemaine.com /?page_id=119. Accessed July 23, 2011.

———. 2009j. "Questions and Answers about Question 1." http://www.standfor marriagemaine.com/?page_id=259. Accessed February 26, 2010.

———. 2009k. "Why Marriage Matters." http://www.standformarriagemaine.com /?Page_id=115. Accessed February 26, 2010.

———. 2009l. "Don Mendel Radio Ad." http://www.standformarriagemaine.com/?p =700. Accessed February 26, 2010.

Stanton, Glen. 2008. "Love, Power, and Sound Mind." Church Communication Network Simulcast. Transcribed by Yvonne T. Boggs, December 13, 2009.

Starr, Kevin. 1973. *Americans and the California Dream, 1850–1910*. New York: Oxford University Press.

———. 1985. *Inventing the Dream: California through the Progressive Era*. New York: Oxford University Press.

———. 2009. *Golden Dreams: California in an Age of Abundance, 1950–1963*. New York: Oxford University Press.

Stefancic, Jean, and Richard Delgado. 1996. *No Mercy: How Conservative Think Tanks and Foundations Changed America's Social Agenda*. Philadelphia, PA: Temple University Press.

Stein, Arlene. 2002. *The Stranger Next Door: The Story of a Small Community's Battle over Sex, Faith, and Civil Rights*. Boston, MA: Beacon.

———. 2013. "What's the Matter with Newark? Race, Class, Marriage Politics, and the Limits of Queer Liberalism." In *The Marrying Kind? Debating Same-Sex Marriage within the Lesbian and Gay Movement*. Edited by Mary Bernstein and Verta Taylor. Minneapolis: University of Minnesota Press, 39–66.

Stewart, Therese. 2010. "Redirect Examination of George Chauncey." Transcript of Trial Day Two, January 12. *Perry v. Schwarzenegger*. http://www.afer.org/wpcontent /uploads/2010/01/Perry-Vol-2-1-12-10.pdf. Accessed September 1, 2010.

Stone, Amy. 2012. *Gay Rights at the Ballot Box*. Minneapolis: University of Minnesota Press.

Tadlock, Barry L., C. Ann Gordon, and Elizabeth Popp. 2007. "Framing the Issue of Same-Sex Marriage: Traditional Values versus Equal Rights." In *The Politics of Same-Sex Marriage*. Edited by Craig A. Rimmerman and Clyde Wilcox. Chicago, IL: University of Chicago Press, 193–214.

Talbot, Margaret. 2010. "A Risky Proposal: Is It Too Soon to Petition the Supreme Court on Gay Marriage?" *New Yorker*, January 18. http://www.newyorker.com/reporting /2010/01/18/100118fa_fact_talbot?printable=true. Accessed February 2, 2010.

Teles, Steven. 2008. *The Rise of the Conservative Legal Movement: The Battle for Control of the Law*. Princeton, NJ: Princeton University Press.

Thibodeau, Mike. 2009. "Legislative Record." *One Hundred and Twenty-Fourth Legis-*

lature First Regular Session 34th Legislative Day. http://www.maine.gov/legis/house/records/124hrecindx.htm#may09. Accessed July 17, 2011.

Thomas, Doug. 2009. "Legislative Record." *One Hundred and Twenty-Fourth Legislature First Regular Session 34th Legislative Day.* http://www.maine.gov/legis/house/records/124hrecindx.htm#may09. Accessed July 17, 2011.

Thompson, David H. 2010a. "Cross Examination of Nancy Cott." Transcript of Trial Day Two, January 12. *Perry v. Schwarzenegger.* http://www.afer.org/wpcontent/uploads/2010/01/Perry-Vol-2-1-12-10.pdf. Accessed September 1, 2010.

———. 2010b. "Cross Examination of George Chauncey." Transcript of Trial Day Two, January 12. *Perry v. Schwarzenegger.* http://www.afer.org/wpcontent/uploads/2010/01/Perry-Vol-2-1-12-10.pdf. Accessed September 1, 2010.

———. 2010c. "Cross Examination of Michael Lamb." Transcript of Trial Day Five, January 15. *Perry v. Schwarzenegger.* http://www.afer.org/wpcontent/uploads/2010/01/Perry-Vol-5-1-15-10.pdf. Accessed September 1, 2010.

———. 2010d. "Cross Examination of Gary Segura." Transcript of Trial Day Seven, January 20. *Perry v. Schwarzenegger.* http://www.afer.org/wp-content/uploads/2010/01/Perry-Vol-7-1-20-10.pdf. Accessed September 1, 2010.

Trahan, David. 2009. "Legislative Record." *State of Maine One Hundred and Twenty-Fourth Legislature First Regular Session Journal of the Senate.* http://maine.gov/legis/senate/124th-records.html. Accessed July 17, 2011.

Tucker, Jill. 2008. "Class Surprises Lesbian Teacher on Wedding Day." *San Francisco Chronicle,* October 11. http://www.sfgate.com/news/article/Class-surprises-lesbian-teacher-on-wedding-day-3191209.php. Accessed May 29, 2013.

Tyler, Bob. 2008. "ABC Protecting Marriage." Simulcast, October 20. Transcribed by Laura L. Springate, December 16, 2009.

U.S. Census Bureau. 2015. "Maine Quick Facts." http://quickfacts.census.gov/qfd/states/23000.html. Accessed August 20, 2015.

Wakefield, Floyd, Ken Brown, and Robert Peterson. 1972. "Argument in Favor of Proposition 21." In *Proposed Amendment to the Constitution: Propositions and Proposed Laws Together with Arguments,* 56–57. http://library.uchastings.edu/ballot_pdf/1972g.pdf. Accessed April 6, 2012.

Walker, Vaughn R. 2009a. "Hearing on Motion for Preliminary Injunction." Transcript of Trial Proceedings, July 2. *Perry v. Schwarzenegger.* http://www.afer.org/wpcontent/uploads/2009/12/2009-07-02-AFER-Hearing-Transcript.pdf. Accessed April 1, 2011.

———. 2009b. "Hearing on Motion to Intervene." Transcript of Trial Proceedings, August 19. *Perry v. Schwarzenegger.* http://www.domawatch.org/cases/9thcircuit/Perry_v_Schwarzenegger/District%20Court/Answers/PvS_DN_39_Answer_of_AG_Brown_to_Complaint_061209.pdf. Accessed April 1, 2011.

———. 2009c. "Hearing on Motion for Summary Judgment." Transcript of Trial

Proceedings, October 14. *Perry v. Schwarzenegger.* http://www.afer.org/wpcontent /uploads/2009/12/2009-10-14-AFER-Hearing-Transcript-MSJ.pdf. Accessed April 1, 2011.

———. 2010. "Trial Proceedings." Transcript of trial proceedings. *Perry v. Schwarzenegger.* http://www.afer.org/our-work/hearing-transcripts/. Accessed September 1, 2010.

Warner, Michael. 1999. *The Trouble with Normal: Sex, Politics, and the Ethics of Queer Life.* Cambridge, MA: Harvard University Press.

Weber, Robert Phillip. 1990. *Basic Content Analysis.* 2nd ed. Newbury Park, CA: Sage.

Weinstein, Netta, William Ryan, et al. 2012. "Parental Autonomy Support and Discrepancies between Implicit and Explicit Sexual Identities: Dynamics of Self-Acceptance and Defense." *Journal of Personality and Social Psychology* 102, no. 4: 815–832.

Werum, Regina, and Bill Winders. 2001. "Who's 'In' and Who's 'Out': State Fragmentation and the Struggle over Gay Rights, 1974–1999." *Social Problems* 48, no. 3: 386–410.

Westin, Carol. 2009. "Legislative Record." *State of Maine One Hundred and Twenty-Fourth Legislature First Regular Session Journal of the Senate.* http://maine.gov/legis /senate/124th-records.html. Accessed July 17, 2011.

Weyrich, Paul. 2004. "The Arlington Group." Renew America. http://www.renew america.com/columns/weyrich/041203. Accessed June 14, 2011.

White, Chip. 2008. "Yes on 8 Campaign Slams New No Ad with Jack O'Connell: O'Connell's New Ad Is Only 96% a Lie." http://www.protectmarriage.com/article /yes-on-8-campaign-slams-new-no-ad-with-jack-oconnell. Retrieved from Internet Archiver September 10, 2010.

White, Chip, and Sonja Eddings Brown. 2008a. "Proposition 8: Who's Really Lying? Public Records Show Proposition 8 Supporters Want Gay Marriage to Be Taught in Public Schools—'The Earlier the Better.'" http://protectmarriage.com/article /proposition-8-who-s-really-lying. Retrieved from Internet Archiver September 10, 2010.

———. 2008b. "Prop. 8 Supporter Violently Attacked for Distributing Lawn Signs." http://www.protectmarriage.com/article/prop-8-supporter-violently-attacked -for-distributing-lawn-signs. Retrieved from Internet Archiver September 10, 2010.

———. 2008c. "Opponents of Traditional Marriage Engage in Dirty Tricks." http:// www.christiannewswire.com/news/517048279.html. Accessed May 16, 2016.

Whittington, Keith E. 2000. "Once More unto the Breach: Post-Behavioralist Approaches to Judicial Politics." *Law and Social Inquiry* 25: 601–634.

Wickenheiser, Matt. 2008. "Groups Mobilize for Gay Marriage Battle: Advocates on Both Sides Lay Groundwork to Push for Laws to Allow or Ban Same-Sex Marriages." *Portland Press Herald,* December 14, A5.

———. 2009. "No on 1 Campaign Has an Edge in New Poll, but Both Sides of the Same-Sex Marriage Issue Say It Will Come Down to Who Gets Out the Vote." *Portland Press Herald,* October 15, A1.

Wilson, Joshua. 2013. *The Street Politics of Abortion: Speech, Violence, and America's Culture Wars.* Palo Alto, CA: Stanford University Press.

Wilson, L. H., Jack Schrade, and Robert Snell. 1964. "Argument in Favor of Proposition 14." In *Proposed Amendment to the Constitution: Propositions and Proposed Laws Together with Arguments,* 18–19. http://library.uchastings.edu/ballot_pdf/1964g.pdf. Accessed April 6, 2012.

Wilson, Pete, Ward Connerly, and Pamela A. Lewis. 1996. "Argument in Favor of Proposition 209." *California Ballot Pamphlet: General Election, November 5, 1996.* http://vote96.sos.ca.gov/bp/209yesarg.htm. Accessed March 30, 2012.

Wittman, Carl. 1970. *A Gay Manifesto.* New York: Red Butterfly.

Yanow, Dvora. 2006. "Neither Rigorous nor Objective? Interrogating Criteria for Knowledge Claims in Interpretive Science." In *Interpretation and Method: Empirical Research Methods and the Interpretive Turn.* Edited by Dvora Yanow and Peregrine Schwartz-Shea. New York: M. E. Sharpe, 67–87.

Yes for Marriage. 2006. "Vote Yes for Marriage." https://www.youtube.com/watch?v=jE_DbI9s8KA. Accessed July 24, 2015.

YesForMarriage.com. 2008. "Why We Need a Marriage Amendment." https://www.youtube.com/watch?v=iHaTxXiwQvA. Accessed July 24, 2015.

Zemans, Frances Kahn. 1983. "Legal Mobilization: The Neglected Role of the Law in the Political System." *American Political Science Review* 77: 690–703.

Zia, Helen. 2010. "Testimony." Transcript of Trial Day Five, January 15. *Perry v. Schwarzenegger.* http://www.afer.org/wp-content/uploads/2010/01/Perry-Vol-5-1-15-10.pdf. Accessed September 1, 2010.

Cases Cited

Andersen v. King County, 138 P.3d 963 (Wash. 2006)

Arizona State Legislature v. Arizona Independent Redistricting Commission, 576 U.S. ____ (2015)

Baehr v. Lewin, 74 Haw. 530 (Haw. 1993)

Baehr v. Miike, 80 Haw. 341 (Haw. 1996)

Baker v. Nelson, 409 U.S. 810 (1972)

Baker v. Vermont, 744 A.2d 864 (Vt. 1999)

Baskin v. Bogan, 766 F.3d 648 (7th Cir. 2014)

Bostic v. Schaefer, No. 14-1167, 2014 WL 3702493 (4th Cir. 2014)

Bowers v. Hardwick, 478 U.S. 186 (1986)

Burwell v. Hobby Lobby, 573 U.S. ____ (2014)

Bush v. Gore, 531 U.S. 98 (2000)

Chambers v. Ormiston, 935 A.2d 956 (R.I. 2007)

Citizens for Equal Protection v. Bruning, 455 F.3d 859 (8th Cir. 2006)

Conaway v. Deane, 401 Md. 219 (Md. 2007)

Forum for Equality v. McKeithen, 893 So.2d 715 (La. 2005)

Gill et al. v. Office of Personnel Management, 699 F.Supp.2d 374 (D. Mass. 2010)

Goodridge v. Department of Public Health, 798 N.E.2d 941 (Mass. 2003)

Gratz v. Bollinger, 539 U.S. 244 (2003)

Grutter v. Bollinger, 539 U.S. 306 (2003)

Hernández v. Robles, 855 N.E.2d 1 (N.Y. 2006)

High Tech Gays v. Defense Industrial Security Clearance Office. 895 F.2d 563 (9th Cir. 1990)

Hollingsworth v. Perry, 570 U.S. ____ (2013)

In re Marriage Cases, 43 Cal.4th 757 (Cal. 2008)

In re Marriage of J.B. and H.B., 326 S.W.3d 654 (Tex. App. 2010)

Kerrigan v. Commissioner of Public Health, 289 Conn. 135 (Conn. 2008)

Kitchen v. Herbert, No. 13-4178, 2014 WL 2868044 (10th Cir. 2014)

Lawrence v. Texas, 539 U.S. 558 (2003)

Lewis v. Harris, 188 N.J. 415 (N.J. 2006)

Li and Kennedy v. State of Oregon, 110 P.3d 91 (Or. 2005)

Lockyer v. City and County of San Francisco, 2004 Cal. 10498 (Cal. 2004)

Maynard v. Hill, 125 U.S. 190 (1888)

Merrick v. Board of Higher Education, 103 Or. App. 328. (Or. App. 1989)

Morrison v. Sadler, 821 N.E.2d 15 (Ind. Ct. App. 2005)

Obergefell v. Hodges, 576 U.S. ____ (2015)

Parker v. Hurley, 414 F.3d 87 (1st Cir. 2008)

Peña v. Superior Court, 50 Cal. App. 3d 694 (Cal. App. 3d, 1975)

Perry v. Brown, 671 F.3d. 1052 (2012)

Perry v. Schwarzenegger, 704 F.Supp. 2d. 921 (N.D. Cal. 2010)

Planned Parenthood v. Casey, 505 U.S. 833 (1992)

Reitman v. Mulkey, 387 U.S. 369 (1967)

Roe v. Wade, 410 U.S. 113 (1973)

Romer v. Evans, 517 U.S. 620 (1996)

Schuette v. Coalition to Defend Affirmative Action, 572 U.S. ___ (2014)

Sevcik v. Sandoval, 771 F.3d 456 (9th Cir. 2014)

Standhardt v. Superior Court County of Maricopa, P.3d 451 (Ariz. App. 2003)

Strauss v. Horton, 46 Cal.4th 364 (Cal. 2009)

United States v. Windsor, 570 U.S. ____ (2013)

Varnum v. Brien, 763 N.W.2d 862 (Iowa 2009)

Washington v. Glucksberg, 521 U.S. 702 (1997)

West Virginia State Board of Education v. Barnette, 319 U.S. 624 (1943)

Index

Note: page numbers in italics refer to figures or tables.

abortion
  ballot measures and, 162, 173n4, 191n5
  Supreme Court on, 190n2
ADF. *See* Alliance Defending Freedom
Advocate (periodical), 30–31
AFER. *See* American Foundation for Equal Rights
affirmative action
  ballot measures on, 162–163, 173n3, 191n6
  right to decide policy on, as issue, 2
African Americans
  and California Proposition 8 campaign, 84–86, 185n16
  and rights, requirements for valid claim to, 176n16
"All Families" (TV ad), 135
Alliance Defending Freedom (Alliance Defense Fund; ADF), 10, 51, 95, 97, 105–106, 107–108
American Center for Law and Justice, 10
American Civil Rights Institute (ACRI), 162
American exceptionalism, 53
American Foundation for Equal Rights (AFER), 95
American Psychiatric Association, on homosexuality, 22, 177n4
American Values Committee, 49
antidiscrimination laws
  Bryant campaign against, 25–29
  Cincinnati movement to repeal, 36
  Colorado movement to repeal, 35–36
  as goal of gay rights movement, 24–25, 45
  history of, 25
  Maine movement to repeal, 36
  Oregon movement to repeal, 35
antigay movement
  development into national movement, 34
  factions within, 41–42
  image as defenders of traditional American values, 9, 37, 42, 73, 155
  inchoate state of in 1970s, 33
  moderates' rejection of homophobic rhetoric of, 34
  morality-based strategies, 34–35
  tactics adopted by, 34
anti-same-sex-marriage movement
  conservative legal organizations supporting, 51
  constitutional amendment drive by, 46, *47*, 180n4
  funding of, 49, 50
  mobilization after *Baehr* decision, 45
  national organizations in, 49–51
  See also conservative arguments against same-sex marriage
Arizona, Proposition 102 campaign (2008), 61
Arizona State Legislature v. Arizona Independent Redistricting Commission (2015), 2
Arlington Group, 49

Baehr v. Lewin (Hawai'i Supreme Court, 1993), 44–45
Baker v. Nelson (Minnesota Supreme Court, 1972), 44, 96, 98, 186n26

Baker v. Vermont (Vermont Supreme
    Court, 1999), 47, 77, 181n7
Baldacci, Jim, 125
ballot measures
    on abortion, 162, 173n4, 191n5
    and citizen votes versus true
        preferences, 16–17, 165–166
    and civil rights law, 161
    conservative defeats in, 110, 150
    conservative preference for, 13, 161,
        163–164
    conservative use of moral appeals in,
        64–66, 65, 67, 69
    conservative use of populist claims in,
        61–62, 62, 63–64
    conservative use of rights-based
        arguments in, 56–59, 58, 73
    conservative victories in, 4, 14, 42,
        46–47, 69, 109, 110, 112, 173n2
    and cultural conflicts, 160–163
    first pro-same-sex marriage effort, 16,
        144, 148
    history of, 160–161, 190–191n3
    left's use of, 191n4
    limited access to in New England, 111,
        113, 147, 187n1
    power of to decide fundamental
        rights, as issue, 2, 69
    rational ignorance of voters and, 7,
        94–95, 109, 133, 152
    rights-based arguments used by
        conservatives in, 3–5, 47
    on same-sex marriage, by state, *167–168*
    states allowing, 175n11
    as venue for debate on fundamental
        rights, 16–17, 165–166
    versus initiative, 173n1
    See also Maine
Blankenhorn, David, 99–100, 187nn29–30
Bowers v. Hardwick (1986), 40, 180n26
Briggs, John, 29–32, 60, 154, 177n10

"Broken Promises" TV ad (2012), 58–59
Bryant, Anita
    Briggs and, 29
    campaign against antidiscrimination
        ordinance, 25–29, 60, 177n8
    as divisive figure, 28
    on gay and lesbian deviance, 13, 19,
        26–28, 151
    gay rights advocates' campaign
        against, 32, 178n12
    moderate voters' outrage at, 33
Burwell v. Hobby Lobby (2014), 60, 15

California
    anti-same-sex marriage ballot
        measures (*see* California
        Proposition 8; California
        Proposition 22)
    as bellwether for cultural conflicts, 72
    citizen initiatives and referendums,
        history of, 75
    court cases on same-sex marriage, 77,
        78, 79
    current Democratic dominance in, 76,
        79–80
    and fundamentalist Christian
        movement, 183n5
    gay marriage debate in, history of,
        77–79, 108–109
    gay rights movement in, 23, 30, 32, 72
    history of, 74–75
    individualistic political culture in, 74,
        109
    legalization of same-sex marriage
        backlash from, 79
        by California courts in *Perry v.
            Schwarzenegger*, 79, 104
        legislative attempts at, 77, 78, 184n7
        national impact of, 110
        by Supreme Court in *Hollingsworth
            v. Perry*, 73, 104, 110

New Right emergence in, 72, 76–77

postwar development of, 76, 183n4

progressive movement in, 75

as test case of institutional frameworks' influence on discourse, 72–73

California Proposition 6 (on homosexual teachers), 29–32

California Proposition 8 (2008) (anti-same-sex marriage), 79–95

assumption of deviance underlying conservative arguments on, 90–92, 109

California's refusal to defend in federal court, 95

challenge to in California Supreme Court, 95

challenge to in federal court (see *Perry v. Schwarzenegger*)

conservative arguments for, 3–4, 28

conservative claims of victimhood in, 15, 89–90

conservative self-perception as culture warriors, 15, 81, 86–90, 109

in context of same-sex marriage debate, 77

initial public reluctance about, 79–80

judicial activism arguments in, 83–84

and legalization of same-sex marriage, backlash from, 79

message discipline of Yes on 8 campaign, 83, 154

minority groups, effort to persuade, 84–86

mobilization of anti-same-sex marriage base, 80–82

as model for future conservative campaigns, 16, 110, 111, 112, 128, 147

and moderate voters, campaign to persuade, 82–84, 92

No on 8 statements and TV ads, 92–93

opponents' efforts to debunk parental rights arguments, 92–95

organizations supporting, 50, 51

parental rights arguments in, 84, 89, 92–95, 109, 151

passage of, 46

populist appeals in, 86–90, 93, 156, 185n17

public ignorance about issues and, 94–95, 109

rights-based appeals of conservatives in, 87–89

backfiring of, 15, 73–74, 102–104, 110

rights language used by opponents of, 86–87

spending on, 46, *167–168*

suspect-class status of gays and lesbians as issue in, 179n21

threats and intimidation against supporters of, 89–90

title of, 79, 184n10

versions of, in draft, 184n8

Yes on 8 TV ads, 83–84, 85, 89, 91, 93–94

California Proposition 14 (1964) (on fair housing), 161

California Proposition 21 (1972) (anti-busing measure), 161–162

California Proposition 22 (2000) (anti-same-sex marriage statute), 77–78, 186n21

California Proposition 64 (1986) (on HIV/AIDS), 34

California Proposition 187 (1994) (on undocumented immigrants), 173n5

California Proposition 209 (1996) (on affirmative action), 162–163

Catholic Church, and gay rights, 50, 118–119, 138, 148, 177n9

censorship of gay and lesbian films and
literature, 21–22, 176–177n2
CFV. *See* Colorado for Family Values
Christians, gay rights as threat to, 4. *See
also under* religious
church networks
and anti-same-sex-marriage
movement, 50
Briggs's Proposition 6 initiative and,
29, 32
Bryant campaign against
antidiscrimination ordinance
and, 26
and California New Right, 77, 183n5
and California Proposition 8
campaign, 80–82
in campaign against same-sex
marriage, 28
opposition to same-sex marriage in
Maine, 118–119, 128, 138
"special rights" arguments and, 36
Church of Latter-Day Saints, 50
Cincinnati, antigay movement in, 36
civil rights law
ballot measures used to dilute, 161
Supreme Court leniency on local
interpretations of, 160
civil rights model of gay rights
African American responses to, 185n16
and homosexuality as choice, 81
special rights counterarguments to,
36–37, 87
civil rights movement
limited success of, 158–159
rights-based discourse in, 158
"Clear" (TV ad), 135
Colorado
and abortion law, 162
antigay movement in, 35–36
Colorado Amendment 2
Colorado Supreme Court vacating of,
38, 179n23

conservative arguments used to pass,
14, 19, 35–36
passage of, 36
U.S. Supreme Court vacating of
(*Romer v. Evans* 1996), 19, 38–40
Colorado for Family Values (CFV), 34,
35–36, 38
compelling government interest
Colorado Amendment 2 and, 40,
179n23
as issue in *Perry v. Schwarzenegger*, 73,
98–102, 104
Supreme Court rejection of morality
as, 40, 104, 179n24, 180n26
"Consequences" (TV ad), 128
conservative arguments against same-sex
marriage
assumption of deviance underlying,
4–5, 9, 41–42, 90–92, 107–108 (*see
also* nonthreatening gay persona,
as strategy)
as masked, 4–5, 18–19, 73, 152–153,
165
moderate voters' rejection of, 4, 13,
19, 32, 34, 37, 42, 92, 132, 151, 152,
154, 165
parental rights arguments and,
57–58, 60, 90–91, 103–104, 109,
129–130, 132, 134, 142–143
Supreme Court rejection of, 40, 104,
179n24, 180n26
traditional family arguments, 66–67
avoidance of overt homophobia after
1990, 13, 19, 37, 151, 154
persistence of, despite courts'
rejections, 9–10, 108, 149, 155–156
See also constitutional arguments;
majority rights, same-sex
marriage as claimed threat
to; moral appeals; populist
appeals; rights-based appeals by
conservatives

conservative legal organizations, 51
conservatives
  characteristic beliefs of, 174n7
  opposition to rights revolution, 10,
    160
  populism of, 164
  recent gains by, 10–11
  sincerity of, 176n15
constitutional amendments prohibiting
    same-sex marriage
  federal efforts toward, 46, 180n4
  states' passage of, 46, 47
  See also California Proposition 8;
    Colorado Amendment 2
constitutional arguments, 53
  described, 53–54
  in frame analysis, 52
  as percentage of appeals, in all venues,
    55, 56, 56, 57
  subframes of, 53–54
  See also minority group ("suspect
    class") status of gays and
    lesbians
content analysis, 52. *See also* frame
    analysis, of institutional shaping
    of conservative discourse
Cooper, Charles, 97, 99
courts
  as arenas of reason
    and consideration of fundamental
      rights, 164–165, 166
    courtroom procedures and, 6
    and failure of conservative
      arguments, 4–5, 15, 42, 59–60,
      60–61, 70, 109–110, 152–153
    and unmasking of discriminatory
      stereotypes, 5
  conservative avoidance of rights-based
    arguments in, 3–5, 43, 56–57, 57,
    59, 69–70, 149, 150
  in *Perry v. Schwarzenegger*, 73, 96,
    102, 109–110

  reasons for, 4–5, 42, 59–60, 60–61,
    70, 109–110, 152–153
  conservative opposition to rights
    revolution and, 160
  conservative use of moral appeals in,
    64, 65, 66–67, 69
  conservative use of populist claims in,
    61, 62, 62–63, 70
  conservative use of rights-based
    arguments in, 56–59, 58
  and cultural conflicts, 160
  ideological preferences of judges and,
    98, 186–187n27
  and institutional norms, 164
  and killing of alternative legal
    meanings, 10, 108, 155
  left's view of as protectors against
    tyranny of majority, 164
  likely conservative turn to after
    Obergefell, 159
  limited enforcement power of,
    175n12
  perception of as antidemocratic
    institutions, 2, 64, 164
  as receptive to same-sex marriage, 69,
    150
  rejection of arguments against
    same-sex marriage, conservative
    persistence despite, 9–10, 108,
    149, 155–156
  rejection of gay rights as special rights
    arguments, 37–40
  state, legalization of same-sex
    marriage by, 44, 45, 47, 47–48, 79,
    104
  See also elites: gay rights as
    imposition by; judicial activism,
    conservative claims of; litigation
cultural conflicts
  ballot measures and, 160–163
  California as bellwether for, 72
  courts and, 160

cultural norms, gays and lesbians'
     relation to, as issue, 41. *See
     also* gay and lesbian deviance;
     gender and sexual norms; sexual
     impulses, ability to control
culture warriors, anti-same-sex marriage
     self-perception as
  in California Proposition 8 campaign,
     15, 81, 86–90, 109
  and gay rights as special rights, 9, 37,
     42, 73, 155
  in Maine Question 1 campaign (2009),
     130–132

debate, shaping of by institutional norms,
     2–7, 69–70, 149, 150–153, *169*
  constitutive impact on identities of
     activists on both sides, 52
  courts and, 164
  in cultural debates beyond same-sex
     marriage, 159–166
  implications for social movements,
     150–151
  instrumental impact on same-sex
     marriage debate, 52
  See also frame analysis, of institutional
     shaping of conservative
     discourse
Defend Our Children, 29–30
Defense of Marriage Act (DOMA), 45, 48
democracy, and fundamental rights, 1–2,
     64, 164
discrimination against gays and lesbians
  history of, 18, 19–22
  sexual deviance as justification for, 18,
     19–22
  See also antidiscrimination laws
Dobson, James, 26, 33, 49, 51
due process clause
  importance to gay rights movement,
     39–40
  in *Lawrence v. Texas* (2003), 179–180n25

  in *Perry v. Schwarzenegger* (2010), 95
  See also equal protection clause;
     rational basis standard

economic rights arguments against
     same-sex marriage, 53
elites
  ballot measures as constraint on, 1
  control of New England political
     institutions, 111–113, 115, 126, 147
  gay rights as imposition by, 156, 164
  in California Proposition 8
     campaign, 87, 93, 156
  credibility of, 64
  in Maine Question 1 campaign
     (2009), 189n14
  opposition between elite and
     popular values and, 62
  parental rights debate and, 152
  Perry v. Schwarzenegger (2010) and,
     105, 109
  as subframe of populist appeals, 53
  varying use of argument by venue, 62,
     63–64
  See also judicial activism; populist
     appeals; victimhood,
     conservative claims of
elite venues
  success of leftist causes in, 163–164
  success of marriage equality advocates
     in, 3, 42, 135–136, 150
  See also courts; legislatures
Emrich, Bob, 125, 138, 139, 188n8
enforcement power, of courts, as limited,
     175n12
Equality Maine, 117, 135, 137, 188n6
equal protection clause
  in *Lawrence v. Texas* (2003), 179–180n25
  in *Perry v. Schwarzenegger* (2010), 95
  in *Romer v. Evans* (1996), 38–40
  in same-sex marriage arguments,
     178n17

Supreme Court rejection of morality as reasonable cause for discrimination, 40, 104, 179n24, 180n26
  as tool in gay rights struggle, 39–40
  See also due process clause; rational basis standard
"Everything to Do with Schools" (California TV ad), 84, 89
"Everything to Do with Schools" (Maine TV ad), 129

Falwell, Jerry, 26, 51
family, gay and lesbian, focus on in Maine 2012 Question 1 campaign, 16, 112, 136, 137–138, 140–144, 148, 157
family, traditional, as critical for proper childrearing
  arguments for, 66–67, 121
  assumption of gay and lesbian deviance underlying, 66–67
  counterarguments to, 182n18
  as issue in *Perry v. Schwarzenegger* (2010), 99–100, 101–102, 187n28
  lack of evidence for, 64, 65–66, 67, 70, 182n19
  as type of moral appeal against same-sex marriage, 53
  varying use of argument by venue, 64–67, 65
  See also parental rights arguments
Family Research Council (FRC), 66, 67–68
"Finally the Truth" (TV ad), 84, 93–94
Fitzgibbon, Scott, 128, 129
Florida Amendment 2 (2008), 65
Focus on the Family, 33, 49, 50–51, 118
frame analysis, of institutional shaping of conservative discourse
  documents used in, 54–55, 181–182nn12–15
  frames used in, 52–54, 181n11

methodology, 51–52, 55
  See also constitutional arguments; moral appeals; populist appeals; rights-based appeals
FRC. *See* Family Research Council
freedom of speech arguments
  and accommodations for religious beliefs, 60, 107, 133, 143, 159
  as type of rights-based appeal, 53
Freedom to Marry, 140–141
Fuller, Charles, 183n5
full faith and credit clause, and same-sex marriage, 45, 54, 77–78
fundamental rights
  courts versus ballot measures as venue for debate on, 16–17, 164–166
  gay rights movements' efforts to invoke, 39
  power of as legal argument, 38
  power to decide issues in, as issue, 1–2
  same-sex marriage as, as issue, 39, 96–97, 98
  and strict scrutiny standard, 38–40

Garlow, Jim, 4, 87, 90
gay and lesbian deviance
  as assumption underlying conservative arguments, 4–5, 9, 41–42, 90–92, 107–108, 149, 151, 171 (*see also* nonthreatening gay persona, as strategy)
  as masked, 4–5, 18–19, 73, 152–153, 165
  moderate voters' rejection of, 4, 13, 19, 32, 34, 37, 42, 92, 132, 151, 152, 154, 165
  parental rights arguments and, 57–58, 60, 90–91, 103–104, 109, 129–130, 132, 134, 142–143, 151–152
  Supreme Court rejection of, 40, 104, 179n24, 180n26
  traditional family arguments, 66–67

gay and lesbian deviance, *continued*
  Bryant on, 19, 26–28
  claimed predation on children, 19, 21,
      26–27, 29–30, 41–42, 68, 90–92,
      103, 104, 151
  conservative fear of legal penalties for
      expressing views on, 106–107
  and discrimination and violence, 13
  fear of, as expression of secret
      admiration, 185n19
  gay rights movement challenges to
      claims of, 24
  as justification for discrimination,
      18, 19–22, 35 (*see also* antigay
      movement)
  religious arguments against same-sex
      marriage and, 154–155
  as type of moral appeal against same-
      sex marriage, 53, 65, 67
  See also sexual impulses, ability to
      control
gay and lesbian political and economic
      power, as issue, 36, 178–179nn18–
      19
gay and lesbian rights
  as claimed threat to majority, 4, 9, 19
  gay and lesbian identity as issue in, 41
  impact of recent victories in, 157–159
  litigation as effective tactic for, 5
  necessity of presenting
      nonthreatening identity and, 16,
      31, 41, 42, 144–146, 148, 158
  See also majority rights; special rights
      arguments
gay bars, police harassment of, 20–21,
      22–23
gay liberation/gay power movement
  challenges to gender and sexual norms
      by, 24, 41, 146, 177n7
  opposition to non-threatening image
      of gays and lesbians, 146, 158

gay rights movement
  Bryant campaign against, 25–29, 60,
      177n8
  in California, 30, 32
  "homophile" movement, 23–24
  factions within, 31, 41
  goals of in 1970s, 24–25
  HIV/AIDS epidemic and, 32–33
  origins of, 13, 18, 20, 23, 72
  radicalization of in 1960s, 24
  Stonewall riots and, 22–23
  strategies adopted by, 24, 30–32, 177n7
  See also antidiscrimination laws; gay
      liberation/gay power movement;
      marriage equality movement;
      nonthreatening gay persona, as
      strategy
gays and lesbians in the United States,
      history of
  as context for same-sex marriage
      debate, 18
  Depression-era crackdown on
      homosexuality, 20
  discrimination and, 18, 19–22
  laws against homosexuality, 20
  listing of homosexuality as mental
      disorder, 22, 68, 81, 177nn3–4
  social ostracizing of exposed
      homosexuals, 21
  urban gay subcultures, emergence of,
      20
gender and sexual norms
  gay liberation movement challenges
      to, 24, 41, 146, 177n7
  Kinsey Report and, 177n5
Goodridge v. Department of Public Health
      (Massachusetts Supreme Court,
      2003), 45, 48, 63

"Have You Thought About It?" (TV ad),
      84, 91

Hawai'i, and same-sex marriage, 44–45, 180n1

Hays Code, 21

High Tech Gays v. Defense Industrial Security Clearance Office (1990), 99

HIV/AIDS epidemic
antigay movement's views on, 34
California Proposition 64 and, 34
impact on gay rights movement, 32–33, 45
and moral appeals against same-sex marriage, 53
and radicalization of gay and lesbian community, 33
and sexual promiscuity of gay men, critiques of, 33

Hollingsworth v. Perry (2013), 73, 77, 104, 110

Hollow Hope (Rosenberg), 175n12

homosexuality
church policies on, before 1980s, 26, 177n9
and incidence of mental and physical illness, 68
as learned behavior, 22, 27, 68, 81, 179n20 (*see also* mental disorder, homosexuality as)

human rights, gay rights as, as strategy, 31. *See also* fundamental rights

Human Rights Campaign, 140–141

Idaho, antigay movement in, 35

immigration policy, referendums on, 173–174n5

impartiality, as legal standard, 5–6

In re Marriage Cases (California, 2008), 77, 79, 83, 87

institutional norms, shaping of debate by. *See* debate, shaping of by institutional norms; frame

analysis, of institutional shaping of conservative discourse

institutions, as mobilization of bias, 5

interest group publications
conservative use of moral appeals in, 64, 65, 67–69
conservative use of populist claims in, 61–62, 62, 63–64
conservative use of rights-based arguments in, 56–59, 58

Iowa, legalization of same-sex marriage, 47

"It's Already Happened" (California TV ad), 84, 91

"It's Already Happening" (Maine TV ad), 129

"I Was Fired" (TV ad), 140

judicial activism, conservative claims of, 10
in California Proposition 8 campaign, 83–84, 87
in *Perry v. Schwarzenegger* (2010), 104–105
as populist appeal, 53
and refusal to accept court rulings, 155–156
varying use by venue, 61–63, 62

Kennedy, Anthony, 1, 38–39, 40

Kerrigan v. Commission of Public Health (Massachusetts Supreme Court, 2008), 47, 66

Latinos/as, and California Proposition 8 campaign, 85, 86

law
freeing of from religious principles, 6
on homosexuality, history of, 20
as inseparable from politics, 8, 175n13

law, *continued*
  legal meaning, construction of outside
      formal legal institutions, 8
  legal order of United States, as plural, 8
  and legal positivism, 6
  mobilization of by social movements,
      7–8
  rationality and impartiality as
      standards in, 5–6
Lawrence v. Texas (2003), 40, 45, 179–
      180n25
legal positivism, 6
legal precedents, arguments against
      same-sex marriage from, 54, 63,
      96–97, 186n26
legislative propositions, states allowing,
      175n11
legislatures
  anti-same-sex marriage legislation by,
      45–46, 47, 49, 51, 77, 180n1, 180n5
  focus on reelection and partisan
      self-interest in, 6–7, 112–113, 119,
      126–127, 147, 153
  rights-based appeals in, 6–7, 125–126
  See also Maine bill LD 1020
Leno, Mark, 78, 184n7
liberals, characteristic beliefs of, 174n7
litigation
  conservative legal organizations, 51
  as effective tactic for gay and lesbian
      rights, 5, 19, 69
  victory in versus social change, 8,
      175n12
  See also courts
*Lockyer v. City and County of San
      Francisco* (California, 2004), 78

Mabon, Lon, 34–35, 154
Maine
  antigay movement in, 36, 50, 118–119,
      125–126, 178n16

citizens' initiatives and people's veto,
      15, 116–117, 147, 188n3
Democratic political dominance in,
      15–16, 112, 117–118, 136, 147, 153,
      188n7
history and political culture of,
      115–116, 135
legalization of same-sex marriage, 48
      (*see also* Maine bill LD 1020)
marriage equality movement, history
      of, 117, 188n6
referendum on repeal of gay rights law
      (2005), 117
Republican victories in 2010 elections,
      136, 137, 189n18
Maine bill LD 1020 (pro-same-sex
      marriage), 117–127
  conservative arguments against,
      119–120, 121–123, 123–125, 125–126,
      153
  conservative efforts to amend, 123–124,
      188n10
  conservative letters to legislature on,
      119–120
  election of 2010 and, 136
  legislative debate on, 122–125, 126–127,
      153
  opposition to, mobilization of, 118–
      119
  passage of, 125, 147, 153
  public hearings on, 120–122
  Question 1 ballot measure as response
      to, 112, 119, 129
  religious liberty protections in, 120
  repeal of, 112, 128, 136
Maine Question 1 campaign (2009)
      (anti-same-sex marriage)
  anti-same-sex marriage arguments in,
      28, 128–130, 147, 151
  California Proposition 8 campaign as
      model for, 16, 128, 147

conservative claims of victimhood in, 130–131

hyperbole of anti-same-sex marriage arguments in, 133–134

influence of California Proposition 8 campaign on, 110

marriage equality advocates' arguments in, 132–136, 147–148

as response to passage of LD 1020, 112, 119, 127

success in repealing LD 1020, 112, 128, 136

threats and intimidation against supporters of, 130–131

voter turnout, 189n18

Maine Question 1 campaign (2012) (pro-same-sex marriage), 136–148

and accommodations for religious beliefs, 143

anti-same-sex marriage arguments in, 151

appeals to older voters, 190n21

conservative strategy in, 138–140, 148

as first pro-same-sex marriage ballot measure success, 16, 144, 148

funds raised in, 138–139

and legalization of same-sex marriage, 112

mobilization of support for, 136–138, 148

Portland Diocese decision not to participate in, 138, 148

pro-marriage equality strategy in controversial aspects of, 16, 144–146, 148

face-to-face conversations, 137–138, 148

presentation of gays and lesbians as nonthreatening, 142, 143, 148, 157, 190nn21–23

responses to parental rights arguments, 142–143, 156–157

turn to family theme in, 16, 112, 136, 137–138, 140–144, 148, 157

success of, 143, 148

voter registration laws and, 189n18

majority rights, same-sex marriage as claimed threat to, 4, 9, 19. *See also* special rights arguments

Malone, Richard, 118, 121, 125, 138

marriage. *See also* same-sex marriage, legalization of

as God-given institution, 53, 119–120

heterosexual perception of meaning of for gays and lesbians, 141

as institution to tame sexual impulses, 91

opposition to institution in gay community, 44, 146, 158, 180n3

right to define, as issue, 1, 62–63, 69, 88–89, 97–98, 119–120, 123–124, 140, 186–187n27

socioeconomic factors in attitudes toward, 158

traditional, as foundation of moral society, 121, 123, 125

undermining of by same-sex marriage, 84

marriage equality movement. *See also* Maine Question 1 campaign (2012)

court victories of 2003, 45

equal protection arguments of, 178n17

history of, 44–49

local government issuing of same-sex marriage licenses, 45–46

and Maine 2009 Question 1 campaign, 132–136, 147–148

mobilization of after *Baehr* decision, 44–45

origins of, 44

marriage equality movement, *continued*
    "Six by Twelve" campaign, 48, 181n8
    strategy of, 186n22
    success of in elite versus popular
        venues, 3, 42, 135–136, 150
Massachusetts
    citizen initiatives in, 187n1
    and same-sex marriage, 45, 47, 122, 123,
        132, 139
Mattachine Society, 23
Maynard v. Hill (1888), 66
Mendel, Don, 129, 131, 139–140
mental disorder, homosexuality as
    APA and, 22, 177n4
    and medical/psychological treatment,
        22, 68, 81, 177n3
Merrick v. Board of Higher Education
        (Oregon Court of Appeals, 1989),
        178n13
methodology of this study, 11–13
Michigan, and affirmative action, 162
Milk, Harvey, 30, 178n11
Minnesota, and same-sex marriage, 44,
        46, 63–64, 96, 97, 186n26
minority groups, and California
        Proposition 8 campaign, 83,
        84–86
minority group ("suspect class") status
        of gays and lesbians
    conservative understanding of rights
        and, 53
    constitutional arguments denying, 54
    impact of not having, 39
    as issue, 14, 36–37, 38, 99, 100, 101, 109,
        179n21
Mississippi, and abortion law, 162
moral appeals
    in California Proposition 8 campaign,
        80–81
    conservative avoidance of after 1990s,
        13, 19, 37, 151, 154
    described, 53
    in frame analysis, 52
    in Maine, 124
    by marriage equality advocates, in
        Maine, 134–135
    as percentage of appeals, in all venues,
        55, 56, 56, 57
    subframes of, 53
    varying use of by venue, 64–69, 65
    See also family, traditional, as critical
        for proper childrearing; gay and
        lesbian deviance; slippery slope
        arguments
moral decay, conservative concerns
        about, 20, 121
morality, Supreme Court rejection of as
        compelling government interest,
        40, 104, 179n24, 180n26
moral questions
    legal positivism and, 6
    right to decide, as issue, 2, 10
Motion Picture Production Code. *See*
        Hays Code
Mutty, Marc, 118, 125, 131, 133–134

National Organization for Marriage
        (NOM), 49–50, 139
Native Americans, and rights of citizens,
        176n16
New England
    ballot initiatives, limited access to, 111,
        113, 147, 187n1
    early marriage equality movement
        victories in, 111
    elite-centered political institutions in,
        111–112, 113, 115, 126, 147
    history and political culture of, 113–115
    and same-sex marriage debate, 112, 113,
        147
New Hampshire, legalization of same-
        sex marriage, 48

new institutional approach to social
science, 5, 7, 150, 174–175n9.
See also debate, shaping of by
institutional norms; frame
analysis, of institutional shaping
of conservative discourse
New Right
and ballot measures, 161, 163–164
emergence of, 72, 76–77, 160, 176n17
and moral decay, concern about, 121
opposition to rights revolution, 10
Newsom, Gavin, 78, 83–84, 183–184n6
Nixon, Richard M., 76, 183n3, 185n17
NOM. *See* National Organization for
Marriage
nonthreatening gay persona, as strategy
controversial aspects of, 16, 31, 41, 42,
144–146, 148, 158
in defeat of California Proposition 6,
30–32
and efforts to invoke fundamental
rights, 39
in Maine Question 1 campaign (2012),
142, 143, 148, 157, 190nn21–23
success of, 24
North Carolina, constitutional
amendment prohibiting same-
sex marriage, 46
North Dakota, and abortion law, 162

Obama, Barack, 85, 185n15
Obergefell v. Hodges (2015)
and debate on same-sex marriage, 1,
157
dissenting opinions, 1, 63
and due process protection, 180n25
equal protection strategy and, 40,
180n25
impact on gays and lesbians, 157
invalidation of state laws by, 2
Kennedy opinion, 1

and legalization of same-sex marriage,
49
likely conservative strategy following,
159
right to redefine marriage as issue in,
63
on stigma of unmarried gay parents,
67
O'Connor, Sandra Day, 179–180n25
Olson, Theodore, 95, 102, 187n31
"One Thing" (TV ad), 65
Oregon
antigay movement in, 34–35, 178nn13–
14
and same-sex marriage debate, 35, 65,
178n13

parental rights arguments
arguments against, 132–134, 142–143,
147–148, 152
assumption of gay and lesbian
deviance underlying, 57–58, 60,
90–91, 103–104, 109, 129–130, 132,
134, 142–143, 151–152
California education policy and,
92–94, 185–186n20
in California Proposition 8
campaign, 84, 85, 89, 92–95, 105,
109, 151
effectiveness of, 130
in Maine same-sex marriage debate,
122, 128–130, 131, 139–140, 142–143,
147, 151, 153
Perry v. Schwarzenegger (2010) and,
102–104
as type of rights-based appeal, 53
varying use by venue, 57–58, 58
Parker, David and Tonia, 89, 122, 139
"Parkers" (TV ad), 139
Parker v. Hurley (Massachusetts, 2008),
89, 139

Perry v. Schwarzenegger (2010), 95–108
appeals of, 104
conservative critiques of, 104–108
and conservative rights-based
arguments, backfiring of, 15,
73–74, 102–104, 110, 153
defense arguments
from ballot measure, decision not
to use, 73, 96, 102, 109–110
on compelling government interest,
73, 98–102, 104
on marriage, court's lack of
authority to define, 97, 98,
186–187n27
on same-sex marriage as non-
fundamental right, 96–97, 98
defense expert witnesses,
ineffectiveness of, 99–101, 105
defense team for, 95, 186n25
ideological preferences of judges and,
98, 186n24
judges' rulings in, 98, 101–102, 104, 153
marriage equality advocates'
arguments in, 73
plaintiff emphasis on homophobia
underlying Proposition 8
arguments, 103–104, 107–108, 110
plaintiff witnesses, 101, 105–106
selection of judge for, 186n24
suspect-class status of gays and
lesbians as issue in, 99, 100, 101,
109
political activism, rights as resources in,
8–9, 176n14
politics, law as inseparable from, 8,
175n13
populist appeals
in California Proposition 8 campaign,
86–90, 93, 156, 185n17
in conservative critiques of *Perry v.
Schwarzenegger* (2010), 105

conservatives' use of, 164
in court argument, 61, 62, 62–63, 70
described, 52–53
in frame analysis, 52
in Maine same-sex marriage debate,
123–124, 189n14
as percentage of appeals, in all venues,
55, 56, 56, 57
in *Perry v. Schwarzenegger* (2010), 97
subframes of, 52–53
varying use by venue, 61–64, 62
See also elites: gay rights as imposition
by
Prentice, Ron, 84
privacy, as gay rights strategy, 31
progressive movement
and ballot measures, support for, 2
in California, 75
in New England, 113, 114–115
"Prop. 8 Has Nothing to Do with
Schools" (TV ad), 93
Protect Marriage Coalition, 83, 95, 102,
104, 107, 138, 186n25

radical elements in gay community
challenge to gender and sexual norms
by, 24, 41, 146, 177n7
downplaying of by gay rights
strategists, 30–31
opposition to marriage as institution,
44, 146, 148, 180n3
resentment of moderate strategy, 31, 41
rational basis standard, 38–40, 98–99,
179n24. *See also* compelling
government interest
rationality, as legal standard, 5–6
Reagan, Ronald W., 31–32, 76
reality, construction of, as contested
social process, 12
referendums. *See* ballot measures
religion, freeing of law from, 6

religious arguments against same-sex marriage
  in California Proposition 8 campaign, 80–81, 154–155
  interest group use of, 69, *171*
  in Maine, 119–120, 121–122
  as moral arguments couched in rights language, 9
religious beliefs as motive for opposing gay rights, 34
  history of, 26
  HIV/AIDS epidemic and, 34
religious freedom arguments against same-sex marriage, 38
  and accommodations for religious beliefs, 60, 107, 133, 143, 159
  in California Proposition 8 campaign, 81–82
  in Maine same-sex marriage debate, 120, 122, 123, 128, 140
  as type of rights-based appeal, 53
  varying use by venue, *58*, 58–59
  See also special rights arguments
religious right
  history of, 26
  opposition to same-sex marriage, 9, 25, 38, 49, 50–51, 80, 128, 130, 138
  and religious accommodations, 60, 159, 174n8
  See also church networks
Rhode Island, legalization of same-sex marriage, 48
rights
  conservative conception of, 53
  conservative use of for retrenchment, 149, 153–156
  as contingent resources, 9, 11, 18, 19–20, 81, 91, 146, 156–157, 176n16, 180n27
  as resources for political activism, 8–9, 11, 176n14

rights-based appeals
  in civil rights movement, 158
  limited effectiveness of, 158–159
  symbolic political power of, 8–9, 70–71, 154
rights-based appeals by conservatives
  adoption of after 1990s, 13, 19, 37, 151, 154
  and antigay movement as defender of traditional values, 9, 37, 42, 73, 155
  avoidance of in court settings, 3–5, 43, 56–57, *57*, 59, 69–70, 149, 150
    in *Perry v. Schwarzenegger* (2010), 73, 96, 102, 109–110
    reasons for, 4–5, 42, 59–60, 60–61, 70, 109–110, 152–153
  in ballot initiatives, in Maine, 126
  in California Proposition 8 campaign, 14–15, 81–82, 87–89, 91
  in civil rights debate, 161
  in conservative critiques of *Perry v. Schwarzenegger* (2010), 105–107
  conservative understanding of rights and, 53
  in frame analysis, 52
  in Maine same-sex marriage debate, 16, 120, 122–126, 139–140, 153
  mixed-methods approach to, 12
  as percentage of appeals, in all venues, 55, *56*, 69
  and personalizing of consequences of gay rights, 9, 87, 109, 130, 155
  in referendums, 3–5
  as strategy to broaden appeal, 8–9, 37, 82–83, 103, 109, 126, 154
  subframes of, 53, 57–59, *58*
  success of in same-sex marriage debate, 46–47
  texts versus author's intention in interpretation of, 12–13

rights-based appeals by conservatives, *continued*
  use in ballot measure campaigns, 14, 56–59, *58*, 73, 149, 150
  use in courts, 56–59, *58*
  See also special rights arguments
rights-based appeals by marriage equality advocates
  in California Proposition 8 debate, 86–87, 156
  in Maine same-sex marriage debate, 86–87, 134–135
rights revolution of 1960s–1970s, 159–160
  conservative opposition to, 10, 160
Romer v. Evans (1996), 19, 38–40, 99

"Safe Schools" (TV ad), 129
same-sex marriage, legalization of
  and accommodations for religious beliefs, 60, 107, 133, 143, 159
  as claimed imposition of different moral system, 106–107
  conservative strategies following, 159
  impact on gays and lesbians, 158–160
  limited interest in before 1990s, 44–45, 180n3
  at state level, 44, 45, 46–47, *47*, 47–48, *48*, 180n1
  by Supreme Court, 48–49
  See also California: legalization of same-sex marriage; *Obergefell v. Hodges* (2015)
same-sex marriage debate
  in California, history of, 77–79
  and fundamental rights, as issue, 39, 96–97, 98
  history of gays and lesbians in United States as context for, 18
  identity of gays and lesbians as issue in, 9
  length of, 1

lessons from, 149–159
Obergefell as an end of, 1
as ongoing within gay community, 45
scholarship on, 11
spending in, 47, 181n6
See also anti-same-sex-marriage movement; marriage equality movement
San Francisco
  gay rights activists in, 18, 23, 72
  issuing of same-sex marriage licenses (2004), 78, 183–184n6
Save Our Children, Inc., 26, 27
Scalia, Antonin, 40, 45, 180n26
school teachers, homosexual, campaigns to remove, 27, 29–32
Schubert, Frank, 110, 139, 184n9
Schubert and Flint Public Affairs, 79, 83, 85, 93–94, 128, 139, 184n9
Schuette v. Coalition to Defend Affirmative Action (2014), 2
Schwarzenegger, Arnold, 78
separation of powers arguments, as type of populist appeal, 62–63
sexual impulses, ability to control
  claimed lack of in gays and lesbians, 18, 20, 81, 91–92
  as criterion for full citizenship, 18, 19–20, 81, 91, 146, 176n16
sexual impulses, history of laws on, 19–20
sexual promiscuity of gays and lesbians
  as argument against same-sex marriage, 67–68
  critiques of within gay community, 33
"Six by Twelve" campaign, 48, 181n8
slippery slope arguments
  interest group use of, 69, *171*
  in Maine, 123
  as type of moral appeal against same-sex marriage, 53
  varying use of by venue, 65, 67–68

social movements
    institutional influence on debates and,
        150–151
    mobilization of law by, 7–8
social science
    interpretive, on social construction of
        reality, 11–12
    See also new institutional approach to
        social science
sociolegal scholarship, 7–8
sodomy laws, 24–25, 40, 45
Southern Baptist Church, 49, 177n9
special rights arguments, 14, 34–37
    abandonment of as strategy, 178n17
    and antigay movement as defender of
        traditional values, 9, 37, 42, 73,
        155
    argument of, 36–37
    assumption of gay and lesbian
        deviance underlying, 37
    in California Proposition 8 campaign,
        87–89, 91
    and Colorado Amendment 2, 19,
        35–36
    development of, 34
    as effort to broaden appeal, 37
    and gay rights as selfish minority
        demand, 124–125
    in Maine Question 1 campaign (2012),
        140, 157
    marriage equality movement
        arguments and, 136
    and presentation of gays and lesbians
        as nonthreatening, costs of, 144
    rejection of by courts, 37–40
    and rights as zero-sum game, 9, 37, 42,
        87–88, 156
    See also minority group ("suspect
        class") status of gays and lesbians
Stand for Marriage Maine, 118, 127–128,
    131, 132, 188n8

state governments
    anti-same-sex marriage legislation by,
        45–46, 47, 49, 51, 77, 180n1, 180n5
    constitutional amendments
        prohibiting same-sex marriage,
        46, 47
    legalization of same-sex marriage, 44,
        45, 46–47, 48, 180n1
    pro-same-sex marriage ballots
        measures, 47
    See also California: legalization of
        same-sex marriage
State Referendum League (Maine),
    116–117
Stonewall Inn riots, 22–23
Strauss v. Horton (California, 2009), 77,
    95
strict scrutiny standard, 38–39
Supreme Court
    on abortion, 190n2
    on accommodations for religious
        beliefs, 60
    on affirmative action, 162
    on appeal of *Perry v. Schwarzenegger*
        (2010), 104
    on California anti-busing proposition
        (*Peña v. Superior Court*, 1975),
        161–162
    on California fair housing law
        (*Reitman v. Mulkey*, 1967), 161
    Colorado Amendment 2, vacating of
        (*Romer v. Evans*, 1996), 19, 38–40
    legalization of same-sex marriage
        in California (*Hollingsworth v.
        Perry*, 2013), 73, 104, 110
    leniency regarding local civil rights
        law, 160, 190n2
    and power to rule on fundamental
        rights, as issue, 1–2
    and rights revolution of 1960s–1970s,
        159–160

Supreme Court, *continued*
    rightward shift after 1980s, 160
    and same-sex marriage debate, 44
    sodomy laws, vacating of (*Lawrence v. Texas*, 2003), 25, 45
    and strict scrutiny standard, 38–40
    vacating of Defense of Marriage Act (*United States v. Windsor*, 2013), 48
    See also *Obergefell v. Hodges* (2015)
suspect class designation. *See* minority group ("suspect class") status of gays and lesbians

Tam, Hak-Shing William, 107–108
texts, interpretation of, words versus author's intention in, 12–13
"Threat to Marriage" TV ad, 63–64
"The Top Ten Harms of Same-Sex Marriage" (FRC pamphlet), 67–68
"Top 10 Myths about Homosexuality" (FRC pamphlet), 68–69
traditional values, antigay movement image as defenders of, 9, 37, 42, 73, 155. *See also* family, traditional, as critical for proper childrearing

United States v. Windsor (2013), 40, 48, 180n25

Varnum v. Brien (Iowa, 2009), 47
Vermont, legalization of same-sex marriage, 47, 48, 77, 181n7

victimhood, conservative claims of
    in California Proposition 8 debate, 15, 89–90, 106, 108
    fear of legal penalties for expressing antigay views, 106–107
    gay rights as special rights and, 4, 9, 15, 37, 73, 149, 155
    in Maine same-sex marriage debate, 130–131, 139–140
    threats and intimidation and, 89–90, 130–131
voters
    moderate
        and California Proposition 8 campaign, 82–84, 92
        and defeat of California Proposition 6, 31–32
        rejection of homophobic rhetoric, 13, 19, 32, 34, 37, 42, 92, 132, 151, 152, 154, 165
    rational ignorance of, 7, 94–95, 109, 133, 152

Walker, Vaughn, 95–96, 97–98, 100–101, 104–105, 186n24
Washington, same-sex marriage issue in, 143
Washington v. Glucksberg (1997), 97
West Virginia State Board of Education v. Barnette (1943), 60
"Why We Need a Marriage Amendment" TV ad, 61
Worthlin, Robb and Robin, 89, 129